Children and young people's cultural worlds

This book is part of the series *Childhood* published by The Policy Press in association with The Open University. The four books in the series are:

Understanding childhood: a cross-disciplinary approach (edited by Mary Jane Kehily)

ISBN 978-1-447-30580-4 (paperback)

ISBN 978-1-447-30927-7 (ebook)

Children and young people's cultural worlds (edited by Sara Bragg and Mary Jane Kehily)

ISBN 978-1-447-30582-8 (paperback)

ISBN 978-1-447-30925-3 (ebook)

Childhoods in context (edited by Alison Clark)

ISBN 978-1-447-30581-1 (paperback)

ISBN 978-1-447-30924-6 (ebook)

Local childhoods, global issues (edited by Heather Montgomery)

ISBN 978-1-447-30583-5 (paperback)

ISBN 978-1-447-30926-0 (ebook)

This publication forms part of the Open University module E212 Childhood. Details of this and other Open University modules can be obtained from the Student Registration and Enquiry Service, The Open University, PO Box 197, Milton Keynes, MK7 6BJ, United Kingdom (Tel. +44 (0845 300 60 90, email general-enquiries @open.ac.uk).

www.open.ac.uk

Children and young people's cultural worlds

Edited by Sara Bragg and Mary Jane Kehily

Published by
The Policy Press
University of Bristol
Fourth Floor, Beacon House
Queen's Road, Clifton
Bristol BS8 1QU
United Kingdom
www.policypress.co.uk

in association with
The Open University
Walton Hall
Milton Keynes MK7 6AA
United Kingdom

First published 2003. Second edition published 2013

Edited and designed by The Open University.

Typeset by The Open University.

Printed in the United Kingdom by Bell & Bain Ltd, Glasgow.

British Library Cataloguing in Publication Data:
A catalogue record for this book is available from the British Library.

Library of Congress Cataloging-in-Publication Data

A catalog record for this book has been requested

ISBN 978-1-447-30582-8 (paperback)

ISBN 978-1-447-30925-3 (ebook)

2.1

Contents

Series preface

The books in this series provide an introduction to the study of childhood. They provide a cross-disciplinary and international perspective which develops theoretical knowledge about children and young people, both in the UK and overseas. They are core texts for the Open University module E212 *Childhood*. The series is designed for students working with or for children and young people, in a wide range of settings, and for those who have more general interests in the interdisciplinary field of childhood and youth studies.

The series aims to provide students with:

- the necessary concepts, theories, knowledge and skills base to understand the lives of children and young people

- relevant skills of critical analysis

- critical reflection on and analysis of practices affecting children and young people

- an understanding of the links between children's experiences on a global and local level

- an understanding of the analytical, research and conceptual skills needed to link theory, practice and experience.

The readings which accompany each chapter have been chosen to exemplify key points made in the chapters, often by exploring related data, or experiences and practices involving children in different parts of the world. The readings also represent an additional 'voice' or viewpoint on key themes or issues raised in the chapter.

The books include:

- **activities** to stimulate further understanding or analysis of the material

- **illustrations** to support the teaching material

- **summaries** of key teaching points at appropriate places in the chapter.

The other books in this series are:

Kehily, M. J. (ed) (2013) *Understanding Childhood: A Cross-disciplinary Approach*, Bristol, Policy Press/Milton Keynes, The Open University.

Clark, A. (ed) (2013) *Childhoods in Context*, Bristol, Policy Press/Milton Keynes, The Open University.

Montgomery, H. (ed) (2013) *Local Childhoods, Global Issues*, Bristol, Policy Press/Milton Keynes, The Open University.

Professor Mary Jane Kehily

Series Editor

Contributors

Sara Bragg

Sara Bragg is Senior Research Fellow at Brighton University and previously worked at The Open University, the University of Sussex and the Centre for the Study of Children, Youth and Media at the Institute of Education, London. She has researched and published on young people and sexualisation; sex education; child and youth culture, consumption and media education; participation and 'student voice'; school ethos; and on 'creative' research methods and creative learning.

Mary Jane Kehily

Mary Jane Kehily is Professor of Childhood and Youth Studies at The Open University, UK. She has a background in cultural studies and education, and research interests in gender and sexuality, narrative and identity and popular culture. She has published widely on these themes.

Heather Montgomery

Heather Montgomery is a Reader in the Anthropology of Childhood at The Open University, UK. She has carried out research with young sex workers in Thailand and written extensively on issues of children's rights, global childhoods and representations of childhood.

James Ash

James Ash is a lecturer in media at Northumbria University. He is a social scientist working at the intersections between human geography and media. His work investigates the relationship between bodies and technologies, and how technologies shape and alter the practices, experiences and capacities of those who use them. His research is currently concerned with the relationship between screened digital images and the human body.

Lesley Gallacher

Lesley Gallacher is a lecturer based in the Moray House School of Education at the University of Edinburgh. She has a background in human geography. Her research interests fall broadly into two categories: materials, bodies and spaces in early childhood; and the international reception of Japanese popular culture. Lesley has published on socio-spatial relations in childcare settings, the practices of reading manga and methodological issues in childhood research.

Martyn Hammersley

Martyn Hammersley is Professor of Education and Social Research at The Open University. His early research was in the sociology of education. Later work has been concerned with the methodological issues surrounding social and educational enquiry. These include objectivity, partisanship and bias, and the role of research in relation to policymaking and practice. More recently he has investigated ethical issues in social research and how the news media represent social science research findings.

Anoop Nayak

Anoop Nayak is Professor of Social and Cultural Geography at Newcastle University, UK. His research interests are in the fields of racism, ethnicity, migration and asylum; youth and cultural studies; masculinities, education and labour; and whiteness, nationalism and new theories of social class. His current research explores the politics of race, asylum and migration, and the future of multiculturalism.

Tara Woodyer

Tara Woodyer is a lecturer in geography at the University of Portsmouth. Following completion of her PhD, Tara joined the Department of Geography at the University of Exeter in 2009 as a Teaching Fellow. In 2011, she was awarded an ESRC Postdoctoral Fellowship, which she completed at Exeter alongside a period as Visiting Scholar in the Centre for Children and Children Studies at Rutgers University (Camden) in the USA.

Introduction

This book offers a critical, cross-disciplinary introduction to the cultural worlds of children and young people. Each chapter draws on a range of international examples to explore children and young people's cultural experiences in particular places and contexts. The book as a whole explores the idea of cultural worlds as a distinct feature of childhood and youth. Each chapter considers different aspects of children's culture and how they take on meaning for the children and young people involved and their impact upon adult understandings of childhood. In approaching childhood as *cultural* this book adopts a particular understanding of culture as *everyday social practice*. Conventionally, the concept of culture is defined either as the arts, music and literature, or as the shared, traditional beliefs and values of social groups. By contrast, our perspective suggests that culture emerges from and can be observed and studied in day-to-day engagements with the social world.

To take up a perspective developed by writer and cultural critic Raymond Williams (2001 [1961]), we seek to point out that culture is *ordinary*. This conceptualisation of culture has its roots in Williams's working-class childhood on the Welsh borders. Williams refers to the everydayness of culture as a *way of life* that makes sense to individuals involved in that community. But how can this understanding of culture be applied to children and childhood? The chapters in this book observe and discuss the many ways in which children make sense of the world around them and insert themselves into that world through everyday cultural activity. Collectively, the chapters suggest that children are active and eloquent narrators of their own lives. Through negotiations with the social world and the exercise of agency, children and young people give shape to personal biographies that actively ascribe meanings to events. In this way children develop their own *cultures* of relatedness, seeing themselves in relation to others and finding points of connection and belonging in the peer group. The book develops an awareness of how children's cultural worlds may be shaped in relation to broader social structures and practices found in the adult world. Much of the book provides an 'insider' perspective on children's culture, whilst also raising questions about the extent to which researchers can ever fully access this perspective.

This book seeks to understand the distinctiveness of children's cultural worlds. A central aim is to examine how children and young people in the early twenty-first century encounter and creatively adapt to a range of cultural phenomena in an increasingly mediated, commercialised and globalised world. The book highlights the diversity of children's experiences, focusing on children of different ages and living in different cultural contexts. Several key themes are developed throughout the book: children's engagement with the media and information technology; children and young people's activities online and offline; adult perceptions of, and responses to, children and young people's cultural activities; the role of friendship in children and young people's cultural worlds; processes of globalisation and commercialisation in children and young people's cultural lives and how adults can learn about and understand children and young people's cultural worlds.

Chapter 1, by Sara Bragg, Mary Jane Kehily and Heather Montgomery, considers the significance of childhood innocence as a concept that is deeply embedded in adult ideas about childhood. The ideal of innocence is a powerful feature in adult notions of childhood, acting as a touchstone for 'the child' who inhabits an imagined state of purity. Childhood innocence is woven into the fabric of children's cultural worlds and can be seen as underpinning many of the artefacts of childhood – literature, art, the media, toys and clothes. The chapter unravels the concept of childhood innocence in ways that reveal the complex and contradictory character of the idea. Asking the question, 'what is innocence?', the chapter discusses the various meanings and connotations of innocence and how they can be seen at work in visual images of children from different time periods. The chapter considers childhood sexuality and particularly the work of Freud and Foucault as explanatory accounts of children as desirous and sexual beings. Engaging with children's cultural worlds directly challenges the idea of children as innocent subjects. Children's own activity, visible in play, friendship and interactions with media culture for example, offers insights into children and young people as aware, knowing and worldly.

In Chapter 2, Tara Woodyer provides a critical introduction to the concept of play in order to explore its role within children's lives in a range of international contexts. The chapter develops a perspective on childhood as socially constructed. This is illustrated by a focus on materiality and embodiment. The chapter begins by examining different approaches to children's play, incorporating a historical perspective and also exploring the links between play and learning, emotion and the development of social understanding. It looks at the folklore tradition in children's play, including material from both historical and contemporary ethnographic studies of children's playground games. The chapter also examines the social dynamics of children's play, exploring issues of imagination, exclusion and gender. Toys are an important part of children's play and the chapter considers this aspect of the material cultures of childhood. The final part of the chapter discusses play through the lifecourse, which complicates the automatic association of play with childhood.

Children's friendships come into full view in Chapter 3. Anoop Nayak examines the nature of friendship and the significance of friends in children's lives. The chapter describes the changing nature of friendships during the childhood years and the effects of social context on the development of friendship networks and peer relationships. Illustrative material is drawn from children's talk with and about friends as a way of offering an insight into children's perspectives on friendship. The chapter recognises that children's friendships provide a site for companionship, pleasure and support, but that they can also be fraught with difficulty, and discusses some of the negative experiences associated with children's friendship. Later parts of the chapter consider multicultural friendships and how new developments in the digital age, such as Facebook and other social networking sites, might be changing the nature of children's friendships.

Lesley Gallacher and Mary Jane Kehily concentrate on the teenage years in Chapter 4, on youth culture. Introducing the idea of youth cultures as a distinctive feature of young people's social activity, the chapter explores the relationships between cultures and subcultures through a range of historical and international examples. In particular, it develops case studies of skinheads, hip hop and Japanese Lolitas. Through these case studies, the chapter explores how aspects of identity, including gender and ethnicity, are embedded within, or excluded from, particular subcultures. The chapter also looks at the globalisation and commercialisation of subcultures and explores what happens when they are taken up outside of their original cultural contexts. Through this discussion, the chapter considers how useful it is to think in terms of discrete youth cultures or subcultures. Overall, the chapter examines why youth cultures matter to the young people involved and how aspects of these experiences may endure as the participants grow up.

In Chapter 5, James Ash turns our attention to new media technologies and participatory cultures. This chapter builds upon ideas introduced in Chapter 4 by exploring the various, often creative ways in which children and young people engage with media, and particularly with new media technologies. The chapter considers what 'new media' are and how they are different from 'old media'. It examines the kinds of 'participatory' and 'remix cultures' associated with children and young people's use of new media technologies, in which they interact with, pastiche or modify existing cultural goods and media forms to produce their own texts. The chapter critically interrogates the idea that this is a recent development, by exploring a range of historical examples (such as collecting behaviours and fan fiction writing) and more contemporary examples associated with Web 2.0 technologies such as YouTube. The chapter examines the tensions between commercial practices and children and young people's 'remixing' behaviours (including some discussion of the ethics of remix) and considers how corporations have adapted to take advantage of children and young people's activities. The chapter also considers the problems posed by the emergence of a 'digital divide' between those with access to and expertise in using new media technologies and those without.

In the final chapter of the book, Martyn Hammersley provides a methodological commentary on studying children's cultural worlds online and offline. The chapter begins by examining the variety of online data that is now available, and some of the issues that arise in using it, including limits to its value, and its similarities to, and differences from, other kinds of data. It discusses diverse forms of discourse analysis, and what is involved in applying these to online and offline data, focusing particularly on the notion of 'forms of talk'. It explores the concept of 'virtual communities' and compares virtual with offline communities, such as those that make up subcultures. The chapter comments on the porous nature of the digital world, and how the virtual can be accommodated by methods for which online and offline data are combined.

We would like to thank all those who played a part in the development of this book, particularly Lesley Gallacher for her work in the early phases of the project and the consultant authors for their contribution. We are grateful to Professor Chris Philo, who commented insightfully on draft chapters in his capacity as external assessor.

Sara Bragg and Mary Jane Kehily

The Open University, 2012

References

Williams, R. (2001 [1961]) *The Long Revolution*, Toronto, Encore Editions, Broadview Press.

Chapter 1

Childhood, culture and innocence

Sara Bragg, Mary Jane Kehily and Heather Montgomery

Contents

In this chapter, you will:

- explore the concept of childhood innocence and its many meanings
- look at how the concept is evident in culture, including in visual representations of children
- analyse the relationship between childhood innocence and market forces
- examine the ways in which childhood sexuality has been theorised by Sigmund Freud and Michel Foucault
- evaluate the evidence that children are becoming increasingly sexualised
- consider the negotiation that goes on between adults and children over constructions of innocence, especially in relation to sexuality.

1   Introduction

The idea of childhood innocence is a powerful cultural theme. Whether talking about play, children's use of the internet or video games or their move from childhood into adolescence and beyond, the idea of innocence is pervasive; it goes to the heart of how childhood is conceptualised and understood and permeates discussions of children's cultures. Yet innocence is also a highly complex and contested concept with many different meanings. This chapter will explore the multiple connotations of the term and investigate what functions it serves in thinking about childhood, about society and about adult identity and roles. You will examine whether innocence is a quality that adults expect of, and even impose on, children and the consequences for children deemed less than innocent. Finally, the chapter will discuss recent debates over the premature sexualisation of girls. Drawing on a range of different sources, but especially on images of children, this chapter will interrogate the meanings and role of children's innocence in contemporary culture.

2   What is innocence?

When asked what expressions or qualities they associate with 'childhood', many people are likely to say 'innocence'; the link between the two words is so common as to be largely taken for granted. The idea of childhood innocence has been woven into the very texture of children's cultural worlds: it can be traced in literature, art, media, cinema and advertising, as well as in the material artefacts of children's lives, such as their toys, games or clothing. It also informs laws, policy making, architecture and education. However, it is not an easy or straightforward concept and has many, sometimes contradictory, shades of meaning.

Activity 1   What does innocence mean to you?
Allow about 15 minutes

Think about what innocence means to you in relation to children and write down as many different associations as you can.

Then write down where these associations come from: are they based on your experiences as a parent; your knowledge of children as a professional; your memories of being a child; your religious beliefs? Do they come from fiction, poetry, newspapers or popular sayings?

Comment

There are several ways of looking at innocence. It can be viewed as the opposite of evil or (in Christian theology) as a lack of sin. In legal terms, it can be understood as the opposite of guilt. Innocence might imply ignorance, especially of certain forms of knowledge that adults believe children should not have – about drugs and sex, for example, or hatred or grief. It might also suggest a guileless or even gullible form of naivety. Some may see innocence as children's natural, universal state, while others think that it is dependent on the historical and cultural context, and means different things at different times. Innocence might be associated with purity and virtue, in particular with sexual purity, and may also call to mind more unsettling associations – child beauty pageants, 'schoolgirl' paraphernalia (long socks, short skirts, pigtails or bunches), the semi-clad teenagers pictured in fashion magazines.

Where these ideas and associations come from is harder to pin down; each of them has long and different histories, and is reflected differently in the law, in religion, in literature, paintings, advertisements, the media and, of course, in personal experience. It is usually impossible to pick out a single source for these ideas; rather, the point is that ideas of innocence are central to how childhood is understood in all aspects of life, whether in art and literature or in the daily practices of family life.

Figure 1 John Everett Millais (1829–1896) *Cherry Ripe*, 1879 – an image of quintessential child innocence which was immensely popular and much reproduced as a print in the late nineteenth and early twentieth centuries

Innocence is valued as a sign that children are uncontaminated and have not yet come into contact with sexuality, the market, money, capitalism or politics. Accordingly, it requires adult protection, although perceptions of the extent of children's incapacity, and of what children should not be allowed to do as a result, vary considerably across time and place. Innocence is also valued for what it reveals about adults. A belief in childhood innocence not only suggests a belief in innocence as an innate quality possessed by children, but also acts as a form of redemption for adults and a way in which they can reconnect with what they have forever lost. In his poem *Ode: Intimations of Immortality from Recollections of Early Childhood*, William Wordsworth (1770–1850) describes the child in near-ecstatic terms:

> But trailing clouds of glory do we come
> From God, who is our home:
> Heaven lies about us in our infancy!

(Wordsworth, 1939 [1807])

Wordsworth, like other Romantic poets and painters of the late eighteenth and early nineteenth centuries, stressed the magical or utopian state that children inhabit. He portrayed children as instinctual, closer to nature, living in the moment and imaginative in a way that rational, jaded or cynical adults see as impossible or unreal. This world is necessarily and forever lost to adults but, it is suggested, through children and by celebrating and protecting children's innocence, adults can rediscover a sense of wonder and recapture joy.

Activity 2   Reading A
Allow about 40 minutes

In Reading A at the end of this chapter, Marina Warner discusses many different ideas that inform understandings of childhood innocence. Read 'Little angels, little devils: keeping childhood innocent' and then summarise the main features of five or more ideas that inform our understanding of childhood innocence.

Comment

Warner identifies a number of different ways in which adults conceptualise children as innocent, including the following.

- **Children are 'naturally' innocent.** Children are naturally innocent, pure and virtuous. They are uncontaminated by the adult world of corruption that exists beyond their immediate experience and poses an ever-present danger to their young minds and bodies.
- **Children are blank slates.** Children are innocent because they are blank slates. Like Kaspar Hauser, they have no knowledge, no experience and no wickedness or indeed any sense that others might wish them harm.

The above fac-simile is taken from one of the earliest signatures of Caspar Hauser, after his arrival at Nuremberg.

Figure 2 Kaspar Hauser (approximately 1812–1833) was a young German boy who claimed to have grown up in isolation in a darkened room; he was seen by many at the time to embody children's natural innocence

- **Children are agents of redemption.** Children's innocence is redemptive. Children, as seen in characters such as Peter Pan, the boy who never grew up, will always have the innocence, the lack of cynicism and childish wonder that adults have discarded.

- **Childhood is the basis of adult identity (psycho-analytical understandings of the child).** Psychoanalytical theories emphasise the links between the child and the adult. Childhood is the key to an adult's identity. The child's experiences shape the adult psyche. Any psychological injury done to a child will lead to a damaged adult.

- **Children exist in a separate state.** Children are innocent because they are outside society. They have no knowledge of life, or of social organisation. They exist in a special uncorrupted state, separate from the adult world.

- **Children should not be consumers.** Commonly, children's innocence is seen as being lost when they enter the economic marketplace as consumers, being bought or 'pestering' their parents to buy them goods aimed specifically at a child market.

Warner's article briefly mentions all these ways of looking at childhood innocence and, of course, many of these ideas are linked and interrelated at particular moments. You may well be able to think of several more and you may not agree with the ones she has emphasised. However, she is undoubtedly right to point to the tensions and unease that ideas about children's innocence raise, as well as their prevalence in contemporary culture.

2.1 Sheltered innocence

As Activity 1 and Reading A have suggested, it is very hard to untangle the various meanings and connotations of 'innocence'. One theme which does emerge, however, is the changing role of children in the marketplace, as consumers of goods and services, as well as active participants in the world of media technologies – a participation which can lead to clashes with adult authority. Cultural historian Gary Cross (2004) identifies 'sheltered innocence' as a central ideal of contemporary childhoods. Sheltered innocence, Cross argues, reflects the Victorian belief that childhood was a precious time in children's lives and the profound shift in adult–child relationships that occurred during the nineteenth century. 'Far from the workplace, in the warmth of the domestic circle, the child would become the parents' handiwork, chiseled into a secure and unique individual, free from the premature influences of the market' (Cross, 2004, p. 23). It was only in the nineteenth century, Cross claims, that modern understandings of childhood as a separate, protected state could become a reality, at least for some children, and the process of what Viviana Zelizer (1985, p. 11) has called the 'sacralization' of childhood began. During this period, in some sections of the minority world, the value of children gradually shifted from the economic to the emotional; children who were once economically valuable became emotionally priceless. No longer required to bring home a wage to contribute to the family, their perceived innocence was part of the currency that they brought to the adult–child relationship. Cross emphasises the variety of factors which caused this shift in perceptions of children and discusses the relationship between the ideological and the economic. He shows how adults' emotional investment in children, and belief in keeping them innocent and distanced from adult roles and responsibilities, must be understood in the context of the emergence of industrial capitalism, growing affluence, and the collective provision of education, health and welfare.

In contemporary settings, adults' beliefs in sheltered innocence can be seen in the way that parents try to exclude malign influences from their children's lives. This might involve not allowing children to walk to school on their own due to fears of accidents or abduction. It might involve restricting television viewing or computer game playing, only allowing children to watch non-commercial TV channels or DVDs, avoiding certain brands or choosing only particular toys so that girls are not allowed to play with Barbie dolls and boys are forbidden to play with guns. Some of these practices to protect childhood innocence evoke what has been described as an adult nostalgia for a lost golden age of childhood innocence. In this unspecified and ever-shifting past children were free to play in a simple and unburdened world and not exposed through the media to the oppressive and dangerous excesses of adult culture. As Affrica Taylor (2010) notes, people often look back with amusement on their parents' media-related anxieties, whilst being convinced that their own concerns about internet or violent video games respond to real and pressing issues. We explore these issues in more detail in Chapter 5. It is also worth noting that such practices reflect adults' views and understandings of what is appropriate for children rather than children's own ideas. Children may be more ambivalent about being excluded from aspects of the adult world or from the cultural (commercial) worlds of their peers, and may find ways to subvert such restrictions. Indeed, studies of children's own cultural practices often reveal a knowingness and self-awareness at odds with adults' understandings of children's guilelessness. Children are quite capable of playing on adults' perceptions of innocence when it suits them, as is explored below.

Recent scholarship, however, has challenged the idea that childhood innocence is diametrically opposed to consumer culture. In fact, as Cross and others argue, childhood innocence has been increasingly defined and experienced through consumer culture, both positively and negatively. Using US advertisements from the nineteenth and early twentieth centuries as examples, Cross argues that emphasis gradually shifted from the pure to the 'cute'. Cuteness was a more vital, exuberant, robust notion of innocence, celebrating children as naturally 'impish', demanding, spontaneous, fun-loving and adventurous. All these were qualities that incited spending whilst simultaneously reassuring parents that this would not spoil children, but merely satisfy their entirely natural desires, longings and curiosity. Parents were free to recover their own lost worlds of wonder through what Cross refers to as the 'wondrous innocence' of their children's encounter with commercial novelty, vicariously enjoying their offspring's carefree play. Such ideas are still evolving today as traditional and newer holidays such as Christmas, Easter and Halloween have become increasingly focused around the child and consumption, involving gift giving or novel experiences. Yet the relation between innocence and consumer culture has ambivalent consequences. The cycle of consumption never stops and Cross argues that there is constant incitement to buy more and more in a futile quest to reproduce 'the first time' – the child's gasp of delight at desires wholly fulfilled.

Trying to protect children's innocence may seem like no bad thing – it shows love and an attempt to uphold cherished cultural ideals. But protecting innocence is not always possible and when life delivers experiences that cannot be controlled, such as bereavement, illness or disability, parents often experience guilt at their failure to shield children in the way some understandings of 'sheltered' innocence demand. Furthermore, while protecting a child's sheltered innocence keeps children away from aspects of the adult world of sexuality, work or commerce, it is highly dependent on having the resources to provide a certain type of childhood. Alison Pugh's (2009) US-based research into families' responses to consumer culture offers some powerful examples of how circumstances shape parents' abilities to protect their children's innocence. The low-income, mostly African American or Latino, parents in her study lived in neighbourhoods where 'danger was palpable' (Pugh, 2009, p. 144); the multiple hazards they confronted on a daily basis ranged from fast-moving traffic, drug dealing and associated gun crime, gangs and pimps, to fly-tipping and discarded needles. In this context, providing items like Game Boy or Nintendo that would keep children happily entertained at home was an act of love and care for their safety as well as a way of protecting certain aspects of their innocence. Nevertheless, these choices have been heavily criticised and condemned as poor parenting practices which contribute to childhood obesity and ill-health.

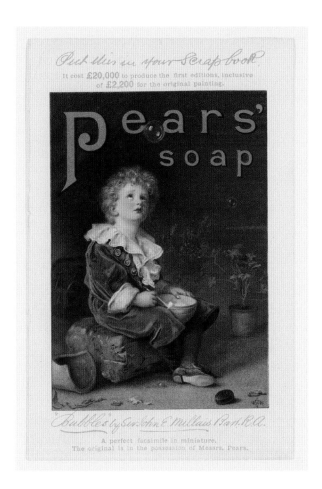

Figure 3   Originally an 1886 painting by Sir John Everett Millais (1829–1896), of his grandson, this picture was bought by Thomas J. Barratt of the A. & F. Pears Soap company and turned into one of the most successful marketing images of all time – now usually referred to as 'Bubbles'. The child's innocence here is equated with physical cleanliness and purity, and is one of the most obvious examples of how a child's innocence is commodified and used to sell products

There is also an argument that children are best protected by empowering them through knowledge, not through relying on their innocence. If children know about the world and how to avoid particular pitfalls, this may be more advantageous to them than shielding them from any unpleasantness or difficulty. Yet those who argue that children should be taught about, for example, sex through sex education at school or should learn about death or natural disasters, often face accusations that they are encroaching on childhood innocence, telling children things that they do not need to know as yet and do not have the experience to cope with. Jenny Kitzinger has suggested that 'the twin concepts of innocence and ignorance are vehicles for adult double standards: a child is ignorant if she doesn't know what adults want her to know, but innocent if she doesn't know what adults don't want her to know' (Kitzinger, 1990, p. 169).

Children who have 'fallen' from the state of innocence, because they have committed crimes or because they have sexual knowledge, experience or feelings, even as a result of abuse, may be made more vulnerable by the emphasis on sheltering the innocent and denied protection and care as a result. Joanne Faulkner argues, 'The unpalatable truth is that the value of a child's innocence depends upon their capacity to be protected. Children born to conditions of poverty and abuse, children who need to work – in short, children deprived of the privilege that would confer innocence upon them – unsettle the parameters of our understanding … We deem underprivileged children threats to childhood innocence more generally, as bad seeds from whom we need to quarantine our own, more fortunate children' (Faulkner, 2011, p. 6). In his study of care provision in Ireland in the 1970s, Harry Ferguson claims that children entering care due to parental cruelty were blamed, using the ideology of a particular kind of Catholicism, for having had their childhood innocence 'contaminated'. 'They were treated as the moral dirt of a social order determined to prove its purity and subjected to ethnic cleansing' (Ferguson, 2007, p. 123).

Summary of Section 2

Ideas about innocence are so intricately linked to ideas of childhood that innocence is often seen as an inherent and necessary feature of childhood.

Ideas about children's innocence are complex and sometimes contradictory. It can be seen as a lack of knowledge, particularly of sex and violence; a lack of experience of the adult world, especially in relation to issues such as sex, money, work, grief or hatred; as lack of evil or sin; as synonymous with purity and virtue; or related to lack of knowledge of economics and consumerism.

There are contested ideas about how best to protect children: children may not always be protected by relying on their innocence; it can be argued that empowering children through knowledge offers better protection.

3   Images of childhood innocence

One way to examine different ideas of childhood innocence is by looking at images of children from different periods of history in paintings, on television or in advertisements. Images can indicate how concepts and ideals of childhood have changed over time. For example, reproduced below are two oil paintings of children. The first (Figure 4) was painted in 1756 by English portraitist, Thomas Gainsborough, and is called *The Painter's Daughters Chasing a Butterfly*. The second (Figure 5), by American artist John Singer Sargent, is called *Garden Study of the Vickers Children*, from 1884.

Figure 4   Thomas Gainsborough (1727–1788), *The Painter's Daughters Chasing a Butterfly*, 1756

In the Gainsborough painting, the children are presented in a woodland setting, as children of nature, following a butterfly (a symbol of ephemerality and frivolity). Nature here is the teacher, not adults or parents, and the children's innocence and natural goodness are suggested by the harmony between them and in the way the older one appears to be looking after the other. Yet there are also hints of danger

Figure 5 John Singer Sargent (1856–1925), *Garden Study of the Vickers Children*, 1884

and difficulty in the rather stormy sky and the darker colours of the landscape surrounding them. While the innocent child in nature is idealised and celebrated, there is also the implication that childhood has to come to an end and the innocence will be lost. The butterfly is a symbol of the impermanence of childhood, and the picture suggests that innocence inevitably gives way to experience, making this image an elegy to childhood as much as a celebration.

The second painting, by Sargent, was produced nearly 130 years later and shows a rather different image of innocent children. Although this is called 'a garden scene' and the children are outdoors, the space seems in some way enclosed. The children are watering the exotic, expensive flowers, one of which is in a pot; the natural world appears constrained and domesticated. The children's neatness suggests good behaviour and order instead of the freedom implied in the Gainsborough painting. There are strict gender roles in this painting: the boy looks directly at the viewers, engaging their attention, while the girl looks down, focusing on the task. However, this is not simply the sentimentalised vision of childhood often associated with this era. Conventionally, whiteness and lilies or other flowers often signify innocence, sexual purity and chastity, qualities which also do not last forever. Here, although the children are still young, the white lilies are already in full bloom and almost overpower the children in the picture, conveying a more ambiguous message about the loss of childhood and of innocence.

Images are rarely simple, and you will have your own readings of and responses to the paintings, which may differ from the commentary we offer here. However, as the rest of this section will show, almost all images of children and childhood carry some commentary on their innocence.

Activity 3   Reading B

The interconnections between representations of children and ideas of innocence are explored in more detail in the second reading associated with this chapter. Turn now to Reading B, 'Pictures of innocence', by Anne Higonnet. Read it through and make notes in response to the following questions:

- Why does Higonnet claim that there is a special relationship between images of childhood and ideals of childhood innocence?
- Why does she claim that images can be dangerous?

Comment

Higonnet argues that, as an 'invented cultural ideal', innocence required representation, and that the visual was particularly powerful because 'the immediate visibility of pictures has always had a privileged ability to shape our understanding of our bodies, our physical selves'. Childhood innocence was 'considered an attribute of the child's body'. In Activity 1 in this chapter, you may have already noted how hard it is to think of innocence without conjuring up particular images, whether oil paintings, contemporary photographs or snapshots of children you know. Pictures – which Higonnet suggests we should think of as 'visual fictions' – have come to define how we understand childhood innocence and our sense that childhood and innocence are naturally linked. She goes on to claim that, recently, images of the innocent child have been replaced by those of the 'knowing child', and that modern audiences view images of children very differently. (Activity 5 will explore this further.)

Absolute and rigid ideals are rarely sustainable, and this has proved to be the case with images of childhood innocence. While the poets and painters of the late eighteenth-century Romantic era can be seen as celebrating the redemptive qualities of the child, contemporary images are viewed with more suspicion and concern, perhaps reflecting changes in childhood in minority-world societies. In particular, pictures of naked children on public display cause great anxiety, with the motives of both the photographer and the viewer being called into question. In Higonnet's analysis, modern images of children have come to challenge Romantic ideals of innocence and unsettle established notions of childhood, such that it becomes impossible to look at them without thinking about issues of abuse and the sexualised child.

Like Gary Cross mentioned above, Higonnet draws attention to the 'commodification' of innocence; and elsewhere in her book (Higonnet, 1998) she shows how images of the innocent child have been used to market a whole range of products. However, while the market certainly has had important impacts on how childhood innocence is conceptualised, images of children in advertisements, television and film are not always employed to sell a product. They are also used widely in charity campaigns to comment on the concept of childhood and on the gap between the ideal and lived experience of many children.

Barnardo's is a leading children's charity based in the UK which supports and promotes the well-being of disadvantaged children. In October 1999, Barnardo's launched an advertising campaign in newspapers and magazines designed to raise awareness of their work with young people. Children were portrayed in a variety of 'adult' situations: homelessness, drug and alcohol abuse, prostitution, suicide and prison. Although such advertisements are more common now, this set of images was one of the first to use such shock tactics to raise money and to confront threats to childhood innocence so directly.

Activity 4 Damaged children

Allow about 20 minutes

Figure 6 and Figure 7 are taken from the Barnardo's advertising campaign discussed above. Look at the advertisements and complete the following tasks:

*   Make a note of your responses to each advertisement. Include initial reactions and thoughts that may occur to you when you have had a little time to reflect upon the image.

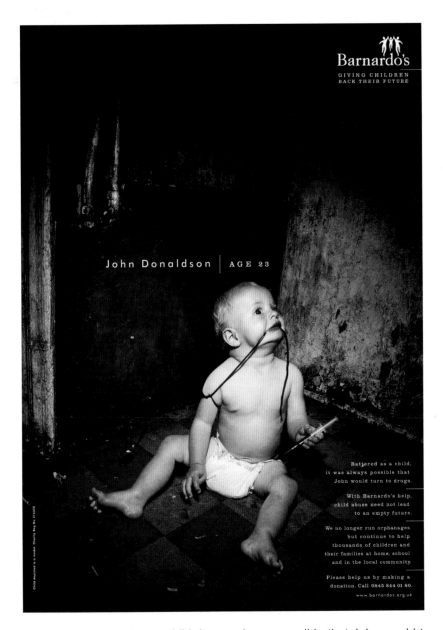

Figure 6 'Battered as a child, it was always possible that John would turn to drugs. With Barnardo's help, child abuse need not lead to an empty future'

- Try to suggest some reasons for your responses.

Comment

Your responses to the advertisements may have included initial feelings of shock and revulsion. The Barnardo's advertising campaign, particularly

Figure 7 'Neglected as a child, it was always possible Kim would be an easy victim for pimps. With Barnardo's help, an unhappy childhood need not mean an empty future'

the image of a baby injecting drugs, aroused a great deal of controversy. The Advertising Standards Authority received numerous complaints from individuals and organisations that considered the advertisement to be shocking and offensive. In the face of public protest Barnardo's replaced the image with one of a happier baby without the syringe and tourniquet.

But why is the image such a shocking one? It could be argued that the power of the image lies in the fact that it deliberately and self-consciously transgresses boundaries. While it is generally accepted that adults have knowledge of the world of drug use, it is usually assumed that children should be protected from such knowledge. To see a baby who is not only exposed to the reality of drug use but actually participating in it, is a violation of generally held sensibilities about appropriate knowledge and behaviour. Yet all drug users were, of course, once babies and this is the point that the Barnardo's advertisement makes very forcefully; that children's environment and experiences have a bearing on their adult life. From the perspective of the charity, the link between abused childhood and troubled adulthood calls for intervention and change summarised in the Barnardo's logo, 'Giving children back their future'. The Barnardo's advertisements suggest several things: that children deserve to have a future and that they represent the future; that childhood should be a time of innocence when children are protected from harmful knowledge about drugs and sex; that these children exist in a cycle of abuse, which suggests that damaged children lead to damaged adults who may, in turn, damage their own children.

The age issue here is crucial. One of the reasons that these images are so effective is the contrast between the innocent child and the damaged adult that the child might become. It is interesting therefore to consider the effects these images might have if the children were to be replaced by adolescents, so that instead of a baby with a tourniquet and a syringe, there was a picture of a 16 year old. Although legally still a child, an adolescent is less likely to be constructed as innocent, and adolescence is not always constructed as a period of innocence – indeed it could be characterised as a period of 'guilty knowledge' of sex, drugs and rebellion. Small children (in this case, a two year old and a six year old) are vulnerable, needing adult protection, and are innocent of the consequences of their actions. A two year old would not knowingly inject heroin. Teenagers, however, are more problematic: they might choose to take heroin, and a picture of a teenager with a needle in their arm may well elicit disgust and fear rather than sympathy. Innocence is not, therefore, a universal quality of childhood but one which is assigned on the basis of adult understandings.

Summary of Section 3

It is through images of children that ideals of innocence are most obviously displayed.

Images can indicate how ideas about childhood have changed over time.

Innocence has been 'commodified' and used to sell a variety of goods and services for well over a hundred years.

Some images, such as those made for the charity Barnardo's, interrogate the gap between ideals and reality for many children, and stress the catastrophic effects of knowledge and experience on children.

4 Childhood and sexuality

So far this chapter has looked generally at innocence, but it is clear from all the discussions that ideas (and fears) about sexuality are never far away from any analysis of innocence. This section will explore in more detail the relationships between childhood, sexuality and innocence. It will focus on two great twentieth-century thinkers, Sigmund Freud (1856–1939) and Michel Foucault (1926–1984), whose views have had a significant impact on how childhood sexuality is viewed and understood; it is impossible to discuss children and sex without taking into account their theoretical frameworks. Freud, the originator of psychoanalysis, popularised the notion of the innately sexual child along with concepts such as the Oedipus complex, the death wish and penis envy, which have become well known, even among those who have not read his work. Foucault was a French philosopher whose work is extremely influential in the social sciences and beyond because it highlights the issue of power in relation to sexuality.

4.1 Sigmund Freud

Freud understood sexuality as part of the developmental process and claimed that children had sexual natures and sexual drives. Writing at the end of the nineteenth and into the early twentieth century, Freud rejected the notion of the child as an asexual being without sexual feelings or motivations. He claimed that far from being a time of asexual innocence, early childhood was a time of sexual conflict, repression and tension. He saw childhood activities such as thumb sucking or genital manipulation as sexual responses and as part of a child's growing sexual nature. In 1905 he published 'Three essays on the theory of sexuality' which looked broadly at issues of sexuality and which sought to show the links between early childhood experiences and adult behaviour and personality. In the second essay, 'Infantile sexuality', he argued that sexual feelings were present in the child from the moment of birth and rejected the idea held by his contemporaries that sexual experiences and sexual feelings began only at puberty. He wrote:

> One feature of the popular view of the sexual instinct is that it is absent in childhood and only awakens in the period of life described as puberty. This, however, is not merely a simple error but one that has had grave consequences, for it is mainly to this idea that we owe our present ignorance of the fundamental conditions of sexual life. ... So far as I know, not a single author has clearly recognized the regular existence of a sexual instinct in childhood; and in the writings that have become so numerous on the development of children, the chapter on 'Sexual Development' is as a rule omitted.
>
> (Freud, 1953 [1905], p. 173)

In this essay, Freud went on to argue that everyone, from birth onwards, was driven by sexual or bodily pleasure, even though the instinctual efforts made by infants and young children to gain pleasure were frequently punished and thwarted by parental and social control. Children therefore experienced their childhoods as a series of conflicts that had to be dealt with and overcome. In other work, Freud showed how unresolved conflicts at various stages of sexual development could lead to conditions such as mental illness or hysteria in adult life; but he also fundamentally challenged the idea that there is any such thing as a 'normal' sexuality (Freud, 1953 [1913]).

Freud labelled the earliest stage of infant development the oral one, in which the infant sought release and obtained his or her pleasure through sucking. The anal stage followed this, during which pleasure was linked to release through defecation. Afterwards the young child developed an interest in his or her genitals and acknowledged them as a source of pleasure, understood by Freud as the phallic stage of development. Furthermore, he claimed that during the phallic stage of development (occurring around the age of five), male children went through a particular phase of psychosexual development characterised by the Oedipal conflict. This occurred when the boy began to be

Figure 8 The work of Sigmund Freud (1856–1939) still challenges conventional views on child sexuality

jealous of his father as his mother's sexual partner, desiring the exclusive love of his mother and unconsciously wishing for his father's death. This, however, also aroused in the boy the fear of the father's anger, and the fantasy of castration by the father as punishment for his desires: a fear Freud called castration anxiety. The Oedipus complex was usually resolved by the child internalising the father's rules, repressing both attraction for the opposite-sex parent and hatred of the same-sex parent and understanding that he could not sexually possess his mother and should turn his attention towards other objects of desire. He then entered a 'latency' period when sexual motivations became less obvious and would not become as significant again until puberty, when bodily development and genital changes occurred.

Freud's views were controversial when first published and have been continuously debated ever since. Some claim that Freud saw human sexuality as inherent and biological, driven by instincts that paralleled the animal world and that could be found in all humans wherever they lived. Anthropologists have then argued that this is not the case, that there is no evidence for Oedipal conflicts (for example) in societies with very different child–parent relationships, and studies of cross-cultural child-rearing have not shown evidence of the Freudian developmental stages (Montgomery, 2009). Most social scientists now accept that far from being 'natural', sex is a social behaviour that only makes sense to people within a specific context; but many argue that the complexity and richness of Freud's work supports this view rather than a reductive notion of universal, natural, sexuality. In relation to children and sex, sociologist Stevi Jackson has argued: 'Our feelings about children and sex are not a natural response to people of a particular age but result from the way childhood is defined within our society' (Jackson, 1982, p. 22). Attitudes towards, for example, children's masturbation depend on the gender of the child, and on class, epoch and culture, and show the difficulties of talking about children's expression of sexuality as if this were a biological fact. Is a child who gains some sort of pleasure from putting their hands between their legs indulging in a sexual act or one of bodily self-exploration? Or both? The answer to this question depends on adult perspectives: what people understand and experience as sexual behaviour may be different in different societies. It is not possible therefore to make universal statements about the nature of children's sexual awareness or sexual behaviour as every society draws on different (and often contested) discourses concerning appropriate expressions of children's sexuality and behaviour.

4.2   Michel Foucault

The Freudian notion of the innately sexual child was heavily critiqued by Michel Foucault, a French philosopher and historian, whose work on power and knowledge has had a wide influence across the social sciences. Foucault's writings on sexuality are among his best known, but he also wrote extensively on medicine, the prison system and psychiatry. Foucault argued that ideas about sexuality are cultural and historical constructs, which therefore change over time and place. He understood sexuality as the product of particular ways of speaking and thinking which he referred to as discourses. He argued that discourses about sexuality are embedded in the processes and practices of social institutions (such as the law or the church or the education system). He claimed that they do not describe or capture in language a pre-existing reality, but instead constitute that reality. They establish horizons for thinking, interpreting and acting that make it more difficult to frame alternatives; they define some things as 'true' or certain, and others as false. In this respect they are always articulated within power relations.

Figure 9 Michel Foucault (1926–1984), along with Freud, was one of the key thinkers of the twentieth century

In *The History of Sexuality* (1976), Foucault examines the sexuality of children as a key feature in the development of educational provision and social policy in western Europe. He saw schools as sites in which large numbers of young people interact and where their sexual conduct could therefore become a matter for surveillance and intervention. Foucault shows how schooling in the eighteenth and nineteenth centuries was preoccupied with sex, as displayed in the architectural layout of the buildings, disciplinary procedures and organisational structures. Here, the sexuality of children was addressed directly: 'the internal discourse of the institution – the one it employed to address itself, and which circulated among those that made it function – was largely based on the assumption that this sexuality existed, that it was precocious, active and ever present' (Foucault, 1976, p. 28).

Foucault throws down a challenge to those who suggest that in the past, sex was 'repressed' and not spoken of, or that children were thought of as asexual:

> It would be less than exact to say that the pedagogical institution has imposed a ponderous silence on the sex of children and adolescents. On the contrary, since the eighteenth century it has multiplied the forms of discourse on the subject; it has established various points of implantation for sex; it has coded contents and

qualified speakers. ... The sex of children and adolescents has become, since the eighteenth century, an important area of contention around which innumerable institutional devices and discursive strategies have been deployed.

(Foucault, 1976, pp. 29–30)

Foucault suggests that the sexual activity of schoolboys, once labelled and categorised, was created as a public problem requiring vigilance, moral guidance and medical intervention. On the grounds that sexuality was a thing to be known and spoken about in the 'public interest', there was a proliferation of discourses around sex in fields such as religion, medicine and criminal justice, through which there emerged a number of sexual categories such as the 'hysterical woman', the 'homosexual', the 'masturbating child' and the sex worker. From this perspective, the sexual conduct of a population becomes an object of classification, administration and regulation. Foucault goes on to argue that in the modern era, discourses of sexuality offer a complex means of policing the person and have ambivalent effects. Sexual categories such as 'the homosexual' can be seen as actively generated by discourses of sexuality, and as defining individuals by their sexual activity rather than by any other aspect of their lives. Once created, however, they can then become sexual *identities*, the basis for political organising and demanding rights, such as in lesbian and gay liberation movements of the 1960s. In other words, we should not see discourses of sexuality as purely oppressive or negative. Instead of debating whether children and young people are 'really' sexual, or thinking of sexuality as a 'forbidden' topic, we should consider how children and young people's sexuality is in fact forever being talked about, and focus on questions of who speaks about it, within which institutions and according to what kind of 'rules'.

Summary of Section 4

Children's lack of sexual experience is central to adult constructions of them as innocent, although whether they are, in reality, asexual has been much debated.

Freud argued that all children are inherently sexual, although his views are still much contested.

Foucault suggested that ideas about sexuality are created through discourses – particular ways of thinking, speaking and categorising sex.

Foucault argued that, beginning in the eighteenth century, modern systems of government did not repress sexuality (as is often claimed) but developed new ways of talking about sex, categorising sexual activity and defining people in terms of their sexual identity. All of these developments produce new forms of control and regulation, but also new identities and possibilities for action.

5 Policing children's innocence

Associating childhood innocence with sexual ignorance becomes a rationale for keeping sex away from children. On some levels, protection is obviously beneficial. There are, and always have been, a small number of adults who are sexually attracted to children and children may not have the power or knowledge to resist them. Yet adult strategies to keep children sexually innocent walk a line between protection and control – a theme that runs through many discussions of children's innocence. Stevi Jackson and Sue Scott (2004) argue:

> Children and sex are seen as antithetical, both being defined as special and bracketed from the 'real' world. Thus there is little focus on becoming sexual as a process; rather it is seen as a matter of leaping a chasm between 'innocence' and 'knowledge'.

> (Jackson and Scott, 2004, p. 235)

Egan and Hawkes (2008) point to the historical precedence of endeavours to regulate childhood sexuality for the protection of all children. They claim that efforts to manage and control children's sexuality produce the paradoxical logic of assuming the child as asexual or innocent while introducing strategies for the regulation of premature expressions of sexual knowingness. They identify the contradictory configuration of childhood as a state of fragile purity, ever susceptible to contamination by the outside world, as an enduring theme in the history of childhood since the nineteenth century.

However, attempts to prevent children from learning about sex are rarely wholly successful, as children are often more curious and knowing about sex than adults admit. There has been a limited amount of research into how children think about sex – not surprising given the sensibilities involved – but there has been some work looking at how families deal with sexuality in the media and how ideas about childhood innocence are used and negotiated by both parents and children. In their study of young people, sex and the media, David Buckingham and Sara Bragg (2004) explored how these ideas were played out in daily domestic life. In reply to questions about sexual activity on the TV, children and parents gave the following responses:

(Girl, 10)   'They keep being stupid about things like that [kissing on TV], I'm like "mum and dad, it's not that rude. I mean, get a grip, it's not that rude!" [laughs]' (Buckingham and Bragg, 2004, p. 191).

(Girl, 17)   'some of the things that you'd laugh at, your parents go "Why do you know about that?"... I would rather leave them with a nice little mental image of me being twelve, if that is what they want' (p. 193).

(Boy, 14)   'on They Think It's All Over [a television quiz show] or something, when they say something, I'll laugh and my mum just looks at me thinking like "oh, he knows what that means." ... Sometimes when I watch it upstairs with my brother, I laugh then, but when I'm downstairs I try to not laugh at some of the things which I shouldn't really know' (p. 193).

(Girl, 12)   'But sometimes I'll be watching something downstairs on the TV with me mum and it might have like a bit of sex in it and my mum and me just have a giggle about it but if me dad's there he'll go "huh, huh" [throat clearing noise] like that and just turn over (…) with me and my mum it's different because like we're both girls and we just have a laugh about it but when it's just like me and my dad we're just like – no way. I can't laugh at anything' (p. 194)

(Father, talking about his son as a toddler)

'He used to come in here and watch pretty girls on the telly didn't he? And then you weren't supposed to watch him watching. One ... advert, he'd be right up the telly [mimes tongue hanging out] .... Yeah, real pretty girl on. And then, you know, he'd notice that he ... that he likes pretty girls and then he'd go, "my thing keeps standing up". I said "Oh don't worry about it"' (p. 204).

In this research, younger children often rejected being positioned as innocent, claiming instead to be in the more desirable position of 'knower', like the ten-year-old girl in the first quote. Teenagers, however, claimed that in front of their parents they performed innocence, by suppressing indications of the 'true' state of their knowledge, such as the sources of humour in TV ribaldry, as they believed it was expected of them. This also depended on the gender of their parent, as the 12-year-old girl quoted above suggests. For their part, parents seemed to find it hard to relate to their daughters as sexual beings. Boys' sexuality seemed easier to talk about, even if it was interpreted from an adult perspective, as in the case of the father of the toddler who discusses his son's excitement through the lens of an adult heterosexual male. What each of these quotes suggests is how ideas about innocence and appropriate knowledge about sexuality come into play, sometimes consciously manipulated in response to particular situations by different family members, at different times.

5.1   The sexualisation debate

Discussing children's sexuality is fraught with difficulties and ambivalence. This is most visible in analyses of teenage girls' sexuality, which problematise ideas about sexual purity and challenge the precarious boundary between a charming, flirtatious and innocent child and a sexualised, alluring adolescent:

As a child, sexuality is forbidden to her, and it is that very ignorance that makes her the most perfect object of men's desire, the inexperienced woman. Thus the fascinating exchange between knowledge and ignorance reaches beyond the boundary between

girl and woman and towards the forbidden attraction of innocence
itself.

(Holland, 1992, pp. 137–8)

In Holland's argument, it is the boundary between sexual innocence and
sexual knowledge that is so titillating and which eroticises girls. This is a
difficult and problematic area to deal with as the issue of sexual abuse
is not far from the surface. The issue is evident in the unease many
people now feel when looking at Lewis Carroll's suggestive and
provocative, and sometimes semi-naked, pictures of young girls
(photographed around 1859), including Alice Liddell (his model for
Alice in Wonderland) and Evelyn Hatch, which are reproduced as part
of Activity 5 below. We cannot know the exact nature of the
relationship between Carroll and the girls who posed for him, so why
are they so unsettling?

Activity 5   Erotic or innocent?

Allow about 10 minutes

Examine the photographs below (Figure 10 and Figure 11). Then write
short notes in answer to the following questions:

- Do you think that the girls in these pictures are eroticised?
- What influences your answer? Does it relate to anything in their
  clothes, posture and the way they look at the camera? Or is it
  something about the spectator? It may well be worth looking again at
  Marina Warner's and Anne Higonnet's comments, in Readings A
  and B respectively, about Carroll's photographs.

Figure 10   Evelyn Hatch

Figure 11 Alice Liddell

Comment

In Carroll's picture of Alice Liddell as an urchin, she is posed in a suggestive manner. Her shoulders are bare and her head is tilted coquettishly to one side. Although in no way pornographic, it is suggestive of sexual knowledge and certainly the potential to see this as a seductive image is there. Evelyn Hatch, in the first photograph, is photographed naked and positioned as an adult woman, reclining alluringly on what could be a bed or a floor. She looks straight at the camera with no hint of demureness or reticence. Again, there is nothing intrinsically pornographic in her pose but a naked child displayed in this way disturbs many. The picture is ambiguous and any interpretation of it will depend on your own views of what you consider seductive and your ideas about children's sexuality and adults' portrayal of that.

How can we make sense of these issues? One possibility is that the key to understanding childhood innocence lies in the eye of the beholder. You may recall the point in Marina Warner's article extracted in Reading A, where she says 'It's we who have lost innocent eyes', and she notes that Lewis Carroll's friends were undisturbed by his semi-naked images of their children. According to this view, what adults view as innocent says very much more about adults than it reveals about childhood. All these pictures are ambiguous and it could be claimed that in all of them the girls are eroticised. The question is, however, by whom: the photographer or the viewer?

In 1937, a magazine co-edited by the novelist Graham Greene was prosecuted for libel and forced to close down after it published an article he had written entitled 'Sex and Shirley Temple?'. Shirley Temple (Figure 12) was a dimpled, golden-haired child actor, shown here aged about nine years old. Greene speculated about whether the film studio she worked for deliberately promoted her erotic appeal to 'middle aged men and clergymen'. He was subsequently sued for damages and denounced in court as having committed a 'gross outrage' – although such a suggestion is barely even surprising today.

Figure 12   Shirley Temple was a child star of the 1930s and 1940s, known for her cuteness and dimples. She played roles such as a prostitute, exotic dancer and 'sweetheart' in films that replayed 'adult' narratives with child-only casts

In the twenty-first century, debates about the so-called 'sexualisation and commercialisation of childhood' have intensified and received significant policy as well as media attention, bringing together concerns about the apparent intrusion of the market into children's lives and about the behaviour and appearance of girls in particular (Kehily, 2010). Retailers, television, magazines and the internet have all been cited as guilty parties in the proliferation of sexual material and its presence in the everyday experience of the child. Girls are thought to be at special risk: in 2007 the conservative newspaper the *Daily Telegraph*, for example, ran a story headlined 'The generation of "damaged" girls' (Womack, 2007) which claimed that 'old-fashioned frilly frocks' for girls had been replaced by 'mini skirts, plunging necklines and sequined crop tops' and suggested that over-sexualised clothing promoted girls' need for affection in ways that could lead to eating disorders, low self-esteem and depression.

Such reports link into wider concerns about childhood being 'in crisis' and claims that cultural change has produced a toxic cocktail that is damaging the social, emotional and cognitive development of children (Kehily, 2010). Writers such as Frank Furedi (2001) have suggested that parents have lost confidence in their abilities to raise their children, while Sue Palmer (2007), in an influential book *Toxic Childhood*, contends that technological change and an overemphasis on consumerism in the previous 25 years have had a detrimental impact on modern life. In what many have seen as a melodramatic and sensationalised account, she asserts that children have come to associate happiness with the 'stuff' of consumer culture, such that wanting things, buying things and having things bought for them have all acquired misplaced prominence in their lives, distorting notions of what happiness really is and how it can be achieved. In a (typically judgemental) aside, she remarks that 'when children dressed like dockside tarts throng the streets, it's hardly surprising that paedophilia thrives' (Palmer, 2007, p. 275).

Governments of different political persuasions here in the UK and abroad, have commissioned reports on sexualisation and on children's engagement with the commercial world more generally. The Labour government (1997–2010) commissioned a review on children and new technology (Byron, 2008), and a major independent assessment of the impact of the commercial world on children's well-being, chaired by David Buckingham (DCSF, 2009). The Home Office commissioned 'celebrity psychologist' Linda Papadopoulos to deliver a *Sexualisation of Young People Review* (Papadopoulos, 2010) and the Scottish Parliament also funded research (Buckingham et al., 2010). Soon after it came to power in 2010, the UK Coalition Government commissioned Reg Bailey, the Chief Executive of a Christian pro-family charity, the Mothers' Union, to produce a 'Review of the sexualisation and commercialisation of childhood'. His report, entitled *Letting Children be Children*, recommended regulatory measures to curb those suspected of encroaching on children's innocence: lads' magazines; retailers of sexualised clothing; makers of music videos; and advertisers (DfE, 2011).

The term 'sexualisation' can be used descriptively, to denote cultural shifts characterised by the 'mainstreaming' of sexual material in contemporary society (Attwood, 2009). More frequently, however, it is used in confused, negative and poorly evidenced ways. For instance, the UK Government's Department for Education defined it as 'the imposition of adult sexuality on to children and young people before they are capable of dealing with it, mentally, emotionally or physically' (DfE, 2012). This is normative, implicitly distinguishing between 'healthy', timely or 'appropriate' forms of sexuality and problematic ones. It asserts adult power and rests on an uncertain evidence basis about the 'effects' of contemporary culture on young people.

5.2   Parents' and young people's responses to the sexualisation debate

Despite the adult concern, very limited attention has been paid to what children actually do or how they respond to the 'sexualised' culture which is seen as so damaging to them. An interesting example is provided by looking at the popularity of the Playboy brand's extensive range of merchandise – make-up, jewellery, stationery, bed linen and more. All these objects bear its recognisable bunny logo and were, at one time, often available in children's sections of shops, catalogues and websites. The products became a particular target for campaigners against the sexualisation of childhood, with the charge that they amounted to 'corporate paedophilia' (Rush and La Nauze, 2006). When, in 2009, the Scottish Parliament funded research into 'sexualised goods' in response to these concerns, it was reported as 'going to war' with Playboy and 'bringing it to book' for its practices (Buckingham et al., 2010).

However, the researchers, talking to diverse groups of parents and young people (aged 12–14) around Scotland, were struck by some interesting contradictions in the way parents and children talked about and discussed Playboy. For instance, although Playboy merchandise sells well, hardly anyone in the research sample was prepared to admit (in a context of school interviews or focus groups) to buying the products any more. Yet young people often acknowledged an earlier emotional attachment to the bunny even while claiming it was 'too childish' for them now; or they displaced this on to younger siblings amongst whom they claimed it had continued currency. They described the products in derogatory terms such as 'tacky', 'mingin', 'tarty', 'chavvy' and 'neddy' (Buckingham et al., 2010, p. 63). Nonetheless, some were actually sporting examples of these goods even as they spoke. The authors describe how during a group interview with four friends, three girls loyally backpedalled on their denunciation of Playboy when the fourth pointed out that she herself was wearing a Playboy sweatshirt. According to the latter, who described herself as a 'sporty type' always dressed in 'trackies', her mother had also dropped her own principled objection to Playboy on the grounds that the item was at least pink, and thus a relief from the otherwise entirely blue wardrobe her daughter favoured.

This research also found evidence that parents were less concerned about sexualisation than the media and public debate suggest. If they did permit 'inappropriate' purchases, some parents claimed this was only after relentless nagging by children, or justified it by calling on 'common sense' notions about adolescence, such as 'rebellion against authority', 'getting it out of your system' and 'peer pressure'. However, many also suggested that their lack of concern or refusal to 'just say no' to sexualised products (as campaigners urge) was rooted in overall philosophies of 'good parenting' and 'healthy child development', according to which children need to shoulder some responsibilities in adolescence, as a rehearsal for the adult life into which they would soon emerge. Since in practice the sphere in which they could most conveniently do so was that of clothes and personal care, this meant that parents had consciously opted to allow children to make their own decisions about precisely the kinds of items often cited as agents of 'sexualisation'; as parents repeatedly told the researchers, 'there are worse things they could be doing' (Buckingham et al., 2010, p. 44).

Summary of Section 5

Adults define children as sexually innocent at the same time as introducing strategies for the regulation of sexual knowing.

Adults and children negotiate over constructions of innocence, especially in relation to sexuality; children may well know more than they tell their parents, and certainly claim to.

The sexuality of girls is often seen as particularly problematic and in need of regulation, although the eroticisation of innocence is by no means a recent issue.

What adults view as innocent can reveal more about adults than about childhood, and associations of innocence depend on the eye of the beholder.

There have been growing fears, expressed in the media and by campaigning groups, that children are becoming sexualised too early. Parents' concerns about this may be overstated, however, and children may well react differently than adults to these perceived threats.

6 Conclusion

This chapter has argued that innocence is a complex and controversial notion with different meanings and different values placed on particular kinds of innocence. Innocence features strongly in contemporary constructions of childhood and this chapter has looked at how linkages between childhood and innocence are made. It has focused in particular on images and on debates around the commercialisation and sexualisation of childhood. If childhood is constructed as a time of innocence, then children who are not innocent because they have experience of sex or because they know 'too much' in other ways, become problematic. The innocence (or otherwise) of children is a theme that recurs throughout discussions of children's cultural worlds and is therefore central to this book. It is a multifaceted and often very difficult concept, but it is also one of the bases on which modern childhood is founded and therefore central to the ways in which children are understood and how they understand themselves.

References

Attwood, F. (2009) *Mainstreaming Sex: The Sexualisation of Western Culture*, London, IB Tauris.

Buckingham, D. and Bragg, S. (2004) *Young People, Sex and the Media: The Facts of Life?*, Basingstoke, Palgrave Macmillan.

Buckingham, D., Willett, R., Bragg, S. and Russell, R. (2010) *Sexualised Goods Aimed at Children: A Report to the Scottish Parliament Equal Opportunities Committee*, Edinburgh, Scottish Parliament Equal Opportunities Committee.

Byron, T. (2008) *The Byron Review: Safer Children in a Digital World*, London, DCSF.

Cross, G. (2004) *The Cute and the Cool: Wondrous Innocence and Modern American Children's Culture*, New York, Oxford University Press.

Department for Children, Schools and Families (DCSF) (2009) *The Impact of the Commercial World on Children's Wellbeing*, London, DCSF.

Department for Education (DfE) (2011) *Letting Children be Children: Report of an Independent Review of the Commercialisation and Sexualisation of Childhood*, London, HMSO.

Department for Education (DfE) (2012) 'Sexualisation', *A-Z of Terms* [online], http://www.education.gov.uk/vocabularies/ educationtermsandtags/7143 (Accessed 10 May 2012).

Egan, R. D. and Hawkes, G. L. (2008) 'Endangered girls and incendiary objects: unpacking the discourse of sexualisation', *Sexuality and Culture*, vol. 12, no. 4, pp. 291–311.

Faulkner, J. (2011) *The Importance of Being Innocent: Why We Worry About Children*, Cambridge, Cambridge University Press.

Ferguson, H. (2007) 'Abused and looked after children as "moral dirt": child abuse and institutional care in historical perspective', *Journal of Social Policy*, vol. 36, no. 1, pp. 123–39.

Foucault, M. (1976) *The History of Sexuality*, vol. 1 (trans. R. Hurley), Harmondsworth, Penguin.

Freud, S. (1953 [1905]) 'Three essays on the theory of sexuality', in Strachey, J. (ed, trans.) *The Standard Edition of the Complete Psychological Works of Sigmund Freud*, vol. VII, London, Hogarth Press.

Freud, S. (1953 [1913]) 'Totem and taboo: some points of agreement between the mental lives of savages and neurotics', in Strachey, J. (ed, trans.) *The Standard Edition of the Complete Psychological Works of Sigmund Freud*, vol. XIII, London, Hogarth Press.

Furedi, F. (2001) *Paranoid Parenting*, London, Allen Lane.

Higonnet, A. (1998) *Pictures of Innocence: The History and Crisis of Ideal Childhood*, London, Thames & Hudson.

Holland, P. (1992) *What is a Child?*, London, Virago.

Jackson, S. (1982) *Childhood and Sexuality*, Oxford, Basil Blackwell.

Jackson, S. and Scott, S. (2004) 'Sexual antinomies in late modernity', *Sexualities*, vol. 7, no. 2, pp. 233–48.

Kehily, M. J. (2010) 'Childhood in crisis? Tracing the contours of "crisis" and its impact upon contemporary parenting practices', *Media, Culture and Society*, vol. 32, no. 2, pp. 171–85.

Kitzinger, J. (1990) 'Who are you kidding? Children, power and the struggle against sexual abuse', in James, A. and Prout, A. (eds) *Constructing and Re-constructing Childhood: Contemporary Issues in the Study of Childhood*, London, Falmer Press.

Montgomery, H. (2009) *An Introduction to Childhood: Anthropological Perspectives on Children's Lives*, Oxford, Wiley.

Palmer, S. (2007) *Toxic Childhood: How the Modern World is Damaging Our Children and What We Can Do About It*, 2nd edn, London, Orion.

Papadopoulos, L. (2010) *Sexualisation of Young People Review*, London, Home Office.

Pugh, A. J. (2009) *Longing and Belonging: Parents, Children, and Consumer Culture*, Berkeley, CA, University of California Press.

Rush, E. and La Nauze, A. (2006) *Corporate Paedophilia: Sexualisation of Children in Australia*, Canberra, The Australia Institute.

Taylor, A. (2010) 'Troubling childhood innocence: reframing the debate over the media sexualisation of children', *Australasian Journal of Early Childhood*, vol. 35, no. 1, pp. 48–57.

Womack, S. (2007) 'The generation of "damaged" girls', *Daily Telegraph*, 20 February [online], http://www.telegraph.co.uk/health/1543203/The-generation-of-damaged-girls.html (Accessed 20 June 2012).

Wordsworth, W. (1939 [1807]) 'Ode: Intimations of Immortality from Recollections of Early Childhood', in Quiller-Couch, A. (ed) *The Oxford Book of English Verse*, Oxford, Oxford University Press.

Zelizer, V. (1985) *Pricing the Priceless Child: The Changing Social Value of Children*, New Haven, CT, Yale University Press.

Reading A
Little angels, little devils: keeping childhood innocent

Marina Warner

Source: *Managing Monsters: Six Myths of Our Time*, 1994, London, Vintage.

In 1828 a young man was found in the market square of Nuremberg; he could write his name, Kaspar Hauser, but he couldn't speak, except for a single sentence, 'I want to be a rider like my father'. He had been kept all his life in a cellar alone in the dark until his unexplained release that day. Though he was in his teens when he suddenly appeared, he seemed a symbolic child, a stranger to society, a *tabula rasa* in whom ignorance and innocence perfectly coincided. In his wild state, Kaspar Hauser offered his new minders and teachers a blueprint of human nature – untouched. And in his case, his character fulfilled the most idealised image of original innocence.

He was sick when given meat to eat, passed out when given beer, and showed so little aggression and cruelty that he picked off his fleas without crushing them to set them free through the bars of his cell. ...

Kaspar Hauser was an enigma, and after his mysterious return to the world, his life was never free from strange, turbulent incident: he was suspected of fabrication, he was assaulted and wounded by an unknown assailant, and later, was thought to be the usurped heir to the throne of Baden. His innate gentle goodness couldn't save him: he was attacked, seduced, betrayed, and abandoned by his would-be adoptive father, the Englishman Lord Stanhope. And finally he was murdered, in still unsolved circumstances, in 1833.

There'd been other wild children who'd inspired scientific experiments into human development, but Kaspar Hauser more than any other foreshadows this century's struggle with the question of the child's natural character. And his fate still offers a timely parable about the nostalgic worship of childhood innocence, which is more marked today than it ever has been: the difference of the child from the adult has become a dominant theme in contemporary mythology. In literature this has produced two remarkable dream figures living in voluntary exile from grownup society – Kipling's unforgettably vivid Mowgli, and J.M. Barrie's cocky hero, the boy who wouldn't grow up, Peter Pan. Both reveal the depth of adult investment in a utopian childhood state. This can lead to disillusion, often punitive and callous, with the young as people ... [Children are seen as] the keepers and the guarantors of humanity's reputation. This has inspired a wonderfully rich culture of childhood, one of the most remarkable phenomena of modern society – from an unsurpassed imaginative literature of children today to deep psychoanalytical speculation on the thinking processes and even language of the foetus. But it also has social consequences for children themselves that are not all benign.

Childhood, placed at a tangent to adulthood, perceived as special and magical, precious and dangerous at once, has turned into some volatile stuff – hydrogen, or mercury, which has to be contained. The separate condition of the child has never been so bounded by thinking, so established in law as it is today. This mythology is not fallacious, or merely repressive – myths are not only delusions – chimeras – but also tell stories which can give shape and substance to practical, social measures. How we treat children really tests who we are, fundamentally conveys who we hope to be. ...

The nagging, yearning desire to work back to a pristine state of goodness, an Eden of lost innocence, has focussed on children. On the map of contemporary imaginative pathways, J.M. Barrie stands as firmly as the statue of Peter Pan gives West London children their bearings in the park. He truly became a founding father of today's cult of children when in his famous play of 1904, he made the audience responsible for the continued existence of fairyland: the fairy Tinkerbell drinks poison and Peter Pan cries out to the audience, 'Do you believe in fairies? Say quick that you believe! If you believe, clap your hands!' Barry was so anxious that nobody would clap in reply that he paid a claque [a hired group of clappers] to do so in the first performances, but then found that it was unnecessary.

Adults applaud their loyalty to the world of pretend and children follow. The statement of faith in fairies signals collusion with Peter Pan, the boy who never grew up – it affirms the connection of the adult with that childhood Eden in which the Lost Boys are still living; it defies the death of the child within. But at this point, a double bind catches us in its toils: for the defiance of itself admits the impossibility of Peter Pan and the Lost Boys' state. Grown ups want them to stay like that for their sakes', not the children's, and they want children to be simple enough to believe in fairies too, again, for humanity's sake on the whole, to prove something against the evidence. ...

Yet, even as I speak, I can hear objections flying thick and fast: for every dozen wonderful innocents in literature or popular culture, there are unsettling figures of youthful untruth and perversity: children today, far from holding up the lit lamp of hope like the little girl in Picasso's 'Guernica', have become the focus of even greater anxiety and horror than their mothers, than even their single mothers. …

We call children 'little devils', 'little monsters', 'little beasts' – with the full ambiguous force of the terms, all the complications of love and longing, repulsion and fear. Jesus said 'Suffer the little children to come unto me', and Christianity worships its god as a baby in a manger, but the Christian moral tradition has also held, simultaneously, the inherent sinfulness of children.

Original sin holds up the spectre of innate human wickedness: Whatever glosses theologians put on it, Christian children have been raised to believe that without divine help the species is bound for hell. Grimly, parents and carers confronted child wickedness: in New England, Cotton Mather used to beat his daughter to drive the demons of sin from her, and recommended the practice to his fellow Americans; in 1844, a German pastor wrote the terrifying punitive *Struwwelpeter*, with its scissor man and other bogeys for making little boys and girls be good. …

But the Child has never been seen such a menacing enemy as today. Never before have children been so saturated with all the power of projected monstrousness to excite repulsion – and even terror. …

Today, such doubts match widespread fears, and public grief focuses obsessively on the loss of an ideal of children, of their playfulness, their innocence, their tenderness, their beauty. The child holds up an image of origin, but origins are compounded of good and evil together, battling it out; this conflict spreads rings of disquiet all around. Children are perceived as innocent because they're outside society, pre-historical, pre-social, instinctual, creatures of unreason, primitive, kin to unspoiled nature. Whether this is seen as good or evil often reflects the self-image of the society. …

Although the cultural and social investment in childhood innocence is constantly tested by experience, and assailed by doubts, it's still continued to grow. As psychoanalytical understanding of children's sexuality has deepened, so have attempts to contain it. The duration of the age of expected innocence has been greatly extended since Victorian times, for instance: a good thing, if it can prevent exploiting child labour and adult molestation but perhaps not, in other cases.

Most teenagers will have broken at least one of the many laws that forbid them adult behaviour – like smoking, drinking, clubbing, watching 18-rated films or having sex – thus placing them willy-nilly outside the law, and helping to reconfirm their identity as intrinsically delinquent anyway (something they don't find entirely uncongenial, of course).

At the same time, the notion of child sexuality is encoded in upbringing at a much younger age than before. The modern emphasis on sex difference, on learning masculinity and femininity, begins with the clothing of the infants, and has developed markedly since the end of the First World War. A boy who was dressed in pink ribbons by his father today would very likely be taken away from his care. Yet Robert Louis Stevenson, whose character was hardly disturbed, appears in a daguerreotype around the age of three dressed in fur-trimmed cape, full skirts, hair slide and spit curls … The portraits of the French or English aristocracy and gentry showing children clothed as adults, with jewels and powdered wigs and crinolines and farthingales, were displaying the status of their families; but the little girl in the little black dress, patent pumps, lipstick and earrings who was brought out in the finale of a recent Chanel collection was showing off her body, and looked like a travesty of the sex-free youth children are supposed to enjoy.

Yet even if children today aren't titillatingly dressed, they can still be looked at salaciously. It's we who have lost innocent eyes, we who can only be ironical children. Lewis Carroll's friends were undisturbed by his photographs of their children, while some pederasts today, it seems, are kept very happy by Mothercare catalogues.

Pornography clusters to the sacred and the forbidden like wasps' nests in chimneys: and children have in many ways replaced women. The very term child abuse, of recent, highly symptomatic coinage, implies that there's a proper use for children, and it is not sexual. Yet at the same time, there circulates more disguised kiddie porn than at any other period in history, and more speculation about their internal lives of fantasy and desire. The nineteenth century used femmes fatales with bedroom eyes and trailing tresses, wet-look drapery and floating chiffon on the official buildings and advertisements, but the late twentieth century has seen children emerge as the principal incitements to desire: the nymph or the vamp has yielded pride of place to the nymphet, the urchin and the toddler.

There's probably no way out of this maze of mirrors, at least on this side of eternity, unless, like Islam, we were to ban graven images – especially of children as objects of desire. The consecration of childhood raises the real-life examples of children to an ideal which they must fail, modestly by simply being ordinary kids, or horrendously by becoming victims or criminals. But childhood doesn't occupy some sealed Eden or Neverland set apart from the grown up world: our children can't be better than we are.

Children have never been so visible as points of identification, as warrants of virtue, as markers of humanity. Yet the quality of their lives has been deteriorating [since the 1980s] in this country; one of the fastest growing groups living in poverty are children and their mothers. The same ministers who sneer about babies on benefit, and trumpet a return to basic values cannot see that our social survival as a civilised community depends on stopping this spiralling impoverishment of children's lives. The Child Poverty Action Group estimates that a third of all children are suffering from an unacceptably low standard of living. …[1]

To add to the difficulties, economic individualism has brought us the ultimate nightmare – not just the child as commodity, but the child consumer. Plenty of dinosaur lunch boxes at school, not many books in the library. The wicked, greedy, knowing child grows in the same ground as the industry around childhood innocence: children are expensive to raise, anyway, but all the products made for them unashamedly appeal to their pester power – as consumers of films, hamburgers, the right brand of trainers, video games. The child, as a focus of worship, has been privatised as an economic unit, has become a link in the circulation of money and desire. …

Many of these problems result from the concept that childhood and adult life are separate when they are in effect inextricably intertwined. Children aren't separate from adults, and unlike Mowgli or Peter Pan, can't be kept separate; they can't live innocent lives on behalf of adults,

---

[0] When this was written, Warner was referring to the Conservative governments in power between 1979 and 1997. However, in June 2012, the Child Poverty Action Group website stated: 'there are 3.6 million children living in poverty in the UK today … 27 per cent of children, or more than one in four; child poverty reduced dramatically between 1998/9 and 2010/12 when 1.1 million children were lifted out of poverty …; under current government policies, child poverty is projected to rise from 2012/13 with an expected 300,000 more children living in poverty by 2015/16. This upward trend is expected to continue with 4.2 million children projected to be living in poverty by 2020' (Child Poverty Action Group, http://www.cpag.org.uk/child-poverty-facts-and-figures, accessed 28 June 2012).

like medieval hermits maintained at court by libertine kings to pray for them, or the best china kept in tissue in the cupboard. Nor can individuals who happen to be young act as the living embodiments of adults' inner goodness, however much adults may wish it. Without paying attention to adults and their circumstances, children cannot begin to meet the hopes and expectations of our torn dreams about what a child and childhood should be. Children are our copy, in little: in Pol Pot's Cambodia they'll denounce their own families; in affluent cities of the West, they'll wail for expensive trainers with the right label like their friend's. The one thing that can be said for absolute certain about children is that they're very quick to learn.

We know by now that the man is father to the child [*sic*]; we fear that children will grow up to be even more like us than they already are. Kaspar Hauser the innocent was murdered; now we're scared that if such a wild child were to appear today he might kill us.

Reading B
Pictures of innocence

Anne Higonnet

Source: *Pictures of Innocence: The History and Crisis of Ideal Childhood*, 1998, London, Thames & Hudson.

Pictures of children are at once the most common, the most sacred, and controversial images of our time. They guard the cherished ideal of childhood innocence, yet they contain within them the potential to undo that ideal. No subject seems cuter or more sentimental, and we take none more for granted, yet pictures of children have proved dangerously difficult to understand or control. …

On a troubling edge between accumulated tradition and the unfamiliar, pictures of children in all visual media, including the most popular, must now contend with hopes and fears felt acutely by millions of people. Take the quite ordinary and therefore all the more revealing, case of an advertisement launched in the summer of 1997. The Estée Lauder company introduced its fragrance called Pleasures for Men with a photograph of a man and a boy resting together in a hammock. In many ways the image is traditionally idyllic. Both people are beautiful, and their hammock is slung above a watchful dog; behind them stretches a white picket fence: signs of peaceful, faithful, domesticity. Above all, the image resonates with harmonious family snapshot memories. The Lauder image, however, was apparently not ideal enough. By September of 1997, the original version had been withdrawn from circulation and another put in its place. The only difference between the old and the new versions was the addition of a tiny but densely symbolic detail: a wedding band on the man's ring finger.

Today, all photographs of children hinting at 'pleasure' are suspect, let alone photographs of children explicitly titled 'pleasures for men'. Everyone brings to an understanding of photographs the associations, good or bad, suggested by their cultural climate, and now associations with pictures of children are anxious ones. Advertisements seek the identification of consumers with their images, so it is safe to assume the Estée Lauder company only wanted to appeal to a stylishly updated family ideal. But to be able to call any intimacy between an adult and a child 'pleasure' required negotiating deep concerns that childhood is no longer being experienced the way it used to be, either by adults or by children. At their most tragic, those concerns include a growing recognition of sexual child abuse.

We are living through a major change in our culture's understanding of childhood. But ideas about childhood have changed profoundly before. The last major change, which gathered critical momentum during the eighteenth-century Enlightenment, under the impulse of such influential texts as Jean-Jacques Rousseau's 1762 *Emile*, was not perceived as a threat, though its importance was acknowledged. Now we are going through what feels like a crisis, because any change in our current ideal of timelessly natural innocence is bound to seem threatening, if not entirely negative. The change we perceive also seems dangerously unfamiliar because it is so visual. While pictures did eventually reflect new notions of childhood by the eighteenth century, they certainly had not inaugurated those changes. In a highly visual late twentieth century, however, pictures lead. They offer us the first glimpse of what childhood might seem like in the future. And they have already become the most fraught focal point for resistance to any alteration in the idea of childhood. In the broadest sense, the image we have of childhood now is just that – an image.

Historians date the modern, western, concept of an ideally innocent childhood to somewhere around the seventeenth century. Until then, children had been understood as faulty small adults, in need of correction and discipline, especially Christian children who were thought to be born in sin. Pictures represented children accordingly. Art historians have observed that pictures of children underwent a major transformation during the Enlightenment, but have treated this shift as the discovery of a natural truth, rather than as a brilliant pictorial version of an invented definition. Precisely because the modern concept of childhood was an invented cultural ideal, it required representations. Fictions about lived experience were more consistent, more convincing, and more beautiful than any lived experience could ever be.

Visual fictions played a special role in consolidating the modern definition of childhood, a role which became increasingly important over time. To a great extent, childhood innocence was considered an attribute of the child's body, both because the child's body was supposed to be naturally innocent of adult sexuality, and because the child's mind was supposed to begin blank. Innocence therefore lent itself to visual representation because the immediate visibility of pictures has always had a privileged ability to shape our understanding of our bodies, our physical selves. The same modern period that created the ideal of childhood innocence, moreover, placed its faith in visual evidence. Sophisticated pictures ostensibly based on the eye's empirical observations, or, better still, the camera's optical machinery, could appear at once compellingly beautiful and persuasively real.

The first great movement in the visual history of childhood innocence was led by elite eighteenth-century British portrait painters, among them Sir Joshua Reynolds, Thomas Gainsborough, and Sir Henry Raeburn. Borrowing, distilling, and altering elements from the art historical past, these painters introduced a new vision of the child, a set of visual signals brilliantly embedded in individual pictures, and so basic they could inform all future pictures. I call this vision, this collective image, Romantic childhood. Romantic childhood caught on quickly. After its initiation in the mid-eighteenth century came its diffusion during the nineteenth century. Gradually, the visual invention of childhood innocence permeated popular consciousness, swept along by the proliferation of image technologies which generated more diverse and inclusive types of pictures, artists and audiences. From its origins in elite painting, the image of Romantic childhood spread to popular genre paintings – some of which, such as Sir John Everett Millais's beloved *Cherry Ripe*, were turned into best-selling prints or advertisements – and from there into the mass market of industrially produced illustration. As it was being commercialized, the image of the child was simultaneously being feminized. Most of the women who aspired to painting careers were effectively allowed no other choice of subject. Artists as gifted as Kate Greenaway, Mary Cassatt, and Jessie Willcox Smith were therefore dedicated to perfecting the image of Romantic childhood, not despite but because of its decline in esthetic status.

Photography inherited their work. The visual habits so thoroughly acquired during what is known as the Golden Age of Illustration passed directly into the medium of photography. More convincingly realistic than any other medium, photography made it possible for the ideal of Romantic childhood to seem completely natural. Cheap, easy camera equipment and film processing put pictures of children at almost everyone's disposal, both to look at and to make. The more people saw or made photographs of children, the more axiomatic the image of childhood innocence became. Today, approximately half of all advertisement photographs show children. The most successful commercial child photographers, notably Anne Geddes, sell millions of pictures. Billions of amateur snapshots of children are taken each year –

somewhere between 8.5 and 12.5 billion in the mid 1990s in the United States alone.

Yet it is photography which at the same time has precipitated the current crisis in childhood's image. The conditions of that crisis were latent in the ideal of absolute childhood innocence itself, and have been vividly revealed because of a similarly absolute belief in photography's objective neutrality. In practice, rigid oppositions between childhood innocence and adult passion, particularly sexual passion, are difficult to maintain. Nor can a photographer's subjective participation in the photographic process ever really be eliminated. Intentionally flagrant violations of cultural ideals such as childhood innocence and photographic objectivity do, of course, occur constantly. More subtle and powerful, however, in the long run, are the inadvertent slips allowed by conscious adherence to those same ideals. The most challenging pictures of children have been produced by a combined faith in the child's innocence and the camera's neutrality: photographs which force us, as viewers, to see what our ideals deny, just as they expressed what their own makers could not admit. Take the notorious example of Lewis Carroll, author of *Alice in Wonderland* as well as photographer of little girls. Carroll insisted his camera, being mechanically automatic, could do nothing but capture the truth of childhood, which, he also insisted, was inherently innocent. Somehow, though, Carroll's photographs suggest otherwise. And Carroll's photographs were not the only ones. Ever since the medium was officially inaugurated in 1839, photography has been unsettling the certainties of ideal childhood, marginally at first, and now unavoidably.

As photographic variations on innocence accumulated over time, reaching the most popular commercial mainstream, as well as the canon of photographic history, it became inevitable either that the ideal of innocence would be challenged, or that photography would be accused of endangering that ideal (or both). More and more sexual meanings are now being ascribed to photographs of children both past and present, whether because of what is in the photograph or what is in the eye of the beholder. Neither the esthetic quality of a picture nor its author's explicitly stated purposes can prevent the mutation of its meanings – on the contrary. Great photographs and articulate programs attract multiple interpretations, sometimes layered on each other, as in the case of Edward Weston's hallowed 1925 *Neil* series. The trend to see sexuality in photographs of children accelerated in the late 1970s, leading to scandals over controversial art photographs like Robert Mapplethorpe's, but even more significantly over mass-media commercial photographs like Calvin Klein's notorious 1995 jeans ad campaign. Erotically suggestive images of children – perhaps deliberately erotic – now pervade all media, appearing with increasing frequency in spectacles ranging from fashion photography to Disney movies to intellectually ambitious art works to televised sports and beauty pageants. All the difficulties of a Romantic childhood have surfaced.

When we look at troubling images of children we not only see abstract meanings, but dread real consequences. At every moment in all societies, the connection between some kind of representation, some form of expression, and actual behavior arouses extreme anxiety, social revulsion, and state repression. In late twentieth-century western societies, pictures of children scare us more than any others. It is terrifying to think of a picture causing someone to harm a child, and horrifying to think of a picture causing someone to molest sexually, inflicting a heinous combination of physical and psychological damage.

One reaction against fear has been to protect children by controlling pictures. Law, public criticism, commercial pressure, the withholding or withdrawal of pictures from exhibition or publication, all have been deployed against images. While all these means can have powerful effects, law clearly wields the most force. During the last fifteen years, prohibitions against child pornography have been introduced and constantly expanded in several western nations, most dramatically in the United States. Extremely precise and unassailable measures concerning real children and real actions are mingled in this legislation with measures purporting to protect real children, but in effect censoring the interpretation of images. Most problematically, recent measures have moved child pornography law into zones of completely subjective interpretation. Suddenly, any image of a child in which someone, anyone, sees sexuality can be prosecuted as criminal child pornography. Inherently personal opinion now suffices to send someone to jail for years, or to launch investigations that may never bring even indictments, let alone convictions, but can still shatter reputations, consume years, and cost astronomical legal fees. At first, child pornography laws were aimed at photographs that documented crimes perpetrated against real children; then they targeted photographs suggesting sex acts, whether those acts were simulated or not; next they attacked photographs of child nudity, followed by all remotely suggestive pictures of real children, clothed or unclothed; and as it now stands child pornography law includes in its scope all images of children's bodies, regardless of whether the image represents a real child or not. All computer-generated images are therefore potentially suspect, and so, by logical analogy, are also all paintings, drawings, sculptures, etc. Because some images, especially photographs, look realistic, all images are being treated by child pornography law as if they were themselves real, as if images were the same as actions.

All pictures of children are now suspect, yet the existence of child pornography laws allows us to hope we can easily draw a line between the safe and the dangerous, between the good and the bad. The demonization of something branded 'child pornography' lulls us into ignoring our own quite ordinary complicity in a culture-wide phenomenon. Everywhere we look, the image of childhood is changing, aided and abetted by eager media consumers of all ages. In many different ways, the image of the child is becoming more physical, and more involved in the world of adults. Some of those changes may be negative or exploitive, but the magnitude itself of the transformation indicates a major shift in an entire culture's ideas, not a fringe criminal phenomenon.

Combined with a lack of historical perspective, denial of the present prevents us from coping with irreversible change by fixating us on mythic nostalgia and false culprits. Whether we want to recognize it or not, the visual definition of childhood invented in the eighteenth century is being reinvented. We are now uncomfortably caught between two ways of defining childhood, and neither is easy to live with. In its death throes, the old Romantic ideal reveals its weaknesses and falls prey to ruthless demands for profit and publicity. At the same time, however, another vision of childhood is emerging. Images by a growing number of photographers, many of them the parents of their subjects, represent children who, far from being psychically or sexually innocent, are what I call Knowing children. Unlike Romantic images, Knowing images, for the first time in the history of art, endow children with psychological and physical individuality at the same time as they recognize them as being distinctively child-like. It is difficult to turn from cherished and polished traditions to these new pictures. Being new, they can be abrasive, exploratory, or raw.

Is a Knowing childhood leading us away from a defense of children on the grounds of innocence? Absolutely not. Though new images of childhood call into question children's psychic and sexual innocence by attributing to them consciously active minds and bodies, those images leave intact the concept of children's social innocence, including innocence of adults' socially formed psyches and sexuality. We are, however, being asked to redefine innocence along with childhood. We now have to consider whether a child has to be psychically or sexually innocent to deserve protection, or whether social innocence is all the justification we should ever need to shelter children from adult abuse.

Chapter 2

Play

Tara Woodyer

Contents

In this chapter, you will:

- examine the place of play in the study of childhood and the perspectives that may be employed in the study of children's play
- consider how children's worlds have a distinct character in terms of traditions, lore and games
- describe the changing nature of play over the course of time and the effects of social context on children's play activities
- identify the social dynamics of play
- identify the place of toys in childhood and some of the historical changes affecting children's toys and playthings
- reflect on the role of play throughout life
- consider the role of play in children's lives in a range of international contexts.

1   Introduction

Play can take different forms as the examples below demonstrate. Yet, despite its variegated character, play represents one of the most distinctive features of childhood. It is something that children across the globe have in common.

Dukan (store)

This is a game played by children in a Sudanese village called Howa.

A typical game involved boys and girls setting up a number of small shops nestled in the base of a tree, along a houseyard wall, or in some other shaded area. The wares included the standard dry goods available in Howa and some more exotic imports, all represented by such things as vials discarded from the village dispensary, tomato paste tins, cans and bottle tops, dirt, wads of mud-clay modeled into such things as bread and other foodstuffs, batteries and battery tops, bottles, goat dung, metal scraps, a telegraph pole insulator, shells, wood bits, packages or scraps of packaging, seeds, and shards of glass. ... The medium of exchange was 'china money' (shards of broken crockery and dishes).

(Katz, 2004, pp. 103–4)

Wrestling

Robert stands paused while James runs towards him. In a swift action Robert scoops up his brother, spinning him round on his shoulders before throwing him towards the sofa. As James tumbles to the floor, Robert pounces, straddling his brother. The two struggle, James grabbing his brother in a headlock, prompting him to cry out in submission. James leaps to his feet, punching the air in triumph.

(Woodyer, 2010)

Onika Bonika

This is a game involving three Year 5 boys (9 to 10 year olds) that was video-recorded in a Sheffield (UK) playground in 2010.

The boys stand together, each with one leg outstretched in front of them to form a circle. One boy takes the lead touching each foot in turn as he recites the following rhyme: 'Onika bonika super sonika, onika bonika nobs'. The foot corresponding with the word 'nobs' is withdrawn from the circle. The first time this happens to a player, they withdraw one foot and replace it with the other. The second time the word 'nobs' falls on them they are eliminated from the group. The last remaining player is nominated 'it' and has to chase after the others.

(British Library, 2010)

Figure 1   Onika Bonika

Whilst children differ in the games they play, not least according to age and gender, play is seen to make their world distinct from that of adults. Indeed, for many people it is children's capacity and enthusiasm for play, and the importance attached to being allowed to play, that defines what childhood is about. Adults are often restricted from this world, seen as an unwelcome intrusion or possessing only limited comprehension of the terms of play. But what is actually going on when children play?

Figure 2   Children's enthusiasm for play defines what childhood is about

2 Perspectives on children's play

Figure 3 Innocence and playful exploration

Some of the earliest attempts to explain the importance of children's play emerged from the writers, artists and poets associated with the Romantic movement of the late seventeenth and the eighteenth centuries. William Blake, Samuel Coleridge, William Wordsworth and particularly Jean-Jacques Rousseau imagined children embodying an innate goodness and a natural instinct for playful exploration and free expression, and advocated freedom for the child and nurture through encouragement and support.

This Romantic discourse challenged a more Puritan discourse, which linked children's play to the animal origins of humankind. Rather than harmless pleasures, play involved the expression of base instincts and was therefore a risk to the 'civilising' process. Children had to be saved from the worst excesses of the self through strict training and sound teaching. This mythology of primal forces remained a powerful theme in twentieth-century literature, for instance William Golding's 1954 novel *Lord of the Flies*.

Despite such ambivalence, play is one of the defining features of modern (post-Enlightenment) notions of childhood. The Romantic view of play has come to represent a particular ideological position about the

Figure 4   Expression of base instincts – *Lord of the Flies*

nature and status of childhood itself. The eighteenth-century image of the playful child was reinforced in the nineteenth and twentieth centuries by the economic and social changes brought about by industrialisation, the domestication of home space, changing family ideals centred on the child and the emergence of a market in goods for children, as we saw in the previous chapter.

Activity 1   What is play?

Allow about 10 minutes

We have contrasted two widely differing discourses on play that are underpinned by their respective ideological stance on childhood itself. Think about a range of situations where children of different ages and genders are playing, including the examples in the introduction to this chapter. Do you see these as healthy expressions of playful exploration, or as potentially worrying and dangerous? Do some seem more harmless than others? Note down some reasons for your responses. We will return to these later in the chapter.

Comment

The examples at the beginning of the chapter begin to point to important issues and debates surrounding children's play. The game of dukan played in Howa seems innocent enough, girls and boys coming together rehearsing future roles and activities. The game of wrestling may be more troubling, since it can be seen either as a harmless valve for the release of aggressive feelings, or as legitimising violent behaviour. A perennial concern is whether levels of aggression within play are increasing, perhaps as a result of media influences. However, from a child's point of view, this kind of play-fighting is often highly stylised, with clearly defined and acknowledged boundaries for appropriate behaviour.

The example from Howa is interesting as it prompts consideration of the similarities and differences in play and games across the globe.
I remember playing 'post offices' as a young girl with my Petite Post Office set. In many ways this game was similar to dukan, although it centred on a commercial toy rather than on 'household' and natural objects.

The example of Onika Bonika may remind you of similar playground practices, pointing to processes of continuity and change in play across generations. It also involves rituals of inclusion and exclusion, which can in some cases lead to bullying. Whilst we often think of play as fun and benign, it may not always be a positive experience for those involved. Play produces power relations and social hierarchies among children. Along with the winners there are also losers.

2.1   Different ways of discussing play

Different academic disciplines have quite different interests in play. For example, biologists, psychologists and educators examine how play contributes to growth and development. Psychoanalysts tend to focus on the role of play in emotional adjustment. Sociologists and anthropologists have been more concerned with how children develop an understanding of others and learn about social roles through play. Given these different interests, there are various definitions of what play is and the different forms it can take (Smith, 2010). Some kinds of play have received much more scrutiny than others; for instance, there is a vast literature on children's imaginative or pretend play, but comparatively little on rough-and-tumble play.

One general feature of many academic and clinical approaches is that they analyse play as a means to an end; for instance, considering how it helps children grow into mature, competent, socially integrated adults. This perspective tends to position children primarily as adults in the making. It is worth remembering, therefore, that the purposes of play identified in academic studies may be incidental to the child's own experience of play as fun and as something they value for its own sake.

In this chapter we concentrate on anthropological and sociological ways of discussing play, beginning with how role play helps children develop a sense of self and social understanding.

2.2   Play, self and social understanding

Role play in pretend and make-believe situations is also referred to as sociodramatic play, and has been an area of particular focus in play research. This kind of play is understood to be crucial to children's development of understanding others, learning about social roles and acquiring language.

In an ethnographic study of children's play in a Sudanese village, Cindi Katz (2004) describes how children would mimic the economic activities that both they and their parents engaged in, albeit on a smaller scale. This included tilling small areas of land, building charcoal mounds, constructing shelters, setting up shops and exchanging china 'money' (as in the game of dukan described above). Through these activities, children made sense of their social world and rehearsed future roles.

Role play is also understood to be important to a child's developing sense of self. Through role-play activities, they imagine themselves in different social roles in ways that enable them to develop a reflective sense of themselves as individuals, and how they are seen by others. Katz discusses how the village children used play to engage in activities and enact roles that were uncommon for their elders. For instance, girls would enact collecting firewood alongside tending to household chores, a practice uncommon to the village women. Through their play these children were opening avenues for changing not only their own roles, but also the community's practices, more broadly.

Children's role play is not just about developing a mature sense of self and practising future social roles. By acting out imaginary roles and social contexts children are also able to make sense of the here and now. The following activity aims to help you explore this idea further.

Activity 2   Playing at interviewer
Allow about 10 minutes

I recorded the following example of role play while I was undertaking a study of children's domestic play. I had already interviewed the child here, Matthew (eight years old). He had then been provided with a digital camcorder and asked to document his toy collection. Read the extract and consider the significance of Matthew's new game.

Matthew takes the camcorder on a tour of the house. Having reached his final destination, his bedroom, he scrabbles around to find Gromit, his soft toy dog, and places him on the bed. He keeps the camcorder turned on in his hand as he does so, producing blurry, jerky footage of nothing in particular. He sits Gromit upright, resting him against the wall. He zooms in on his face, saying 'Hello, hello, hello' before zooming out again. As he adjusts the camcorder, he mutters, 'Try to find your whole body. I need to stand back.' He positions himself some distance away on his brother's bed, running parallel to his, and then zooms in, muttering, 'Bit back. There, very good.' He then declares, 'And now I'm going to interview Gromit. What do you think of this house?' In a somewhat comical voice, he adopts the role of Gromit, 'Oh it's very nice isn't it. I like it.' The interview continues, 'How do you feel about this?' Emphasis is placed on the word 'feel' by drawing out the vowels.

(Woodyer, 2010)

Comment

This game is rooted in the present. Matthew is engaged in making sense of the world around him, playing with practices and activities that have been introduced to him through the research. Matthew's role play demonstrates his social understanding. He playfully enacts the power relations embedded in the research encounter, standing over Gromit, capturing him in the camera frame. This game can be seen as an attempt to own the experience by acting it out. It is worth noting that the role play involves skilful levels of imitation. Matthew not only impersonates the interviewer's questions and ways of speaking, but takes great care framing Gromit appropriately in the camera lens. He shows diligence to interviewees' wishes to look good in front of the camera, and the interviewer's wishes for professional footage. When exaggerating the question, 'How do you feel?' Matthew is not just copying the interviewer, but mocking this practice. This use of mimicry demonstrates children's ability to observe, incorporate and make fun of the adult world around them.

In this section we have considered contradictory Romantic and Puritan discourses on play and how these relate to broader understandings about the nature and status of childhood. We have discussed academic and clinical approaches to play, which identify its functions within children's development. These are not the only way of thinking about play. In the rest of the chapter we will be concentrating on attempts to understand play in its own right, as a distinctive feature of children's cultural worlds, and an ongoing activity throughout life. We will be asking important questions about continuity and change in the ways in which children play, and about power relations and social hierarchies within play, how far children's culture is a distinct world set apart from adult society, and the place of toys in children's play.

Summary of Section 2

Children's play can be interpreted from different perspectives using different disciplinary traditions.

Views on the purpose and significance of children's play reflect debates about the nature and status of childhood itself.

Play serves many functions, but it is also important to consider how children, as competent social actors, value play for its own sake.

Play takes many different forms, yet tends to be seen as a distinctive feature of children's cultural worlds.

---

3   Play as a culture of childhood?

The folklorists Peter and Iona Opie pioneered the idea that children's play constitutes a culture of childhood that can be studied on its own terms. Over the course of 30 years or more, they gathered an exhaustive collection of street and playground-based child lore and games. This was seen as evidence for cultural forms unique to children, traditions circulating child to child and a secretive world external to the home and family.

The notion of an autonomous 'culture of childhood' independent of the adult world is a problematic one, debated by folklorists, anthropologists and sociologists. It is at odds with another important concept in understanding childhood, that of socialisation – the process whereby children's behaviour is circumscribed by their surrounding (adult) environment. Sociologists, in particular, argue that the notion of an independent culture of childhood does little to help us understand how children eventually become recognisably adult.

Approaching childhood as a separate culture plays down the social context of children's lives outside of their relations with their peers. This is problematic as the majority of children's time is spent in the company of adults. Arguably, the notion of a 'culture of childhood' is in some ways a fiction generated by researchers. This section addresses features of our contemporary world that problematise the 'culture of childhood' idea.

3.1   Parent–child play

Most ethnographic studies of children's play are conducted in the school playground or similar spaces dominated by children. There is a relative absence of work exploring play with siblings and parents in the home, despite the prevalent emphasis on the importance of parent–child (particularly mother–child) play to 'normal' child development. Moreover, contemporary child-rearing (particularly in middle-class families) increasingly conforms to a particular cultural logic that the sociologist Annette Lareau (2002) calls 'concerted cultivation'. Every parent–child interaction and domestic routine becomes a learning opportunity. There is a growing body of research that describes and compares the various methods used by and promoted to parents in this regard. These include using bedtime stories and dinner table conversations to encourage early reading and the expansion of vocabulary, alongside using everyday domestic tasks such as laying the table or doing the washing to teach basic concepts of sorting, matching and comparing (Walkerdine and Lucey, 1989). These methods also extend to strategies to encourage fantasy and make-believe in the very young as a way to develop fluent literacy:

> With infants, mothers may model pretending for the child, by holding up and making a stuffed animal or doll talk. With toddlers and preschoolers, mothers provide play scripts and embellish their children's early fantasy constructions.

> (Lancy, 2007, p. 279)

Activity 3   A play curriculum?
Allow about 10 minutes

Think about situations where you have played or observed other adults playing with children. Make notes on any elements that might correspond to the logic of 'concerted cultivation', as coined by Lareau (2002), and on the factors that might influence levels of parental involvement in play.

Comment

Whilst I am not a parent myself, my familial relations frequently bring me into contact with young children. When I took the time to reflect on my engagements with these children I was shocked by the extent to which they are shaped by attempts to aid development. I might ask children to count or name the colour of the objects they are interacting with or to tell me what has happened so far in a story as I sit down to read to them at bedtime. These actions are spontaneous and instinctive, rather than consciously educational. Yet they rest on particular assumptions about 'good' parenting and, by extension, 'good' adult–child interactions – that these should be pedagogic, or like teacher–pupil relations in some way.

Parental (particularly the mother's) involvement in play is seen as a prerequisite for educational success and future participation in the information economy. Take the UK as an example: before the 1997 general election, Tony Blair asserted that education would be 'the passion of my government', arguing that 'levering up standards and achievements' was pivotal both to individual prosperity and to reversing Britain's economic and social decline (Blair, 1997, pp. 159, 176). Yet this emphasis on education went beyond the school: the home too has increasingly become a target for educational initiatives, with parents being encouraged to prime children to succeed in academic settings (often by investing in computers and so-called 'educational' software). Buckingham and Scanlon (2003), in an analysis of some of these initiatives, argue that they address and position parents and children in ways that are 'more in keeping with the cultural styles of middle-class families' (p. 9), and note that they often demand considerable time and energy. They therefore offer an ideal that the majority of parents find difficult to achieve, which can result in feelings of guilt and inadequacy. They also promote a particular kind of pedagogy, ignoring the many kinds of 'informal' learning that suffuse children's everyday lives.

It is important to note that mother–child play is by no means a universal phenomenon, which in turn suggests that it is sustained by a range of factors, including economic resources. In the USA, Lareau (2002) has noted that it is less common in working-class than in middle-class households. Drawing on an extensive review of anthropological reports on childhood, David Lancy (2007) argues that mother–child play is very rare beyond minority-world influenced, relatively wealthy and industrialised contexts. The following extract from a report about a Ganda farming community in Uganda is typical:

> If baby games were infrequent, so were hugging, nuzzling, and kissing. We saw no baby being coaxed to kiss or hug. I noted only three mothers who nuzzled and kissed their babies as they held them ... Ganda mothers did not interact with their babies through toys ... [there was] no instance of a mother trying to elicit a response from her baby by dangling a plaything in front of him.
>
> (Ainsworth, 1967, p. 94)

There may be many reasons why there is less mother–child play in such contexts, not least high infant mortality. Restricting communication with the child may reduce the loss felt in such instances. Indigenous theories of child development or folk theory may hold that very young children are not perceptive or cognisant, making communication with them a waste of time and energy.

Even if it is not universal, mother–child play is nonetheless a powerful ideal that has significant implications for how we understand and promote play. The International Association for the Child's Right to Play, for example, is pressing to export the parent–child play movement around the globe:

> Children at play not only require the understanding of adults but also their active support and participation. Parents must find time to play with their children. ... I am especially happy when adults regard the noise of playing children as the music of the future.
>
> (International Play Association, 2005, cited in Lancy, 2007, pp. 279–80)

3.2   The intertwining of work and play

Increasing parental intervention in play makes the notion of a separate culture of childhood harder to sustain. So too does the blending of play, work and learning in the lives of the vast majority of the world's children.

In a rich ethnography of Sudanese village life, geographer Cindi Katz (2004) explores how work and play are intertwined for children, rather than distinct. In this culture dominated by agriculture, animal husbandry and forestry, the passing on of fundamental environmental knowledge is a routine part of everyday life. It occurs through direct oral instruction and demonstration, riddles and songs, apprenticeship and shared adult–child activities. The following rhyme is one example of a riddle or *hajwa* passed down generations:

> Al Simbriya Um Guddoum
> Aysh Aboui Bigoom
> Mitaya Bitgoom Bakir
> Ma' al Asakir
>
> The Abdim's stork with its long bill
> My father's sorghum sprouts
> It will grow tomorrow
> With the dawn

(Quoted in Katz, 2004, p. 63)

Seeing a *simbriya* (or Abdim's stork) means that it will rain soon as these birds arrive during the rainy season. Such practices of exchanging knowledge and skills are important for the continuation of the community's way of life and help shape the children's future social roles.

Activity 4   Reading A
Allow about 15 minutes

Now study Reading A, 'Playful work and "workful" play', in which Cindi Katz describes children's participation in charcoal production in the Sudanese village of Howa. Note the ties between work and play, and the wider social and economic practices and relations they are embedded in.

Comment

Charcoal production is just one example of how work and play are intertwined for the children of Howa. In her ethnography Katz also describes children's practices of herding, fetching water, gathering wood for fuel, agriculture and collecting wild foods. Many of the tasks these children engage in are specifically designated as children's jobs. By the age of ten, most children demonstrate a high degree of mastery of such chores. In more complex tasks – such as farming – where adults assist children, they become competent in discrete aspects of wider processes at an early age. Work and play are critical ways through which children reproduce the social and economic life of the village.

Figure 5   Children combine work and play

3.3   To share or not to share?

By highlighting how play is entangled with work and learning, and often involves different forms of adult engagement or intervention, the examples described so far problematise the notion of a separate culture of childhood. They emphasise the need to consider the wider social context of children's lives outside of their relations with their peers.

But what happens if we examine the question of a separate culture of childhood from the child's point of view? Do children strive for an independent, even secretive world? If they do, what mechanisms are used to establish and maintain it? The following two extracts, taken from my own ethnographic study, provide interesting points for consideration.

Extract 1

Joshua (11 years-old) is able to talk at length about his Yu-Gi-Oh! cards: the different types of cards – monsters, traps, magic and spells, dragon, machine, etc; the uses of different cards in attack and defence situations; their relative ratings; and their rarity. He knows the TV theme tune off by heart, and regularly sings it in the middle of conversations. Joshua explains that trading cards are banned at his school so I ask whether he plays Yu-Gi-Oh! with his mum. 'Yeah, quite often', he laughs. 'Is your mum good at it then?'

I have to admit that I'm still baffled by the game despite his explanations. 'No', he responds firmly. I chuckle. 'She's not' he says proudly. 'She keeps getting that card [he points to a particular card in his collection] and she never uses it to increase her life force by a thousand points.' I ask whether he explains this to his mum. 'No,' he giggles, 'she doesn't watch the TV programme either. She'll never understand it. Adults just don't get it,' he says smugly.

Extract 2

The two boys, Stephen (10 years-old) and Matthew (8 years-old) set up the PlayStation console in the lounge. After an emotional debate, they opt to play Pro Evolution Soccer 6 (a football simulation game, usually referred to simply as 'Pro Evo'). Matthew chooses to play as Chelsea FC whilst Stephen opts for Sheffield United. They demonstrate a clear knowledge of their teams' relative standings in the 'real world', exchanging information about their relative successes, failures and reputations. Chelsea had finished top of the FA Premier League the previous season, whilst Sheffield United had only been promoted to the top league that summer. Stephen's choice of an 'underdog' team is an attempt to make the game more even. He prides himself on having superior gaming skills to his younger brother. ...

> Stephen, playing as the underdog, defeats his brother with relative ease. While Matthew is disappointed, neither boy seems surprised at the outcome. Stephen proudly exclaims, 'I can't wait to tell Dad that Sheffield United beat Chelsea.' The boys set about deciding who will play the next match.
>
> The boys' play is interrupted when they hear the sound of a key in the door. Stephen shouts to his dad, desperate to tell him about Sheffield United's victory. They exchange opinions on United's ability and recollect the team's success, or rather lack of it against their favoured team, Reading FC.
>
> (Adapted from Woodyer, 2010)

Figure 6   The secretive world of play

While Stephen took great delight in sharing aspects of his video game play with his father, Joshua found glee in his mother's incomprehension of the world of Yu-Gi-Oh! As social actors, children make choices about when to share aspects of their culture with parents and other adults. By restricting the study of play to spaces of peer interaction, this feature of children's culture is often neglected.

If we are to understand children's play more fully we need to consider domestic spaces of familial relations and productive spaces where children's play and work are intertwined, alongside child-dominated spaces of peer relations.

Summary of Section 3

The existence of a separate 'culture of childhood', independent of the adult world, is debated by folklorists, anthropologists and sociologists.

Around the world, play is often inseparable from work-based practices that help shape children's future social roles, and so will vary according to socio-economic contexts.

In the affluent and (post)-industrialised contexts of the minority world, children's play is increasingly subject to parental intervention aiming to prime children for success in academic settings and for future participation in the information economy.

Children take delight from sharing aspects of their culture with adults, but also revel in the fact that adults find some elements of this culture mysterious and alien.

---

4   The folklore tradition

The term 'folklore' was coined by William Thoms in 1846 to refer to 'manners, customs, observances, superstitions, ballads, proverbs, etc, of the olden time' (Thoms, cited in Dundes, 1965, p. 5). Childhood tradition formed part of folklore from the start, with Thoms using a children's custom in Yorkshire as his principal example.

Subsequently, Lady Alice Bertha Gomme (one of the founders of the Folklore Society in 1878) conducted an extensive two-volume survey of childhood tradition. Published as *The Traditional Games of England, Scotland, and Ireland* in 1894 and 1898, it did much to establish the study of children's folklore as a valid field in its own right. The books include detailed descriptions and classifications of 800 games and their variants, drawn from her own and others' fieldwork, various literary and other sources, and adult recollections.

Whereas psychological and sociological research has often concerned itself with weighty matters of child development and socialisation, folklorist research has tended to focus on what are often deemed the 'non-serious things of life' (Sutton-Smith, 1970, p. 2). Yet these things form a significant part of children's experience of childhood and should not be dismissed as trivial, as Sutton-Smith and others suggest when they describe them as 'expressive culture'. Bishop and Curtis (2001, p. 8) argue that 'children's play traditions often reveal dimensions of creativity, artistry and complexity in their own right, including carnivalesque, subversive and parodic elements as well as normative ones'. They are at once inherited and improvised, rule-bound and adaptive, collaborative and competitive, universal and local.

4.1   Peter and Iona Opie

Peter and Iona Opie were also members of the Folklore Society. Their studies of children's worlds in the UK are well known and frequently cited. Importantly, they made the transition from collecting adult reminiscences to observing and interviewing children themselves. In the early 1950s Peter and Iona Opie set out to identify and chart the traditions and pursuits of British schoolchildren. Their motives were straightforward: in the light of public concern that such lore was in decline, they wanted to find out how much of it still existed and to record it. In so doing they also wanted to construct an account of how children amused themselves in their own free time at a certain point in history. They used the correspondence columns of the *Sunday Times* newspaper to recruit 151 schoolteachers across the UK who agreed to report on the lives of the 7- to 11-year-old children in their schools. The teachers asked the children to write about the games they played out of school, the rhymes they used, and the rules and conventions that governed the things they did. When the Opies did not completely understand the children's descriptions, the children would be contacted directly for further explanation. The guidelines given to study participants were deliberately broad: 'any game played with a ball', 'any names for people you don't like'. This initial study stage was complemented by observation of playground activities.

With additional subsequent surveys, the Opies produced four volumes: *The Lore and Language of School Children* (1959); *Children's Games in Street and Playground* (1969); *The Singing Game* (1985); and *Children's Games with Things* (1997). The original written contributions are now housed in the Bodleian Library in Oxford, whilst recordings made in school playgrounds are held in the British Library National Archive in London.

4.2   'Children don't play games anymore'

There is a widespread perception that children no longer play 'traditional' games. As the Opies' concerns in the 1950s attest, this is not new: in fact, Samuel Pepys recorded similar sentiments in his diary

Figure 7   Peter and Iona Opie researching children's games

on 25 July 1664, and writers to newspapers and other social commentators have been doing so ever since. In 1883, William Newell introduced his book, *Games and Songs of American Children*, thus:

> This collection represents an expiring custom. The vine of oral tradition, of popular poetry … is perishing at the roots; its prouder branches have long since been blasted, and children's song, its humble but longest-flowering offshoot, will soon have shared their fate.
>
> (Newell, 1963 [1883], p. 1)

The Opies have commented that the belief that traditional games are dying out is itself traditional. Over the years many reasons have been identified for this supposed decline: in the nineteenth century the new National Schools and the coming of the railways were among the culprits; in the earlier part of the twentieth century it was cinema, radio and the gramophone; in the 1950s, television; and most recently pop music and computer games have been held responsible (Opie and Opie, 1997; and see below). More recently, an article in the *Daily Mail* (2009) headlined 'Skipping scuppered!' outlined the results of a survey – carried out, ironically, for a soft drinks manufacturer – in which parents expressed concerns that 'skipping, conkers, hopscotch, British bulldog and climbing trees' were dying out thanks to 'health and safety regulations' in our 'cotton-wool society'. It is possible to view these concerns as an expression of perennial adult anxieties that childhood is not what it used to be.

As Bishop and Curtis (2001) argue, these elegies rarely give any critical consideration to what is meant by the term 'traditional'. For instance, it is often assumed that in earlier times culture was passed down the generations unchanged; or that the traditional is inherently positive and valuable, something we should respect and revere. In the process it is conveniently forgotten that (for example) racist name-calling and viciously violent games are equally as 'traditional' as hopscotch, marbles and group skipping. Another common feature of these concerns stretching across generations is the absence of a basis in research. Yet in fact research has established beyond doubt that playground culture is much more robust than often supposed.

4.3   Continuity and change

That children's play activities should change over time is not surprising given the constant change of population and the influx of new influences this brings. Elizabeth Grugeon's (2001) work on playground cultures illustrates processes of continuity and change. While she was filming games on a visit to a school playground, a group of five nine-year-old girls positioned themselves in front of the camera and sang the following song. Each line was illustrated by exaggerated mimed actions, with much giggling consuming the parts that the girls evidently considered the rudest:

> We are the teenage girls [dance about with exaggerated wiggle]
> We wear our hair in curls [curling actions on either side of head]
> We wear our dungarees
> Up to our sexy knees [hands by knees]
> I met a boy last night
> He paid me 50p [loud slap of hand]
> To go behind a tree
> To have it off with me [action not clear but much mirth]
> My mother was surprised
> To see my belly rise [gesture to indicate large stomach]
> My daddy jumped for joy
> It was a baby boy [mimic babe in arms]
> My mum had fifty tits [much hilarity]

(Adapted from Grugeon, 2001, p. 108)

The idea of 'fifty tits' seems to be a mishearing of 'fifty fits', a phrase that would be unfamiliar to this generation. Grugeon is always keen to trace the provenance of the games she observes and records. She found a more innocent version of the song in the Opies' (1985) publication, *The Singing Game*. It appeared in Glasgow in 1975:

> We are the Barbie girls
> We wear our hair in curls,
> We wear our dungarees
> To hide our dirty knees.
> We wear our father's shirt,
> We wear our brother's tie,
> And when we want a guy
> We simply wink the eye.

(Quoted in Opie and Opie, 1985, p. 478)

Interestingly, when Grugeon asked the girls how they knew 'Teenage girls' and other rhymes she observed them performing, they responded by saying that they made them up at school. The 'rude one' had been told to one group member by an older sister, and another group member by a friend. The girls then 'all put it together' (Grugeon, 2001, p. 112).

These rhymes illustrate the way in which children's lore is not static but constantly changing and evolving. An emphasis on tradition as an ongoing process emphasises that traditional play activities are passed on by social actors rather than an abstract, passive means. This alteration in children's rhymes and games is one explanation for concern about the demise of children's traditional play. It is a replica of past practice rather than evidence for the dynamic incorporation of contemporary influences and experiences into 'traditional' practices that is being sought. In his book, *Out to Play,* Alasdair Roberts urges us 'to remove games from the realm of nostalgia and demonstrate that they are as lively and varied now as they ever were' (Roberts, 1980, p. xi). We need to examine our adult assumptions about contemporary play activities and the effect our personal experience has on our perceptions of them.

4.4   Oral culture and empowerment

The more recent version of the song above should be seen in its wider social and cultural context. It was recorded in July 1997, the same

Figure 8   An enduring pastime

summer that the Spice Girls' song 'Wannabe' was at the top of the pop music charts in the UK. It seemed every young girl from five to 15 years wanted to be a Spice Girl. Indeed, spontaneous renderings of 'Wannabe' accompanied by imitations of the pop stars' personas and dance routines were recorded on the same playground by Grugeon. The Spice Girls' singing and dancing routines were sexually provocative and aggressively loud. Teachers and parents had mixed views, with some schools even banning the Spice Girls from the playground. Grugeon notes that in the playgrounds where the Spice Girls were allowed, there was a confidence and noisy exuberance to the girls' games. This went some way to addressing the commonplace marginalisation of girls in school playgrounds. In the 1980s, girls tended to be excluded to the edges as boys played football in the central space.

From her analysis of songs and games, Grugeon has argued that far from being just a quaint relic of past childhoods, they are 'powerful agents for socialisation, enculturation and resistance' (Grugeon, 1988, p. 167). The text and actions of the songs combine the subversive and the normative, not only transmitting the social order, but also providing the means to challenge it. Normative femininity is powerfully encoded in the songs' predictions of a future of domesticity and childrearing. As 'Teenage girls' clearly shows, new femininities, such as 'Girl Power', are also encoded within them, allowing for subversive acts of resistance. Rather than simply representing a loss of childhood innocence, the provocative nature of such songs references a future where the rules about how women express their sexuality are far broader and more open than in previous generations. These new femininities need to be understood in the context of broader economic, social and psychological changes affecting women in the past five decades. These play texts may be both empowering and reassuring for girls, allowing them to explore adult themes whilst remaining children. They can explore the boundaries of their experience in a safe and conservative environment. The nonsense element of the texts and actions allows this behaviour to be one step removed from everyday life. Examples such as these illustrate how elements of children's playground culture and experience may have wider implications for their engagement with society.

4.5   Playground games for the digital generation

Media technologies are frequently cited as a cause for the supposed demise in traditional games, as we noted above. In April 2006, the *Daily Express* carried the headline 'Skipping? Hopscotch? Games are a mystery to the iPod generation' (cited in Beyond Text, 2011, p. 3). There is no doubt that digital media influences contemporary play activities, but given that children's media cultures are richer and more diverse than ever before, this should come as no surprise. Developments within the global culture industry have given rise to an almost seamless convergence of toys, games and media in the commercial marketplace, which transfers into children's everyday lives. As Goldstein et al. (2004) acknowledge, 'children's culture is now highly intertextual: every "text" effectively draws upon and feeds into every other text' (Goldstein et al., 2004, p. 2). For the psychologist Stephen Kline, the 'stylized narratives' of children's television lack 'psychological depth or intrigue', are 'stilted and hollow', and do not deal 'authentically with real children' or create 'useful parables for the young' (Kline, 1993, p. 315). Children's imaginative play in these contexts, he suggests, is stifled by the 'technicians of the imagination' who generate fictions driven primarily by economic considerations.

In contrast to Kline, Elizabeth Grugeon's analysis of media influences is more positive. She argues that children, 'creatively absorb this material into their play culture, exploring themes and issues that they make their own through imaginative narratives. A look at what these children say and do shows the extent to which these games, far from deadening their imagination, feed and extend possibilities for new narratives' (Grugeon, 2004, p. 82).

Grugeon's collection of primary school trainee teachers' observations provides rich examples of the integration of digital media influences into children's playground cultures. In 2001, Pokémon was one of the most popular playground games for 5 to 11 year olds, as the teacher below, Jane, discovered:

Jane: So what are you playing in the playground then?

Child A: Our Pokémon game. He's a Squirtle and he can squirt water; I'm a Beedrill and I can drill through things.

Child B: What about the ball?

Child A: Oh yeah, the Power Ball. You can throw it at people and make them slow down so you can use your powers on them.

(Grugeon, 2004, p. 75)

Pokémon cards were banned in this particular school. Yet, there were many instances of children absorbing and adapting characters and narratives into their fantasy play. This play involved confident use of the language of the Pokémon world. Children took on particular roles and developed new skills, as another teacher, Clare, noted:

> There was one child who was obviously very knowledgeable about Pokémon and how the battles were decided. This meant that he appeared to take on the role of adjudicator with many of the children approaching him to clear up disputes they had over who had won the battle and arguments about 'fair swaps'. He is a child who is quiet in the classroom, often refraining from raising his hand because he lacks confidence in his own ability.

(Quoted in Grugeon, 2004, p. 76)

The incorporation of media influences into children's play is by no means new. The Opies were clear about the importance of media cultures as a resource for play, documenting the incorporation of ad jingles, TV theme tunes and popular songs. In the 1970s, performances of Abba songs were popular in the playground. In the twenty-first century, children can be seen performing Abba songs derived from the film *Mamma Mia* (2008). Playground games reflect the circulation of media productions, promotions and merchandise. Whilst Pokémon games were still evident in playgrounds in 2002, they became outnumbered by games relating to Harry Potter, as this teacher, Heather, relates:

At the other end of the playground, some eight and nine year-old boys were engaged in dramatic play focused on the super hero, Harry Potter. ... The six boys start to run around the playground accompanied by appropriate sound effects. They seem to have a deep knowledge of the fantasy genre, gained from their reading, but also from media texts. ... After a few minutes, four of the boys throw themselves onto the ground. I am intrigued to understand this development ... I discover that they are playing the characters Harry, Hermione, Ron Weesley, and the twins, George and Fred. The setting is Hogwarts and they are playing a game of quidditch, playing on a broomstick, the aim of which is to look for the 'Golden Snitch'. This involves a special manoeuvre known as the Ronski Feint which involved the protagonist or seeker diving towards the ground pretending they have seen it ... the skill of the leading seeker is, just prior to diving into the ground, to swoop skywards in flight, tricking the other seekers into crashing into the ground.

(Quoted in Grugeon, 2004, p. 78)

When I conducted my own ethnographic study of domestic play in 2006, Harry Potter was still popular. One child spoke of going to the local play park with her friends to play 'magic', using the climbing frame as Hogwarts (the school of witchcraft and wizardry that Harry and his friends attend in the book series). It was also evident that themes from Harry Potter influenced other games such as 'orphans'. The death of Harry's parents at the hands of his arch rival, Lord Voldemort, is central to the Potter tales.

Recent research demonstrates that 'traditional' children's games are not marginalised or threatened by digital media. The inventiveness of playground games and how they might be performed co-exists and is infused with media influences. For example, running and chasing games that are perennially popular among children have been adapted accordingly. The game 'It' has been transformed into 'Croc' (based on a PlayStation game character) and the recent running game 'Mario Karts races' is inspired by the Nintendo Wii title. Given the strength of children's creative engagements with media cultures, there have been calls for a 'transformative pedagogy', a model of literacy that fuses children's cultural interests with school requirements.

Summary of Section 4

Adults have repeatedly lamented the demise of 'traditional' children's games, but this is an oversimplified perception.

Studies of playground cultures illustrate processes of historical continuity *and* cultural change.

The content of play is socially and historically specific, reflecting the wider cultural world in which it takes place.

Children incorporate media influences into their play, and this is by no means new. Playground games reflect the circulation of media productions, promotions and merchandise.

Scholars have debated the merits and drawbacks of media influences on children's play.

5   The social dynamics of play

This section addresses play as a social process. The social and imaginative dimensions of children's play have interested anthropologists, sociologists, cultural psychologists and geographers among others. One pertinent question addressed is the extent to which children's play draws upon and reflects aspects of the cultural worlds that children inhabit. In an anthropological study of the Mehinaku in Brazil, Thomas Gregor (1977) observed several features of children's games that appeared to mirror the structure and values of the adult society. He commented that, like Mehinaku social life itself, children's games were non-competitive and did not involve hierarchies. Consider this description of Mehinaku children at play:

> What is to me the most stirring of the games of role playing is 'Women's Sons' (*teneju itai*). Held at a good distance from the village where the children cannot be seen either by their parents or their other siblings, 'Women's Sons', quite unlike most plaza games, is played by boys and girls together. The age of the players runs from about five to twelve years.
>
> The game begins as children pair off as married couples. The husband and wife sculpt a child from a clump of earth, carving

arms, legs, features, and even genitals. They cradle the baby in their arms and talk to it. The mother holds the child on her hip and dances with it as she has seen her own mother do with younger siblings. After the parents have played with the child for a while, it sickens and dies. The parents weep and dig a grave for the infant and bury it. All the mothers then form a circle on their knees in traditional fashion and, with their heads down and their arms over each other's shoulders, they keen and wail for the lost offspring.

On the occasions that I have seen *teneju itai* played, the children were enormously amused by the entire enactment. When the time came to bury the 'babies', the boys smashed them into pieces and the girls interrupted their ritual crying with bursts of giggling and shrieks of laughter. Nevertheless, Women's Sons provides a tragic commentary on Mehinaku life – death in infancy and early childhood is all too common in the village. The game helps the children prepare for the time when they may lose a sibling and, later on, an offspring of their own. It also teaches them how to express and cope with grief through the medium of ritual crying. A poignant amalgam of tragedy and burlesque, *teneju itai* will help the young villagers to face the bitter fact of death in future years.

(Gregor, 1977, pp. 112–13)

This description vividly illustrates the way in which children's role play relates to and is an integral part of the broader culture. The cultural specificity of 'Women's Sons' reflects a feature of Mehinaku life that can be enacted to the point of parody.

Now compare this with the play of two 12-year-old girls in a bedroom in a south London apartment. The following extract is drawn from video footage created by one of the girls as part of my ethnographic study of children's domestic play:

They begin by setting up the dollhouse on the bed, arranging furniture and small dolls, some of which are from branded ranges like Animal Hospital and The Simpsons, whilst others are non-descript. The play narrative is initially concerned with exploring family life within the domestic space of the home. Then the mother begins to cry out for her baby, anxious that she can't find it in the house. The narrative quickly takes on a more fantastical character as it emerges the baby has been kidnapped by (Lego) spacemen. A search ensues, but is hampered by a river that comes alive and goes wildly out of control, along with an earthquake and a monster attack. In the meantime, there is an explosion back at the house, destroying the building. By this point, almost an hour has passed, and the girls are beginning to tire of their game. Suddenly there is a burst of energy as it is declared, 'Meanwhile, the family are reunited!' As one girl collects all the figures together, the other heads to the bed to gather up the furniture and set the house upright, claiming, 'Meanwhile, the house is fixed!' In chorus they then exclaim, 'And they all lived happily ever after!'

(Adapted from Woodyer, 2010)

Figure 9 Imaginative dollhouse play

The girls' pretend play works with an improvised imaginary script rather than with the rituals and practices of the adult world. It is unlikely that the two girls would have experience of the kind of events and situations they are enacting. Although, it is worth noting that an earthquake and tsunami had struck the Solomon Islands a few weeks previously and it is possible that news footage of this is being referenced here. In this example, play allows the children to act out difficult scenes and emotions, exploring issues and themes that are not directly part of their daily lives, but may touch upon them in subtle ways. The miniature nature of the play provides a sense of containment, allowing scary and threatening narratives to be domesticated. H. G. Wells discusses this element of play in his 1913 book *Little Wars,* which outlines a set of rules for playing with toy soldiers. Comparing his table-top game to the wargame training of the Prussian army, he declares: 'My game is just as good as their game, and saner by reason of its size' (Wells, 2004 [1913], p. 26).

5.1   Play in imaginary worlds

So far in this chapter we have largely considered play as a social activity that centres on roles, relationships and rituals. This is, in part, a reflection of the central role playground cultures take in play research. Play can also be solitary, particularly when located in the domestic space of the home. Children can temporarily withdraw from the realities of the physical world around them by creating fantasy worlds. Although children's imaginative activity is commonplace, the fantasies involved are typically short lived, serving the purposes of the moment. For a smaller number of children, however, the imaginary worlds they create become more elaborate and are sustained for months if not years. These imaginary worlds are sometimes referred to as 'paracosms' (Silvey and MacKeith, 1988).

In the 1970s Robert Silvey wrote an article about the fantasy world that he had constructed during his childhood – The New Hentian States, a federal republic occupying a large island in the South Atlantic. He compiled notebooks on its history and geology, drew maps and wrote newspaper reports on current events happening there. His interest in this world lasted until he was at least 15 years old, and for several years bordered on obsession. In many ways this world was Silvey's private retreat, although it was not secret as it was known to his family.

Silvey placed notices in several British newspapers and magazines requesting others with similar experiences to contact him. These responses have been collected and analysed by the psychiatrist Stephen MacKeith and psychologist David Cohen. The worlds that were revealed took a variety of forms, ranging from elaborate railway systems to Teddyland. Cohen and MacKeith (1992) make some pertinent observations. Firstly, the manufacture of such fantasy worlds is a common phenomenon of childhood that generally begins between the ages of eight and ten, and ends with adolescence. Secondly, contrary to what one might expect, the invention of these lands is not a preoccupation of lonely introverts. Just as many worlds are generated by children who are socially gregarious and actively enlist friends or siblings in their play. Consider the imaginary world created by Daisy (12 years old), a participant in my research:

> Daisy identifies as a witch, a practitioner of 'old magic' in particular. She explains, 'Every day we do magic, since nursery. Well, it started with just me and one friend when we were in nursery and we discovered like this hole in the building and that, that was erm … magic land.' Daisy has crafted a back story to this magic land, that firmly positions her as a magic being: 'In magic land there was a book shop and the book opened and two flowers came out and then two children were born, me and my friend.' She is able to tell if somebody is magic by identifying particular markings on the palm of their hand. She also teaches other school children, both boys and girls, how to do magic, having set up a witch's colony and made preparations for a magic school, the United Deculas School. Although popularity for magic amongst her peers is on the wane: 'Ten people used to do it, yeah about thirteen, fifteen people used to do it until about a year ago and then everyone else found out and started going, "That's so childish" and then loads of people quit.' The 'old' magic she teaches includes making potions, and using enchantments and curses. She explains, 'Now and again we curse our worst enemies, like I was cross with someone and I muttered a curse for them to drop their spoon and they dropped the spoon.' When she's not busy teaching, Daisy spends her time making wooden wands, talismans and clay apparatus, growing herbs for use in potions, and writing magical tales. When she spends time with her close friends they often travel to Ethrole Castle, where they practise power control and the creation of force fields.
>
> (Woodyer, 2010)

Daisy's Magic Land was central to her social identity, not only as a witch, but also as a teacher and purveyor of knowledge. As with the child with substantial Pokémon knowledge, play afforded the development of new roles and skills. Far from being an introvert, Daisy actively enrolled other schoolchildren into her magical world. However, her discussions of their dismissals of magic revealed that it was often only in solitary play that she could fully express herself.

Today, many imaginary worlds have taken on a digital character through the use of simulation video games and online virtual worlds like Sim City and Second Life. Consider the Sim City world created by Joshua (10 years old) in relation to Silvey's New Hentian States:

> The city has 500,000 citizens in it. It's full to the brim, and I don't have any more land to use unless I buy some more. It has a necropolis and there's a major's house and that's my house. I'm the major. And then I've got a military base, yeah, I've actually got five military bases. I granted land to the military and that keeps monsters away and things away like hurricanes and stuff, not really natural disasters, but they can keep them away by force fields.
>
> (Quoted in Woodyer, 2010)

While imaginative play is commonplace amongst children, these virtual worlds are by no means restricted to them. Indeed, the online world Second Life is intended for people aged 16 and over.

5.2   Rituals of inclusion and exclusion

Common-sense notions of play as fun and inconsequential overlook its less harmonious aspects. When a group of children begins to play there are many decisions to make, not least who is to be included and excluded. These decisions are not benign as they may produce power relations and social hierarchies among children. Children may devise many ways of excluding others and in doing so may draw upon forms of sexism and racism embedded in cultural stereotypes and popular prejudices. Play does not occur in a vacuum. It is situated within broader power relations and is often highly normalising and exclusionary.

Whilst childhood may appear as a zone of sameness to adults, it is often a realm of difference from a child's point of view. In a study of young people's experiences of growing up in rural areas, Faith Tucker (2003) reveals the various lines along which children are segregated, including age and gender. This is explored through reference to different groups' social ownership of play spaces. For example, recreation grounds were found to be contested spaces:

> Natalie: Groups of people [hang out at the rec.]. They intimidate you … They just, like, sit there and stare at you. Or they come up to you and say something horrible.
>
> (Tucker, 2003, p. 118)

Gender provides a prime example of rituals of inclusion and exclusion within play. The American sociologist Barrie Thorne (1993) used ethnographic methods to study the social worlds of boys and girls aged 9–10 years in a public elementary school. Thorne describes various rituals of gender division, including playground chasing games involving 'cooties'. 'Cooties' are invisible, contagious 'germs', and Thorne documents how, on the whole, it was girls who were seen as the source of 'cooties'. In one school they were referred to by boys as 'girl stain'. This involved boys treating girls and objects associated with girls as polluting, whilst the reverse did not occur. Thorne's analysis of these games points to the relationship between children's cultural worlds and the broader context of power relations in which they exist:

> When pollution rituals appear, even in play, they … enact larger patterns of inequality, by gender, by social class and race, and by bodily characteristics like weight and motor co-ordination. … In contemporary US culture even young girls are treated as symbolically contaminating in a way that boys … are not. This may be because in our culture even at a young age, girls are sexualised more than boys, and female sexuality, especially when 'out of place' or actively associated with children, connotes danger and endangerment.
>
> (Thorne, 1993, pp. 75–6)

Thorne uses the term 'borderwork' to point to the significance of gender in children's cultural worlds. It is a term used to characterise the ways in which children tend to form single-sex friendship groups that serve to create and strengthen gender boundaries. She suggests that children's play creates a spatial separation between boys and girls that they work to maintain through games and social interactions more generally.

Other researchers have also examined how heterosexuality underpins understandings of gender among both children themselves and their teachers. For instance, Emma Renold (2006) draws upon ethnographic fieldwork in primary schools to argue that creating an identity as a 'normal' girl or boy increasingly involves children in a range of heterosexualised practices, including sexual bullying, relationship cultures of 'girlfriends', 'boyfriends', 'dating' and 'dumping', playground games such as 'Blind Date' and for girls, testing out romance-oriented products and games from sources such as girls' magazines. By their final year of primary school, girls in Renold's study increasingly identified themselves and each other as 'girlie' or 'non-girlie' (an opposition centring on the significance of romance) and as 'single' or 'girlfriends'. Debbie Epstein's earlier studies similarly showed children constructing themselves as heterosexual and gendered by playing games such as kiss chase – or this local variant, 'kiss, cuddle and torture':

> Samantha: And we play this game called 'kiss, cuddle and torture', but we don't really do any of it, but 'cos, like, we catch [the boys], put them like in jail and then, then, when we've got all of them, we'll ask them and they'll go 'torture' …
>
> Louise: We never say torture, we [the girls] always say, give us a cuddle.
>
> (Epstein, 1997, p. 44)

Sociological studies have also examined the perpetuation of racial and ethnic patterns in children's play. Van Ausdale and Feagin (2001) argue that some of the young children in their study used different ethnic markers, such as language and skin colour, to control and establish dominance in social interactions and the social ownership of space.

The creation of boundaries also presents opportunities for transgression, or as Thorne refers to it, 'border crossing'. Whilst, on the whole, most children adhere to gender-defined boundaries, some choose to cross the line, disrupting gender-appropriate behaviour. Border crossing tends to be acceptable among girls or boys who have achieved a position of high status within their peer group. Some children opt for more sustained practices of border crossing, for instance girls who strongly identify as 'tomboys'. Renold argues that for some girls, being a 'tomboy' provided an identity through which they could escape the 'heterosexualised' practices described above, form strong friendships with boys and engage in 'male' activities such as football. Others, however, give more ambivalent accounts of what it involves.

Activity 5   Reading B

Now study Reading B, 'Girls will be boys', in which the journalist Joanna Moorhead reflects on her daughter's experiences as a tomboy. Note the many aspects of behaviour that Miranda – or Alex – has to adapt to, the repercussions for friendship formation and spatial use she faces and the particular role of games and toys in both the assignment and enactment of gender roles.

Comment

Although Moorhead attempts to convey the positive experiences of having a tomboy daughter, one cannot fail to be moved by the heartache Alex experiences when friendships fall apart as her true gender is discovered. In many respects I identify with Alex. As an only child, I spent the majority of my time playing with male cousins and the grandsons of next-door neighbours. I hated wearing skirts as I felt they restricted my ability to engage in the same activities as my male peers. This was awkward at a time when schools did not permit girls to wear trousers. My uncles and cousins are keen football fans and I always felt hard done by when, due to being a girl, I was sidelined in conversations and left behind as they travelled the country going to matches. Moorhead powerfully demonstrates the assumptions embedded in the way society assigns gender roles. Toys and games are shown to play an important role in this. Whilst acting as a tomboy is often regarded as a phase that young girls will grow out off, Moorhead points to the implications gender-based play can have for attitudes and future roles.

The dynamics of power in children's social relationships are complex. The boundaries upon which inclusion and exclusion are based are shifting, and there is often tension and volatility involved in 'borderwork'. Emotions can run high, and play can easily slide into non-play. Tucker documents how children use a variety of strategies to manage this conflict and the rivalry it can entail. This includes children excluding themselves from spaces, either through fear of intimidation or association, only using contested spaces in the presence of adults, and remaining on the move rather than settling in one spot for any period of time:

Megan: People hang around the church gates, and when you walk past it's not nice.

Mary:	You just kind of walk twice as fast and you don't look at them.
Alisha:	You try not to go there.
Mary:	You walk around them. You make sure there's a gap between you and them.
Megan:	You try to avoid it if you can. I sometimes walk the long way round so I don't go near them.
Alisha:	But if you have to go past them, you do it as quick as you can, basically.
Louise:	I walk on the other side of the road.
Katie:	My mum sometimes takes me and my little brother to the rec. Sometimes my friend Chelsea comes too. Then the gang leaves us alone. They don't say stuff if my mum's there.

(Tucker, 2003, pp. 119–20)

Summary of Section 5

Play is culturally specific, reflecting the structure and values of adult society.

Play can be both a social activity and a solitary pastime in which children create their own meanings and develop a sense of identity.

Play produces power relations and social hierarchies among children.

Play activities may draw on larger patterns of social inequality such as gender difference and ethnicity.

Children adopt a variety of strategies to manage conflict and rivalry.

---

6 The place of toys in children's play

Throughout this chapter, the emphasis has tended to fall on the role of child–child interactions within play. However, a number of examples have also spoken of the importance of toys in contemporary play – the influence of the Harry Potter books and Pokémon video games, and the use of Yu-Gi-Oh! trading cards, dolls, teddies and playhouses. As Kline observes, minority-world childhoods have become synonymous with commercially produced toys:

> Toys have become the supreme emblems of the young child's dearest pleasures, a parent's way of saying how special and precious the child is: the very word 'play' now conjures first and foremost the activities that revolve around the relationship between child and toy.
>
> (Kline, 1993, p. 147)

Some examples in this chapter have also pointed to children's ingenuity in creating their own toys where manufactured ones are not readily available. Whilst these examples tend to be drawn from majority-world contexts, it is interesting to note that play for the large majority of British children did not involve manufactured objects until well into the nineteenth century. The likes of hoops, spinning tops, balls and rag dolls were played with, but these were crafted from everyday objects either by the children themselves or their relatives. Manufactured toys were a luxury restricted to a wealthy, privileged minority. Museums housing collections of toys provide a valuable and interesting record of children's playthings through time and across space. However, it is important to be aware that the toys that appear in such exhibits are not necessarily representative of their era or place. The homemade and cheap toys that formed a large part of past children's lives are less likely to have found their way into a museum. Many museum objects, such as ceramic dolls, mechanical soldiers or toy theatres, were often designed for adults and were only rarely played with by children.

It was during the course of the twentieth century that commercial playthings rose to prominence with the expansion of mass-produced factory-made toys. At the start of the century 50 per cent of the toys sold in the USA were imported, mostly from German craft producers. By 1920 this had fallen to 10 per cent as the majority of the toys were now being produced domestically within factories (Kline, 1993). Factory production meant lower costs and wider distribution. Toys were no longer a luxury item restricted to a wealthy minority. A further development in the second half of the twentieth century firmly established the role of commercial toys within play. This was the growth of mass-marketing and the use of television to promote toys. Children's animated television series became extended commercials for

Figure 10   The role of toys in play

entertainment 'spin-offs'. Over the course of the twentieth century, this developed into the practice of integrated marketing – a comprehensive strategic plan based around the seamless convergence of toys, games, media and merchandise.

6.1   Commercialisation of play

At the core of much contemporary popular debate about toys and the nature of children's play is concern about what is seen as an increasing commodification of childhood and commercialisation of children's culture. As Stephen Kline (1993, p. 12) notes, 'the consumerist vector of our society sometimes appears disturbing when we see it reflected and expressed in children's behaviour.' Some people argue that traditional values, discipline and patterns of social relations are being lost; that economic interests rather than a desire to inspire and educate are motivating toy design and development; and that contemporary marketing practices are creating a materialistic mentality, expressed in an 'I want' culture.

A trend towards commercialisation is seen not only in relation to playthings, but also play spaces. Since the 1990s, there has been a dramatic rise in the number of 'commercial playgrounds' in industrialised societies. These include 'stand-alone' soft-play centres and 'add-on' indoor and outdoor playgrounds in a variety of places from family pubs and restaurants to banks and building societies. Whilst this commercialisation has raised concerns about the loss of independent mobility and spontaneous play, these spaces are asserting children's right to play spaces in parts of the built environment that were previously adult domains (McKendrick et al., 2000).

6.2　'Good' and 'bad' toys

The truism that 'play is the work of children, and toys are their tools' (Cross, 1997, p. vi) has informed almost a century of work within the field of child development. However, this work has tended to focus on play as a process of intellectual, emotional and social development rather than the toy. Within this framework, different toys are deemed appropriate, and in some cases necessary, for different stages of development. In the 1950s, the psychologist Beatrix Tudor-Hart (1955) argued that toys encountered at the 'wrong' stage might forestall children's development and thus were potentially harmful. This basic categorisation of toys as 'good' or 'bad' continues to permeate popular understandings of toys. Andrew McClary (2004) has documented the change in tone of media reports on toys since the early twentieth century. In the early years, toys were part of a new and exciting world of technological innovation. Articles in the popular press extolled the delightful and thrilling toys appearing in shops and their potential benefits for children. By the 1950s, however, the tone became more negative: toy guns and action figures were said to incite aggression, Barbie was criticised for her unrealistic figure, children's pestering for the latest craze put parents under pressure, machine-made toys were covered in poisonous paint, and so on.

Such troubles partly account for the rise to prominence of so-called 'educational' toys. These are by no means new, of course: in 1693, the English philosopher John Locke described a friend who placed letters on to the sides of dice and encouraged his children to throw and then arrange them to spell out a word, such that the oldest child 'played himself into spelling, with great eagerness, and … without having been forced into doing it' (Locke, quoted in McClary, 2004, pp. 58–9).

Nonetheless, there is certainly a trend for today's toys to be emblazoned with messages about their 'educational' value, in implicit contrast to their 'non-educational' counterparts. Childcare experts are divided as to what educational toys should teach, some stressing the importance of creativity, others emphasising social awareness. Today's parents are besieged with advice about appropriate toys, not only from experts, but also from toy manufacturers who have exploited the ambiguous nature of the term 'educational' to promote their products. 'But what about fun?' asks McClary, citing in response the words of Eda Leshan, a psychologist and family counsellor:

After years of studying and observing young children – children at play – I'm convinced that they have the answers ... [A child] doesn't ask whether what he's doing is worthwhile. He plays for the sake of play, play as an end in itself.

(Leshan, quoted in McClary, 2004, p. 75)

Leshan's statement suggests that a fixation on intellectual and social development may ignore the broader meanings and emotions attached to toys.

6.3 Toys, creativity and imagination

Studies of children's toys have tended to adopt a method of analysis that approaches them as texts, reading them for the particular messages they convey. Little consideration is given to how they might be received by their intended audience – children. This is especially problematic since the producers and critics of these cultural products are almost by definition not members of that audience. When we approach toys from the child's perspective, we find there is much more going on than is often credited.

Figure 11   Playing Fifa

Activity 6   Reading C

Allow about 15 minutes

Now study Reading C, 'PlayStation, Fifa and footballing cultures'. This involves Stephen and his family (from Extract 2 in Section 3.3) but considers this play in more depth. Playing video games has received bad press in recent years for encouraging aggressive behaviour, inhibiting children's imaginative capabilities and inducing children into a sedentary, solitary lifestyle. This reading points to the often neglected social networks and creative activities that surround gaming.

Comment

Stephen's video game play only makes sense when viewed as but one part of a broader football-centred culture. It is an example of 'genre-blending'. The educationalists, Claudia Mitchell and Jacqueline Reid-Walsh argue that:

> [Children question] the single-item-ness of various popular culture items and the tendency of adults to go after a particular popular culture item in either a celebratory way or in a condemning way, as though children – the players – encounter these objects in the same singular way.
>
> *(Mitchell and Reid-Walsh, 2002, p. 93)*

Similarly, Goldstein et al. (2004) discuss children's abilities to draw upon and move between the various texts – or platforms – that make up contemporary children's culture. They describe the exploratory practices in which children engage as 'heuristic activities par excellence' (Goldstein et al., 2004, p. 3). Stephen used these various platforms to create his own fantasy world where he determined his team's relative positioning in the league table. He shared this fantasy world with his family and friends in the same way that he did the real-world context of English football. Stephen was not only adept at moving between media platforms and play contexts seamlessly, but developed creative ways to extend them. Where he was unable to source particular Shoot Out cards or Merlin stickers, he would create his own using coloured card and pictures downloaded from the internet.

Activity 7   Revisiting a definition of play

Allow about 10 minutes

Now that we are approaching the end of the chapter, return to the initial examples of play that you used in the first activity. Does your reading confirm the views you started with, or might you approach these examples differently? How would you explain to others what is going on in these examples of play?

Comment

Childhood is unique in being a stage of life that we all pass through. Many people assert themselves as an authority on play based on their own personal experience of childhood or casual observations of contemporary children playing. Less consideration is given to how our personal recollections shape our understanding of children's play or the inaccessibility of parts of children's worlds to adults. There is often much more going on when children play than is usually appreciated.

Summary of Section 6

For many children, past and present, toys have been crafted and improvised from natural objects and discarded goods.

Ready-made toys are therefore not necessary to play, although the recent mass-production and marketing of toys has permeated deeply into children's culture.

It is not only playthings, but also play spaces that are commercialised.

Whilst expert opinion on what makes a toy 'good' or 'bad' varies, toys are commonly categorised in this basic way.

Children are creative in their engagements with toys, using them in ways that often go unnoticed by adults.

7   Conclusion

This chapter has explored aspects of lore, games and play that are a distinctive feature of children's worlds. The chapter began by

Figure 12 Play is not just for the young

considering some of the ways in which children's play has been discussed. Play is commonly approached as a learning experience – whether in relation to intellectual, social or emotional development – that prepares children for adult life. The chapter then turned to attempts to describe and understand play in its own right, as a distinctive feature of children's cultural worlds. It questioned the existence of a separate culture of childhood, and pointed to some features of our contemporary world that problematise this notion.

Issues such as historical continuity and cultural change raise questions about the relative merits of personal reminiscence and active research in understanding play activities. Studies conducted at different times and across different geographical locations indicate that play is culturally specific, reflecting the structure and values of adult society. Play is both a social activity and a solitary pastime, through which children create meaning and develop a sense of identity. Whilst play is often considered benign, its effects are not always positive. It produces power relations and social hierarchies among children which can in some cases lead to tension, volatility and conflict.

Commercially produced toys now form a significant part of children's worlds. Questions have been raised about the merits of different toys and their effects on children's development. We drew attention to the way in which an emphasis on playground rather than domestic cultures can skew understandings of children's play. Children spend considerable time at home, in the company of adults; focusing on the school playground may neglect the important role of family members and other adult figures in play. In turn, this may restrict consideration of play to childhood rather than understanding it as an important ongoing activity throughout life.

References

Ainsworth, M. (1967) *Infancy in Uganda: Infant Care and the Growth of Love*, Baltimore, MD, Johns Hopkins University Press.

Beyond Text (2011) *Children's Playground Games and Songs in the New Media Age 2009–2011: Project Report* [online], Swindon, Arts and Humanities Resarch Council, http://projects.beyondtext.ac.uk/playgroundgames/uploads/end_of_project_report.pdf (Accessed 28 June 2012).

Bishop, J. C. and Curtis, M. (2001) 'Introduction', in Bishop, J. C. and Curtis, M. (eds) *Play Today in the Primary School Playground: Life, Learning and Creativity*, Buckingham and Philadelphia, PA, Open University Press.

Blair, T. (1997) *New Britain: My Vision of a Young Country*, Boulder, CO, Westview.

British Library (2010) *Onika Bonika. Playtimes: A Century of Children's Games and Rhymes* [online], London, British Library, http://www.bl.uk/learning/langlit/playground/clips/counting/121181.html (Accessed 28 June 2012).

Buckingham, D. and Scanlon, M. (2003) *Education, Entertainment and Learning in the Home*, Buckingham, Open University Press.

Cohen, D. and MacKeith, S. (1992) *The Development of Imagination: The Private Worlds of Childhood*, London, Routledge.

Cross, G. (1997) *Kids' Stuff: Toys, and the Changing World of American Childhood*, London, Harvard University Press.

Daily Mail (2009) 'Skipping scuppered! The death of playground games, conkers and tree-climbing in our cotton-wool society', *Daily Mail*, 28 July [online], http://www.dailymail.co.uk/news/article-1202580/Skipping-scuppered-The-death-playground-games-conkers-tree-climbing-cotton-wool-society.html#ixzz1z62RpN6L (Accessed 28 June 2012).

Dundes, A. (1965) *The Study of Folklore*, Englewood Cliffs, Prentice Hall.

Epstein, D. (1997) 'Cultures of schooling/cultures of sexuality', *International Journal of Inclusive Education*, vol. 1, no. 1, pp. 37–53.

Goldstein, J., Buckingham, D. and Brougere, G. (eds) (2004) *Toys, Games and Media*, Mahwah, NJ, Lawrence Erlbaum Associates.

Gomme, A. B. (1894) *The Traditional Games of England, Scotland, and Ireland* (vol. 1), London, David Nutt.

Gomme, A. B. (1898) *The Traditional Games of England, Scotland, and Ireland* (vol. 2), London, David Nutt.

Gregor, T. (1977) *Mehinaku: The Drama of Daily life in a Brazilian Indian Village*, Chicago, IL, Chicago University Press.

Grugeon, E. (1988) 'Children's oral culture: a transitional experience', in Maclure, M., Phillips, T. and Wilkinson, A. (eds) *Oracy Matters*, Milton Keynes, Open University Press.

Grugeon, E. (2000) 'Girls' playground language and lore', in Bearne, E. and Watson, V. (eds) *Where Texts and Children Meet*, London, Routledge.

Grugeon, E. (2001) '"We like singing the Spice Girl songs … and we like Tig and Stuck in the Mud": girls traditional games on two playgrounds', in Bishop, C. J. and Curtis, M. (eds) *Play Today in the Primary School Playground*, Buckingham, Open University Press.

Grugeon, E. (2004) 'From Pokémon to Potter: trainee teachers explore children's media-related play, 2000–2003', in Goldstein, J., Buckingham, D. and Brougere, G. (eds) *Toys, Games and Media*, Mahwah, NJ, Lawrence Erlboum Associates.

Katz, C. (2004) *Growing Up Global: Economic Restructuring and Children's Everyday Lives*, Minneapolis, MN, University of Minnesota Press.

Kline, S. (1993) *Out of the Garden: Toys and Children's Culture in the Age of TV*, New York, Verso.

Lancy, D. F. (2007) 'Accounting for variability in mother–child play', *American Anthropologist*, vol. 109, no. 2, pp. 273–84.

Lareau, A. (2002) 'Invisible inequality: social class and childrearing in black families and white families', *American Sociological Review*, vol. 67, no. 5, pp. 747–76.

Mamma Mia (2008) film, directed by Phyllida Lloyd, Universal Pictures.

McClary, A. (2004) *Good Toys, Bad Toys: How Safety, Society, Politics and Fashion have Reshaped Children's Playthings*, Jefferson, McFarland.

McKendrick, J. H., Bradford, M. G. and Fielder, A. V. (2000) 'Making time for a party!: Making sense of the commercialisation of leisure space for children', in Holloway, S. L. and Valentine, G. (eds) *Children's Geographies: Playing, Living, Learning*, London, Routledge.

Mitchell, C. and Reid-Walsh, J. (2002) *Researching Children's Popular Culture: The Cultural Spaces of Childhood*, London, Routledge.

Newell, W. W. (1963 [1883]) *Games and Songs of American Children*, New York, Dover.

Opie, I. and Opie, P. (1959) *The Lore and Language of School Children*, Oxford, Oxford University Press.

Opie, I. and Opie, P. (1969) *Children's Games in Street and Playground*, Oxford, Clarendon Press.

Opie, I. and Opie, P. (1985) *The Singing Game*, Oxford, Oxford University Press.

Opie, I. and Opie, P. (1997) *Children's Games with Things*, Oxford, Oxford University Press.

Renold, E. (2006) '"They won't let us play … unless you're going out with one of them": girls, boys and Butler's "heterosexual matrix" in the primary years', *British Journal of Sociology of Education*, vol. 27, no. 4, pp. 489–509.

Roberts, A. (1980) *Out to Play: The Middle Years of Childhood*, Aberdeen, Aberdeen University Press.

Silvey R. and MacKeith, S. (1988) 'The paracosm: a special form of fantasy', in Morrison, D. C. (ed) *Organizing Early Experience*, New York, Baywood.

Smith, P. K. (2010) *Children and Play*, Chichester, Wiley-Blackwell.

Sutton-Smith, B. (1970) 'Psychology of childlore: the triviality barrier', *Western Folklore*, vol. 29, pp. 1–8.

Thorne, B. (1993) *Gender Play: Girls and Boys in School*, Buckingham, Open University Press.

Tucker, F. (2003) 'Sameness or difference? Exploring girls' use of recreational spaces', *Children's Geographies*, vol. 1, no. 1, pp. 111–24.

Tudor-Hart, B. (1955) *Toys, Play and Discipline in Childhood*, London, Routledge.

Van Ausdale, D. and Feagin, J. R. (2001) *The First R: How Children Learn Race and Racism*, Oxford, Rowan and Littlefield.

Walkerdine, V. and Lucey, H. (1989) *Democracy in the Kitchen*, London, Virago.

Wells, H. G. (2004 [1913]) *Little Wars: A Game for Boys from Twelve Years of Age to One Hundred and Fifty and for that More Intelligent Sort of Girl Who likes Boys' Games and Books; with an Appendix on Kriegspiel*, Kessinger.

Woodyer, T. (2010) *Playing with Toys: The Animated Geographies of Children's Material Culture*, unpublished PhD thesis, London, University of London.

Reading A
Playful work and 'workful' play

Cindi Katz

Source: *Growing Up Global: Economic Restructuring and Children's Everyday Lives*, 2004, Minneapolis, MN, University of Minnesota Press, pp. 82–3.

Children often assisted their fathers and older relatives with charcoal making … Sami participated in charcoal production regularly. Sami was from a relatively poor nontenant household. His father was an older man who earned about half of his annual income from the production and sale of charcoal. Except during the height of the rainy season from July though October, when charcoal was not produced and agricultural work was available, Sami accompanied his father almost daily to cut and gather wood for the production of charcoal and household consumption. They traipsed over an hour away to find adequate supplies of favored species like tulh (*Acacia seyal*) or, more rarely, *hejlij* (*Balanites aegyptiaca*). While Sami and his father cut wood, the latter with considerably more speed and dexterity, Sami's thirteen-year-old sister, Maha, collected felled branches to haul home for household cooking. Besides cutting and transporting wood, Sami and Maha assisted their father every few days when he built an earthen kiln next to their house to carbonize the charcoal. The children also helped their father tend the kiln for the two or three days that the charcoal smoldered and with bagging it for sale either in the village or a nearby town. Even though the children goofed around when they went out each day, their work was not as playful as that of children out only with other kids to collect wood. As assistants to their father, Sami and Maha were not in control of the rhythm of their work or its duration, and unlike the herdboys or children off on their own to do various tasks, these children had few opportunities for 'stolen' moments of unattended spontaneous play. Nevertheless, a different form of play erupted around the edges.

July. The rains were starting and charcoal production would soon be winding down. On a bit of a busman's holiday, Sami spent part of the morning building an extraordinary miniature charcoal mound out of small pieces of wood. Crouching on the ground near his house, he made a small mound of grass and then placed the wood teepee-style around it. He covered the cone in another layer of grass and then sprinkled fistfuls of dirt mixed with dung over the whole thing. The whole enterprise took about ten minutes, whereupon Sami ran to get a burning coal from a neighbor's fire. Touching it to the grass through a small opening he'd left, Sami ignited the comina. As he covered the opening with a doleib stone, Sami announced with great satisfaction that the charcoal would be ready by afternoon. When Sami unpacked the small mound later in the day, he gave the charcoal to his mother – an indulgence she rarely got from her husband's routine charcoal production.

In this activity, Sami, the eternal assistant in making charcoal, had a chance to sequence and control the full range of tasks associated with the activity. His playful work offered a sense of mastery and his workful play produced small amounts of charcoal for his appreciative mother.

Reading B
Girls will be boys

Joanna Moorhead

Source: 'Girls will be boys', 2007, *The Times Magazine*, 4 August, pp. 22–7.

Miranda, my eight year old, is making her first communion in a few weeks' time, prompting a major dilemma. What in heaven's name is she going to wear? We have the perfect dress hanging in the wardrobe – long, white, demure, worn to great acclaim by her older sister on her first communion day four years ago – but when Miranda looks at it, she scrunches up her nose as though she's smelled something foul. 'Mum!' she hisses. 'I can't wear that! It's a dress!'

Miranda is a tomboy – a girl who'd rather be a boy; a girl who seems to feel, as Jo March expressed it in *Little Women*, that she can't quite get over her disappointment at not being born male. Like Jo, Miranda does all she can to redress the problem: she wears boys' clothes (yes, even down to the vests and boxer shorts); she plays boys' games (with, of course, boys); she laughs at boys' humour, and she shouts loudly at the telly during rugby matches with dad, while swigging her Ribena from a beer bottle for maximum masculine effect. She's even chosen a boy's name – Alex – and prefers to be called that.

And boy is she convincing. One of my biggest ethical dilemmas came one sunny afternoon on the common near our home. Miranda had found a new friend and was happily playing football with him; I was lying on the grass having a snooze. Then the other child's dad wandered over. 'Our boys are getting on really well,' he enthused. 'Do you think Alex could come over to play at our house sometime?' Miranda looked up at me, fear in her eyes: please, she was saying, don't break my cover. Freddie thinks I'm a boy, and that's what this new friendship is based on. If I'm a girl, it will be something different. I have rarely hated telling the truth as much as I did on that occasion. Miranda was heartbroken, and the invitation to play never followed …

So what has happened to childhood, if it is so homogenous that the only way to be a girl is to dress in pink frills and play with dolls and plastic kitchens, while boys have monopolised rumbustiousness, den-building and blue gingham shirts and navy shorts? Having Miranda as a daughter has led me, literally, out of the girls' ghetto in the toy shops, the place where I used to hang around with my older daughters poring over My Little Ponies, Sylvanian people and Animal Hospitals, to what I now realise is the more exciting part of the shop, the place where they stack the Scalextric, the Game Boys, the make-your-own-model-helicopter-and-fly-it kits.

Toy shop sexism is subtle, but it is pretty clear one sort of toy is being marketed at one sex, and another at the other. Online toy shops make the differentiation starker: you will find precious few pictures on the internet of little boys playing with Baby Borns and Baby Annabells, or of little girls being fascinated by science experiments and Spider-Man play sets. It all seems slightly odd that at a time when women can aspire to do almost anything men can do – fight in the army, for example, or be a brain surgeon or a helicopter pilot – girls are being dissuaded from playing with the very toys that might ignite an early interest in these directions. Express an interest in 'boys' toys' as a little girl – enjoy, as Miranda does, playing with swords and remote-controlled cars and pirate ships – and you are branded unusual, even odd.

Reading C
PlayStation, Fifa and footballing cultures

Tara Woodyer

Source: *Playing with Toys: The Animated Geographies of Children's Material Culture*, 2010, unpublished PhD thesis, London, University of London.

It is necessary to situate Stephen's videogaming in relation to a passion for football generally, and the various practices and social relations through which this passion is engendered and expressed. Along with his father and brother, Stephen holds a season ticket for Reading FC, and regularly watches them play, both home and away. He actively draws on knowledge gained from experience of these live matches and the practice of following a team's performance in their respective league. (At the time of study Reading FC were in the English Premier League.) His knowledge of teams was not restricted to Reading FC, but extended to his team's competitors, and was particularly seen in relation to popular, high profile teams such as Manchester United and Chelsea. Stephen was an active participant in a broader football culture.

Stephen was an avid 'collector' of football themed Shoot Out cards and Merlin Premier League stickers, which carry information and statistics about Premier League teams and players. These were exchanged with school friends who shared a passion for football, along with posters and cuttings from football magazines. These exchanges were not merely concerned with the sharing of material goods, but with information. This was not only a process of extending friendship, but of expanding knowledge. This knowledge was not restricted to statistics, but also involved chants, taken from the terraces and enacted in exchanges of banter. There was a particular vocabulary, attitude and set of conventions that Stephen drew on and in turn reproduced. Stephen expressed the knowledge gained through his participation in this culture and the practices that sustained it in his gameplay. For instance, he would interject statements such as, 'He scored an own goal against Reading' when particular players' names flashed up on the screen as they gained possession of the ball. He also enacted various chants as he played, chants that related to specific players ('He's M U R T Y, he knows he is, he's sure he is, he's M U R T Y'), chants that related to specific teams ('And it's suuuuper Reading, Super Reading FC, they're by far the greatest team the world has ever seen') and generic chants that are usually aimed at the fans of opposing teams ('Stand up if you're one nil up'). The game allowed Stephen to demonstrate his knowledge and to express his status as a football fan. This was just as important as the demonstration of game based skill. He revelled in the ability to correct his brother's inferior knowledge about particular players, scoffing at his mispronunciation of foreign players' names, or mocking his failure to remain up-to-date with changes in team personnel:

Matthew: [referring to Stephen's comments about Sol Campbell being stupid] So you think an England player's stupid?

Stephen: Ooooooo. He doesn't even play for them any more!

Matthew: [in an accusatory tone] Sol Campbell?!

Stephen: No he doesn't! As soon as Steven Gerrard come in he didn't put him in the first team

Matthew: [mumbles] He still plays for 'em

(Video footage recorded 27th December 2006)

The football related knowledge Stephen demonstrated was not limited to that concerning teams' reputations, players' abilities or strategic play, but also encompassed experiential knowledge of particular stadiums. During a virtual match between Manchester United and Tottenham Hotspur Stephen commented on the home ground, Old Trafford:

Stephen: I sat right up there [...] quite high up [...]

Tara: could you see much?

Stephen: yeah you can see, cos it's a bit high up, you can hard, cos the ground, the height of the ground's quite high up, then you can't see the whole of the pitch cos even the [roofing?] is so long you can't see the whole of the pitch. You can see most of it

(Video footage recorded 27th December 2006)

This is yet another expression of his status as a match going fan, but this knowledge also adds an additional layer of meaning to the game's graphical representation of its tangible counterpart. This allowed a greater sense of attachment to the game and a deeper sense of immersion in the game world. Stephen was able to picture himself being part of the crowd. An understanding of Stephen's mode of engagement in the game requires appreciation of how his gaming practice is positioned in a broader context, situated in relation to wider football related practices. As Wakefield (1999) argues, virtual technologies are not self-contained entities; they have to be seen as socialised. They cannot be considered in isolation from the 'landscapes of translation' in which they are encountered and used. For the combined PlayStation/ FIFA technology, these landscapes of translation include the home in which professional football is domesticated, the school playground in which knowledge about professional football is exchanged and the non-mediated football stadium where professional football is experienced first-hand. These landscapes of translation encompass a variety of objects beyond the console and game, including programmes, trading cards, sticker albums and televisions. The PlayStation technology was not merely socialised as a technology, but as a form of football paraphernalia and a source of football related knowledge. The videogame technology was involved in a circuit of football related knowledge, acting as not only a means through which to express knowledge, but also a means of gaining and clarifying information.

Reference

Wakefield, N. (1999) 'Gender and the landscapes of computing in an internet cafe', in Crang, M., Crang, P. and May, J. (eds) *Virtual Geographies: Bodies, Spaces and Relations*, London, Routledge.

Chapter 3

Children's friendships

Anoop Nayak

Contents

In this chapter, you will:

- examine the changing nature of friendship during the course of childhood
- compare different research traditions in the study of friendship, notably psychological, sociological and anthropological interpretations
- discover examples of the effects that social context has on how friendship is enacted
- reflect on the value of observing children and listening to what they have to say about friendship
- gain an understanding of how friendship is emotional labour that can involve positive and negative experiences
- identify how children's friendship is shaped by processes of gender, class and ethnicity
- evaluate the changing nature of children's friendship through new media such as social networking sites.

1   Introduction

In this chapter we will look at the place of friends and friendship in childhood and at some of the research which attempts to understand the nature of friendship, its changing character and its impact on children's lived experience. In the context of this book as a whole there are two themes to keep in mind. The first is that children's friendships with their peers provide an arena for many aspects of their cultural worlds. For example, children play with friends, they share experiences of television with friends, they go shopping with friends. The second, and related, theme is that within and through their friendships children have opportunities to explore dimensions of experience which can have both formative and lasting effects. For example, within friendships children may experience affection, intimacy, communication, sharing and cooperation. Paradoxically, friendship is also a site for conflict and the experience of what it is to feel jealous, angry and excluded. By comparing themselves with their friends, children may achieve a developing understanding of who they are and what they aspire to become – and even what they aspire not to become. They may further extend their range of emotional experience, both positive and negative. They may find new and different opportunities to be creative and to come to regard themselves as autonomous individuals in their own right. In sum, children's experiences around friendship are closely tied to the development of their personal identity. Such considerations place childhood friendships and peer relationships on a par with the family and the school as highly significant for children's lives and therefore worthy of study.

2   The significance of friendship

Certain rituals, reported by children and collected by Peter and Iona Opie, as part of their study of children's lore, serve to illustrate the abiding significance for children of making, keeping and losing friends:

> The finger of friendship is the little finger. They link the little fingers of their right hands and shake them up and down, declaring:
>
> > Make friends, make friends
> > Never, never break friends.
>
> They quarrel, and their friendship is ended with the formula,
>
> > Break friends, break friends,
> > Never, never make friends,
>
> repeated in a like manner, but, in Croydon, with the little fingers moistened, and in Portsmouth with linked thumbs. They make up again, intoning,
>
> > We've broken before,
> > We break now –
>
> and they separate their little fingers,
>
> > We'll never break any more,
>
> and they intertwine their little fingers again, squeezing tightly (Weston-Super-Mare).

(Opie and Opie, 1959, pp. 324–5)

You may recall similar chants from your own childhood, and they remain in use today – one currently to be heard in Milton Keynes, Buckinghamshire, for example, is:

> Make up, make up,
> Never, never break up.

An important feature of many of the games and activities from childhood so comprehensively catalogued by the Opies is that children engage in them with other children, and in many instances these children would describe one another as their 'friends'. Similarly, as adults, we identify some of those we associate with as 'friends', and in so doing distinguish them from other people whom we might refer to as 'neighbours', 'colleagues' or 'acquaintances' or, more specifically, in terms of their particular role or function, such as 'the postman' or 'Jane's teacher'. 'Friend' has a particular meaning and status – it is not a word that we use lightly – and friends, and the experience of 'friendship', play an important and valued part in our lives at a number of levels. Although the meaning for children of 'friend' and 'friendship' may change over the course of childhood, these early relations are valued by children and typically these relationships are recognised and respected by those with responsibility for them.

Figure 1   Boy alone?

Activity 1   Thinking about friends

Allow about 40 minutes

Think of someone you would currently describe as your friend. Write down some of the features of that relationship which are important to you and which distinguish it from those with people you would not refer to as friends – for example, such features may include the things you do together and the things you talk about.

Now think back to your childhood and identify two significant friends from different points in time – say, when you were eight or nine years old, and then when you were in your mid-teens. The following questions are intended to help you to explore those friendships and what they meant to you. Use them as prompts, recognising that not all of them may be relevant.

- How did you become friends and what was special about these relationships?

- Where did you spend time with these friends – in the family home, at school, in the playground, on the street? To what extent were the things you did together open and public and to what extent were they carried on out of sight of adults?

- Were these friends of the same sex as you? To what extent was gender a factor in the style and nature of the friendships that you had?

- What did your parents think about your friendships? Did they approve of and encourage them, or did they disapprove and try to discourage them? Can you remember why?

- Were there times when you were in conflict with your friends in a significant way? Did the friendship survive? If so, what was it that kept you together as friends?

- Looking back as an adult, how would you describe the influence that these friends had on you at the time? Did that influence endure in any identifiable way?

You may find it interesting and illuminating to ask other people how they would answer these questions – particularly if they are of the opposite gender to you or come from a different social or cultural background. Obviously, to do so would take further time; the allowance given here assumes that you carry out the activity just for yourself.

Comment

The questions in the activity address a number of aspects of friendships which are taken up in various ways in this chapter. As you read about the research and the experiences of others, you should try to relate them to your own personal account, noting the similarities and contrasts and reflecting on their possible implications.

Activity 2   Reading A

Now read Reading A, 'Bad blood', which is an extract from Lorna Sage's autobiography of the same title.

Lorna Sage was born in 1943 and she spent most of her childhood in the village of Hanmer in Flintshire, on the border between England and Wales. Her grandfather was the local vicar and as a young child Lorna lived at the vicarage with her mother while her father was away in the army. After her grandfather's death the family moved into a council house: 4 The Arowry. In this extract Lorna Sage graphically recalls the friendships she, aged eight, struck up with her new neighbours.

As you read, note what these friendships meant to Lorna and how she highlights the negative aspects as well as the positive. How do her memories of friendships at the age of eight and nine compare with your own?

Comment

It was important to the lonely eight-year-old Lorna to have friends of any description, and the move to a new house provided two, as neighbours.

She recalls these relationships as being the source of experiences of intoxicating intimacy. They could also be the site of quarrels and rejections, possibly assisted by tensions associated with there being three of them. And this experience encompassed both being excluded and, in turn, forming an alliance to shut out another. But the abiding memory is of an extended collaboration over a doll's wedding which, nearly 50 years later, is recalled as a piece of idyllic fantasy at work.

The lasting import of social relationships like the ones you recalled in Activity 1, and that Lorna Sage recounts in this reading, suggests that friendships are ways through which children develop a sense of themselves in relation to their society. While there are undoubtedly common features worldwide to the forms that friendship takes and the functions it serves, there are also important variations. The rest of this chapter will attempt to reflect some of this variation through global examples, but it is important to approach the research-based accounts that follow in a critical way and to enquire about the generality of the findings.

Summary of Section 2

Making, keeping and losing friends are important features of children's cultural worlds.

Children's experiences around friendship are closely tied to the development of their personal identity.

Memories of childhood can be a useful starting point for studying friendships, but they should be handled with care.

---

3 Building an understanding of children's friendships

In this section we shall look closely at how academics and child experts have tried to understand children's friendships. There are of course many theories and methods that researchers have deployed with varying success to ascertain the meaning of friendship in children's lives. The purpose in this section is not to take you on a journey through each and every approach but to get you to consider the value of cross-disciplinary perspectives. In particular, we shall examine psychological, sociological and anthropological understandings of children's friendships, which have each inspired traditions and approaches to the study of childhood.

3.1 Children's experience of friendship: psychological understandings

One of the limitations of studying very young children's friendships is that they aren't able to share their ideas about friends. Even after language acquisition small children may be unable to express the complex feelings and emotions that go into the act of friendship. In response, researchers have been drawn to psychology in order to understand the non-verbal ways in which children communicate friendship. This may include tactile behaviour, shared forms of play or mirroring one another.

Influenced by the groundbreaking work of Jean Piaget, psychologists have sought to identify distinct stages in the development of children's friendship. Seen from this perspective, children's ideas about friendship unfold through a sequence of stages which does not vary; each new stage represents a fundamental reorganisation of their understanding. In this respect, say Bigelow and La Gaipa, 'age-related changes in conceptions of friendship can be understood as a specific instance of more basic changes in the development of social cognitions' (Bigelow and La Gaipa, 1980, p. 20). The American psychologist Robert Selman (1980) is another advocate of this view. He put forward the hypothesis that the development of children's conceptions of friendship would relate closely to the more general development of social understanding, in other words the ways in which children construe, interpret and represent other people's points of view. He investigated this hypothesis by telling children stories which centred on a dilemma to do with friendship; for example, where a character promises to be with different friends at the same time. Then he asked them a series of probing questions about such things as the nature of the characters' relationships with one another, how old friendships are maintained and new ones begun, what sort of understanding friends ought to have of one another, and how the dilemma in the story might best be resolved.

From his analysis of interviews with a large number of American children aged between three and 15 years, Selman claimed to find evidence for four stages in the development of their ideas about friendship. In support of his initial hypothesis, these sequences correspond to different levels of skill in taking a social perspective, the assertion being that as children mature and accumulate life experience, they can become more empathetic.

1   **Momentary physical playmate**. For Selman, very young children (3–5 years) define friends in terms of shared activities and geographical associations: they are the children they play with, they live nearby and with whom they may go to the same school.

2   **One-way assistance**. For children at the next stage (6–8 years), a friend is someone who helps you or who does things that please you. Significantly, this is not a reciprocal relation.

3   **Fair weather cooperation**. Selman found reciprocal understanding to be a key feature of children's later friendships (9–12 years). As children try to take account of friends' preferences, conflict and disagreement may appear. This is 'fair weather cooperation' with

little sense of an enduring relationship which can withstand trials and tribulations.

4 **Mutual concern**. By the final stage, children (11–15 years) are able to take the perspective of other people. Friendship is seen as a bond which is built over time and is made strong and stable by expressions of mutual support, concern and understanding. Building this sort of relationship is helped by having friends who share compatible interests, values and personality traits. Minor conflicts can be withstood and when children talk of friendship they refer to *psychological* attributes rather than the physical ones characterising younger children's accounts.

Like Bigelow and La Gaipa (1980), Selman sees children's friendship developing in a linear and systematic fashion. At each stage there is a reorganisation in their understanding of what it means to be a friend, and this is part of a wider development in their cognitive abilities. Rubin (1980) likens this to climbing a ladder and resting at each rung in order to consolidate the new level of interpersonal awareness that has been achieved. Ultimately, psychologists draw attention to the way in which friendship is mediated at a developmental level through a child's age-specific physical and cognitive abilities. Above all, they remind us that what adults might understand by friendship may be experienced entirely differently in children's coming of age.

3.2 Analysing talk about friends: sociological understanding

In the previous section we saw how psychologists require us to interpret children's friendship through their cognitive processes, emotional development and physical capabilities. Sociologists have been keen to explore how children talk about friends and the cultural meaning they endow friendship with. The sociologist Bill Corsaro spent several months closely observing children, aged between three and five years, in a nursery school on the campus of a US university. He made detailed field notes of the children's activities and their social interactions and also video recorded them (Corsaro, 1985). This is an example of an ethnographic approach to studying children, characterised by extensive observation of and involvement in their activities over a period of time. One of Corsaro's interests was in how these young children talked with one another about their friendships and the meanings they ascribed to the word 'friend'. He identified different styles of such talk.

The first way of talking centred on children using reference to friendship in successful attempts to gain access to other children's play. The second covered instances where children talked about being friends because they were playing together. These first two styles together accounted for two-thirds of the references to friendship. They fit closely with the picture that has already been painted by psychologists of friendships at this age, namely that they are based on physical proximity or bonds that are formed by short-lived activities, such as playing together.

Figure 2   Friendship at play

Corsaro's remaining styles, though less frequently observed in the nursery setting, indicate an interesting diversity in the ways that friendship is talked about, even at this comparatively young age. To demonstrate another style, in the following extract Peter tries to get Graham to come and play next to him:

Peter to Graham: Graham – if you play over here where I am, I'll be your friend.

Graham to Peter: I wanna play over here.

Peter to Graham: Then I'm not gonna be your friend.

Graham to Peter: I'm not – I'm not gonna let – I'm gonna tell my mom to not let you –

Peter to Graham: All *right*, I'll come over here.

(Corsaro, 1985, p. 165)

Peter is trying – and failing – to use friendship as a means of social control, attempting to get Graham to play with him in return for being his friend. Corsaro observed that these two boys played together a lot, rather than with other children, and the exchange above illustrates how Peter was keen to protect their joint activities from the intrusions of others.

Corsaro's penultimate style covered those occasions when the children referred to friendship in the course of expressing concern for the welfare of their playmates, most frequently when one of them was absent from the nursery. The final style extends that expression of concern further. Corsaro provides an example of how Jenny and Betty, two three-year-old girls, are able to discuss friendship at a fairly abstract level. Their notion of being 'best friends' is a measure of how much they care about each other, and they also demonstrate their *mutual concern* for how their actions might affect one another's feelings. As we have seen, according to some researchers following psychological and sociological perspectives in the field of children's friendship, this mutual concern is a feature of more advanced levels, when children are 11 years and older.

How come, then, that Jenny and Betty, still only three years old, appear to be operating at that level? Corsaro offers two explanations. First, much previous work with children is based on research in the same tradition as Selman's, where children were interviewed and asked hypothetical ('what if …?') questions, whereas Jenny's and Betty's expression of their friendship is taken from spontaneous talk while interacting with one another. This is a valuable reminder of the need for caution over judging children's competencies on the basis of 'formal' experimental tasks. Second, Corsaro notes that the two girls had a closer relationship than most of the other children in the nursery school and played together a great deal. The fact that they talked about their friendship in the way that they did suggests that children who develop intensive and long-term relations may, through those relations, acquire abstract conceptions of friendship at an early age.

The implications of this are that hierarchical developmental models of children's friendship based solely on age can be overly mechanistic. Allison James has pointed out that any individual child might be at different stages of friendship with different people. She argues:

It is … through its discrete performance that children learn about and experience friendship, which means that the social contexts in which children find themselves, not simply their age, play the greater part in shaping children's understanding of the concept.

(James, 1993, p. 216)

There is a powerful suggestion then that friendship is a profoundly *social* affair that can't be defined solely in terms of mental and physical development. The sociologist Ray Pahl (2000) extends the idea that children's experiences of friendship must be situated within their immediate social context. Pahl regards friends as 'Our social convoy of significant others' (Pahl, 2000, p. 2), something that carries us through life but is mobile and shifting in terms of the different actors we encounter and our varying affiliation towards them. As the social context of friendship changes over time, so too does the meaning of what a 'friend' is. Over an individual's life different friendship groups may cohere around the school, neighbourhood, university, workplace, gym, dance class and so forth. A limitation of many psychological studies of child development is that they tend to fix and compartmentalise childhood into a particular set of life stages, paying less attention to the value of close ethnographic observation and how children actually 'do friendship'. Throughout this chapter we show how observations of children's friendship and their personal understandings of it – which are often symbolically communicated through talk, play, music or fashion – can be pivotal in understanding what we might term the *social practice of friendship*.

Teenagers talking

While young children may have difficulty expressing what friendship means to them, older children can be more forthcoming. In his early book *The Social World of the Child,* William Damon (1977) interviews Jack, an American 13 year old:

Interviewer:	Why is Jimmy your best friend?
Jack:	I don't know, I guess it's because we talk a lot and stuff.
Interviewer:	What do you talk about?
Jack:	Secret stuff, you know, what we think of him or her or whoever. And sports, things we both like to do.

Interviewer:	How did you meet Jimmy?
Jack:	I don't know; hanging around, I guess. We just sort of got friendly after a while.
Interviewer:	When did you get friendly?
Jack:	After we found out we didn't have to worry about the other guy blabbing and spreading stuff around.
Interviewer:	Why would you worry about that?
Jack:	Well, you need someone you can tell anything to, all kinds of things that you don't want spread around. That's why you're someone's friend.
Interviewer:	Is that why Jimmy is your friend? …
Jack:	Yes, and we like the same kinds of things. We speak that same language. My mother says we're two peas in a pod.
Interviewer:	What would you say you like best about Jimmy?
Jack:	Well, you know, we can say what we want to around each other, you don't have to act cool around him or anything. Some of the older kids are always pretending to be big shots, acting real tough. That kind of stuff, it turns me off.
Interviewer:	How do you know who to become friends with and who not to?
Jack:	Well, you don't really pick your friends, it just grows on you. You find out that you really can talk to someone, you can tell them your problems, when you understand each other.

(Damon, 1977, pp. 163–4)

In this passage Jack expresses the value of friendship with Jimmy, a reliable confidant who will not go 'blabbing and spreading stuff around'. Their friendship is based on trust and mutual awareness. The ability to talk and open oneself up to others without fear of repercussions is an essential aspect of their friendship. For Jimmy, one cannot simply select friends, friendship 'just grows on you'. Talk between friends is, then, part of the doing of friendship, a mechanism for 'psychological assistance, secret sharing and the establishment of mutual understanding' (Damon, 1977, p. 164).

Figure 3   Teenagers talking

3.3   Friendship in the majority world: anthropological understandings

In large part the studies referred to in the preceding section come from North America and Europe, as is the case with much of the chapter so far. This is because comparatively little research has been published on the concepts and functions of friendship in Asian, African and Latin American cultures. Is the minority-world experience of friendship as the location for affectionate and intimate relationships between people – both children and adults – universal? One writer on the subject has argued that this particular kind of interpersonal relationship is a 'sociological luxury' which is ill-afforded in many other cultures (Paine, 1974, cited in James, 1993, p. 205).

A central contribution made by anthropologists has been to offer rich ethnographic accounts of everyday life often situated in communities that lie outside of the gaze of the minority-world. These insights are especially useful as they challenge minority world assumptions of what 'childhood', 'friendship' or 'play' might actually mean. In widening the aperture on children's lives we shall turn now to anthropological examples of friendship in southern Africa and rural Bolivia.

Friendship among the !Kung in southern Africa and children in rural Bolivia

The !Kung are a hunter-gatherer society in southern Africa who have a nomadic lifestyle. !Kung communities are small and the people within them are constantly changing. In such settings children form friendships with whoever is available. It is not uncommon to find friendships forming between young children and teenagers and there isn't the preference for friends of the same sex which is so often apparent elsewhere. Friendships are inevitably transitory and dependent on external factors. During the winter, when the !Kung are camped at one of the few permanent waterholes, communities grow in size and children have a greater chance to form friendships. In the summer, on the other hand, people disperse and sometimes travel only in family groups, which restricts the children's opportunities to make friends. For Nisa, an elderly !Kung woman recalling her childhood friendships, the emphasis appears to be more on group activities and shared experiences than on personal preferences and close relationships. The following extract is taken from an interview with Nisa recorded and translated by the American anthropologist Marjorie Shostak:

> A few months later, we left Chotana and went back to live again at our old water hole. All my friends were there, and when I saw them I was happy again. We played and played and danced and sang, played music and sang and danced, and my heart was happy to be with the children I liked.
>
> We used to make believe about everything. We made believe we cooked food and took it out of the fire. We had trance dances and sang and danced and danced and sang and the boys cured us. They went, 'Xai-I! Kow-a-di-li!' They cured us and we sang and danced and danced, danced all day.
>
> Sometimes we played with the children from another village; sometimes we just played by ourselves. Other times, the other children came and found us playing and went back with us to our little village. They'd greet us just as adults do, 'How are all of you?' And we'd answer, 'Eh, we're just fine.'
>
> (Quoted in Shostak, 1983, pp. 124–5)

In societies such as the !Kung where life is organised around hunting and gathering, the proximity of physical danger is another reason for children and young people to be in mixed-age groups. This has the added feature of providing a way of transferring culturally and economically important skills from one generation to the next (Konner, 1981). This example of friendships among the !Kung draws attention to the very different bases for friendship in different societies.

Figure 4 Children use everyday routines to blend friendship with work and play

Critics of minority-world research frequently make the point that patterns of friendship in countries like the USA, the UK, Canada and Australia are founded on a belief system that emphasises personal autonomy and individuality. Children are seen as separate individuals, making and breaking friendships with one or more individuals through the patterns described previously. This atomised account of childhood differs largely from !Kung societies and certain other communities in the majority world. For example, in rural Bolivia children have little spare time for friendship and play as they must carry out domestic tasks. Punch (2000) records how adults use a well-known local superstition *duende* (dwarf) as a control mechanism based on fear to make children work more and play less. She records how the tactic is used to encourage children to return straight home from school and help out with domestic tasks rather than dally with friends along the way:

> There were several different beliefs among participants about who or what exactly the *duendes* were. Some people said they were the rebellious souls of children who had died without being christened. Others said that they were like a mini-devil. Some people thought that the *duendes* existed because of girls who had had abortions. The general image of the *duende* was as a short but plump child-

like figure who wore a large, broad-brimmed hat but no other clothes. ... It was generally believed that the *duende* could be seen only by children, and that it appeared only to children who played too much and were easily distracted.

(Punch, 2000, pp. 50–1)

Of course, none of this means that children didn't play, many would ignore the warnings about the *duende*, fuse work and play and find creative ways of engaging in friendship practices. Rather, what are revealing in such international accounts are the different understandings of what childhood is. Where early childhood is mythologised as a space of relative autonomy in minority-world industrialised nation states, in rural Bolivia the child is also regarded as a worker. Children regularly conduct errands on a daily basis, taking animals out to pasture, fetching firewood for cooking, or collecting water for irrigating crops. At the same time, where childhood in the minority world is often confined to the interior worlds of the school, car and house, children in rural areas of Bolivia freely roam the country and mountainside alone. This meant that despite the restrictions that domestic labour incurs, children are less physically dependent on adults and have a spatial awareness of their surroundings that extends far beyond the confines of much contemporary urban minority-world childhoods. Looking globally, relationships between families and friends are then seen to vary across time and space.

Summary of Section 3

Friendship is a social practice through which children learn about self and others.

Close observation of children and discussions with them can deliver more complex understandings of friendship.

While the nature of children's friendships changes with age, it is not solely age restricted.

Talking is one of the ways in which teenagers participate in friendship and affirm bonds with one another.

Childhood and friendship may have very different meanings outside of the minority world.

> By looking globally you can see how children's friendship varies across time and space.

4   Putting friends in their place

A good starting point for examining children's friendships is to closely examine the everyday spaces they inhabit. In the early years many children tend to live spatially restricted lives in which the home, car or local neighbourhood are formative of their social world. The relatively limited spaces they may encounter in early years can impact upon their friendships which at this point are often structured and mediated by parents. When children are old enough to go to school new types of friendship open up. First though, you'll look at the mundane arenas which many young children occupy on a daily basis – the home, the neighbourhood and, for an unfortunate few, the street.

4.1   Friends at home

When looking at three- and four-year-old children, the point has already been made that friendships often come about because children find themselves in the same place at the same time – what is termed 'propinquity'. Children playing alongside one another in nursery school is but one example. In many social groups parents and carers also play an important part. They often assume that their friends' children, if they have them, will get along with their own children. These are not 'accidental' factors in how friendships are formed, merely a feature of the earlier years of childhood.

When commenting on the friendships to be found among seven year olds in Nottingham in the 1960s, John and Elizabeth Newson (1976) noted that children who lived at one end of a school's catchment area were unlikely to be allowed to go on their own to visit children living at the other end, thus making friendships formed at school more difficult to sustain out of school hours. Similarly, there was a disjunction when children living near one another attended different schools and so had fewer common interests, given the dominant influences of their schools on their everyday lives. As a consequence, they suggest, 'some of those friendships will be the products of use, habit and expedience, rather than the marriage of true minds' (Newson and Newson, 1976, p. 178).

For many parents, too, there is a strong desire that their children should have 'suitable' friends who will be a 'good influence' on them. Evidence from the mothers of these same Nottingham children found that just over a third had already actively discouraged a specific friendship by the time their child was seven, and a further third said that they would act to discourage one if the circumstance arose. The words of one of these mothers set out some of the reasons and some of the dilemmas:

> There's one little boy I'm not so keen on as the others, but I shan't say anything directly; but I would do if it was someone I disliked – if the child were a rough, wandering type of child – wild and so on. I should hate Mark to become wild! So I would just – I think I'd stop him; I might say 'I don't want you to play with him'; I'm not quite sure as to whether I'd do that, or whether I'd be crafty, and always have him busy when this child called. I'm not sure: I might do that.
>
> (Quoted in Newson and Newson, 1976, p. 218)

The attitudes of parents in the 1960s towards children's friendship may not be as starkly different today as we might like to imagine. In interviews with white mothers in London, Bridget Byrne (2006) found that some mothers were highly instrumental in structuring children's friendship through the pivotal role they play in school choice:

> A key concern for the women was to find a school for their children that had the 'right' social and racial 'mix' of students. It emerged that practices around choice of schooling were highly racialised, as well as classed. A school that was seen as being 'too black' or 'too working class' was also viewed as potentially disruptive to their children's education. This disruption concerned not merely questions of qualifications … but also, I suggest, the desire for their children to become raced and classed subjects.
>
> (Byrne, 2006, p. 174)

Looking at the remarks cited by the Newsons and the interpretations offered above by Byrne, you may find it instructive to refer back to your answer to the question in Activity 1 which asked about your parents' approval of your friends. If you have children of your own you might care to reflect on your views on this matter: how have you shaped your children's friendships and what discourses have you drawn on to justify this?

4.2   Friends in the neighbourhood

A further study compared the friendship patterns of 12-year-old children in Monterey and Yuba, two contrasting neighbourhoods in Oakland, California (Berg and Medrich, 1980, cited in Rubin, 1980). Monterey is an affluent, predominantly white neighbourhood with large, widely dispersed houses at some distance from the park and the recreation centre. The children living there reported having only one or two friends, who often lived some considerable distance away from them. They relied on their parents to transport them to see these friends and to take part in social activities which were usually planned in advance. These children said that they chose their friends on the grounds that they had things in common. Yuba, by contrast, is an inner-city neighbourhood populated by low-income, predominantly black families. The 12 year olds here typically had four or five close friends and a yet wider range of friends beyond that. They moved as they chose, mostly in large groups, through the recreation centres, shops and public spaces in the tight-knit neighbourhood.

The researchers noted the similarities between the lives of the children in Monterey and those of their parents: both were relatively formal and scheduled. They also highlighted the ways in which the children developed a view of friendship that emphasised selectivity and psychological compatibility. In similar ways, the Yuba children's social lives conformed to the more inclusive and spontaneous social character of their neighbourhood. The two settings appear to offer children different advantages and disadvantages. Although children in Monterey evidently enjoyed many more material benefits, they were prone to complain that there weren't enough children around and that they were reliant on others in order to carry out their social lives. On the other hand, they may have formed deeper friendships than those of the more inclusive children of Yuba.

In parts of eastern Europe children's friendship can take on a qualitatively different experience. For example, in a Slovak neighbourhood on the outskirts of Bratislava, children were found to spend an enormous amount of time engaged in street-based activities. This is in part because of the construction of the large-scale building of modernist, functional apartments that dominate urban neighbourhoods.

These buildings can house vast numbers of people but the small cubicle, family apartments mean that children usually share bedrooms with siblings and are seldom permitted to invite friends home. In his street-based study, Blazek (2011) found that Slovak children would regularly look after younger siblings, and that most friendships crossed the boundaries of gender and age which more rigidly come to pattern friendships in western European cities.

Before the reunification of Germany in 1990, a team of researchers explored the lives of primary school children in East and West Berlin (Little et al., 1999). After-school adult supervisors in East Berlin encouraged children's cooperation and criticised conflict as immature. In West Berlin, by contrast, parents had primary responsibility for children after school and there was little ideological shaping of children's behaviour. The researchers found that children in East Berlin were more mature in their friendships but less equipped than their West Berlin counterparts when it came to resolving conflict as adults had mediated this for them.

The research from Monterey, Bratislava and Berlin provides some interesting insights into neighbourhood effects on children's friendships. The accounts further suggest that particular sites and spaces are formative of different types of friendship as a consequence of proximity, urban architecture, ideology and culture. The studies reveal the apparently universal importance of friendship wherever we live.

4.3   Friends on the street

Despite the differences in their experiences, the children in Monterey, Berlin and Bratislava were growing up within families and communities which provided them with emotional, social and physical support. For many children, however, their circumstances require them to rely to a much greater extent on one another. What forms does friendship take for the vast number of children living on the street? In 2004, UNICEF reported, 'The latest estimates put the numbers of these children as high as 100 million'; and even more recently, 'The exact number of street children is impossible to quantify, but the figure almost certainly runs into tens of millions across the world. It is likely that the numbers are increasing' (UNICEF, 2005).

Wilfred, Steven and Shane, all in their early teens, are street children in Cape Town, South Africa. They talk about what their three-year-long friendship means and the contexts in which it has particular significance:

Figure 5 Shane, Steven and Wilfred – Cape Town street children

Wilfred: We are good friends. We know each other a long time.
            Sometimes we are bad to each other and sometimes we are
            good to each other. My friends, if they fight with big boys in
            Cape Town then I help him. When I saw him, I have a fight
            and then he help me. And he as well, you see. That's why
            we're together.

Steven: One time I saw Wilfred, he's hungry, then he's about at
            home. Then I don't know Wilfred, then I stay by his house,
            next to his house. Then he come to me, then he ask me
            some bread. Then I give him two slice of bread and that's
            why he's my friend.

Shane: I get the money, then I go to the shop, then I buy me sweets
            and drinks and I take for Steven and for Wilfred with me
            and I say it for him, go and buy it and I'll stay by the shop.
            And it's good. He's my friend.

(The Open University, 2003a)

The picture the three boys paint is one of mutual support, whether in
fights with others or in the sharing of food and drink. When they fight
among themselves the rift is relatively short-lived and the strength of
their friendship prevails. As Wilfred says:

And then we must fight ... And then I'm angry or I'm sad and I
go home and sit there in the road, you see. And I sit in the sun
and I saw him run up and down and don't worry about him. And

the next time they call me and I walk with him. And then when it come, then everything is go down, is go away, like the devil is go away. I wish that Steven come back, you are my friend, OK. And we're all together.

(Quoted in The Open University, 2003a)

Although these three boys rely on one another's friendship to a significant extent, they are not totally dependent on the street for their existence. Shane lives as one of his aunt's large family in a township. Wilfred often stays there too, as his own parents are alcoholic and beat him. Likewise, Steven has a family but is rarely at home as he claims his parents don't care about him. Merle, Shane's aunt, provides her perspective on the interplay between family and friends:

Wilfred and Steven are Shane's friends. I don't actually know a lot about their background or what's the reason that they're out of the house, you see. But they are Shane's friends and because they are Shane's friends they are also like family to us here, you see. So, that, that is just the way it works here.

(Quoted in The Open University, 2003b)

Where there is no family of any sort to provide support and regulation, relationships with the peer group take on an even greater significance. A study of street children in Belo Horizonte, the fourth largest city in Brazil, identified how the gang – known there as the *turma* – provided many of them with the sense of support, companionship and protection that might otherwise have been found within the family (Campos et al., 1994). This support came at a cost. The *turma* had its own strict code of behaviour, and to gain entry prospective members had to steal and prove their willingness to abide by the norms of the group. If they broke the rules they were punished, often in violent and sadistic ways. These children's experiences contrasted with those children who, similarly, worked on the streets but had a home base. For the latter the peer group was important but this was balanced by the influence of their parents and wider family networks. These influences appeared to make for distinctions, too. The researchers found that the home-based street children were less likely to engage in drug abuse and illegal economic activities and they were also more likely to combine their work on the streets with attendance at school.

However, it is not only boys who can be found on the street. Beazley (2002) discusses the plight of street girls in Indonesia who use forms of embodiment to assert their identities. This can involve mimicking male dress codes, cutting their hair short, smoking, doing drugs, using make-up and being aggressively assertive in public, thereby flouting the strict codes of Indonesian femininity. Consider Beazley's interpretation of how street girls signal their identities and affiliations through embodied performance:

> Like the street boys, most of the girls had tattoos, and many of them had the name of their boyfriend tattooed on their hand. As well as tattoos and body piercing, the girls have numerous razor cuts, often in rows up the insides of their arms. These cuts are a sign of their subculture and present a tough and anti-feminine image. ... Almost all the girls had these scarifications on their arms and I read them as a 'social inscription', which can be understood as ... a sign of belonging to their group.
>
> (Beazley, 2002, p. 1676)

To this extent the body is a canvas for the marking of friendship and refiguring of femininity through forms of resistance. As street children are likely to have few, if any, possessions, the body can take on heightened meaning for expressing personal identity and belonging.

Summary of Section 4

In the early years, children's friendships tend to be bound by the mundane spaces they inhabit.

Parents and other adults often play a mediating role in shaping children's friendships.

The characteristics of friendships are culturally specific, reflecting the social practices and values of the culture in which children live.

For vulnerable children, friends may become family, hierarchically organised but also protective.

---

5 Gendered friendships

For most minority-world children patterns of play at school tend to be segregated by gender and reinforced by children, as Allison James notes:

> In this sense, gender has a double significance for children. Its differentiating potential both reinforces and is reinforced by particular forms of play and patterns of friendship which, in turn, generates cultural models of and for particular gendered identities.
>
> (James, 1993, p. 224)

James distinguishes between the tightly bound and structured form of the games that seven-, eight- and nine-year-old girls typically play and the looser team structure of those played by boys which places less emphasis on the personal.

5.1 Girls' friendships

James sees girls' games as reflecting the pattern of intensive one-to-one relationships involving considerable emotional commitment which are characteristic of girls' friendship.

Figure 6   Minna and Elizabeth – 'the most special friendship in Bangladesh'

This sort of girls' friendship is well exemplified by 13-year-old Minna and Elizabeth who come from middle-class homes in Chittagong, Bangladesh. They talk about their close, two-year-long, friendship – what they describe as 'the most special friendship in Bangladesh':

Minna: Elizabeth and I, we're always together and we know each other better than other people know us or we know other people.

Elizabeth: A best friend can understand you best, like when two people stay together for a long time they get to know the people and know their feelings. So it's easier to talk about a problem to a best friend than to talk about it to someone else.

Minna: We agree to each other's decisions always. Yeah. That's what the main thing is. She likes what I like, she dislikes what I dislike, so that's why we're best friends. We're just a photocopy of each other.

(The Open University, 2003a)

Minna and Elizabeth's portrayal has all the appearances of an honest account of their understanding of the basis for their relationship and of its value to them. It is only one version, however, of the sorts of ways in which the particular relationship of friendship – here among girls – may provide the context for wider personal explorations, as the account in Activity 3 reveals.

In a study of children's friendships in a primary school in the English West Midlands, one of the researchers, Mary Jane Kehily, became an 'honorary member' of the Diary Group over a period of seven months. The Diary Group comprised eight 9- to 10-year-old girls predominantly of south Asian heritage who met regularly to discuss issues of mutual interest, including friends, boyfriends and puberty. The girls would decide on a topic of discussion and take it in turns to ask questions of one another. Their self-imposed rules said they had to answer the questions and couldn't give misleading answers. The following extract is from a conversation between three of the girls about Sunil and Ben, the two most desired boys in the class:

Lakbiah: [referring to Sunil]   If he killed me I don't care but I still love him.

Selena: [referring to Ben]   I love him, I love him, I love him.

Lakbia: I don't mind 'cos it's me who likes him. I don't care if he doesn't like me, he's still for me.

Sarah: [to Selena of Ben]   Do you mind, do you mind if you never
                             see him again in secondary school?

Selena: I don't mind, I still know that I love him.

(Kehily et al., 2002, p. 175)

Figure 7 A child's drawing of the interview process, collected by
Mary Jane Kehily

Kehily and her co-researchers regard the Diary Group as offering an
intimate 'fantasy space' where girls can articulate different forms of
desire. Conversations provide opportunities for girls to try out different
identities and to project themselves into situations, including sexual
relations, which may not be part of their actual experience. They
suggest that the discourses the girls engage in demonstrate what it
means to be both a girl and a friend. The rules surrounding secrecy and
honesty mean that those who do not abide by these codes risk being
ostracised from the Diary Group. Kehily describes her status in the

group as that of a 'grown-up girl', 'an invited audience, moral arbiter and source of knowledge about the adult world' (Kehily et al., 2002, p. 168).

Activity 3   The Diary Group
Allow about 30 minutes

Look again at the dialogue above from Kehily's study and subsequent discussion and think about the following questions:

- What does the self-created rule-bound world of the Diary Group impart about girls' friendships?

- What does the notion of a diary suggest and why is talking an important part of girls' friendship?

- What role do fantasy and imaginary relations play in children's worlds?

- What types of friendship work are at play to enable Mary Jane Kehily to become accepted as part of the Diary Group?

Comment

Diary Group discussion on the theme of romance provides an insight into the social world of pre-adolescent girls which indicates that the erotic attachment to celebrities, teachers and boys in the class takes place at the same time. These figures provide a resource for the girls' friendship talk and simultaneously a fantasy space within the group where different forms of desire can be articulated. The discussion indicates that multiple versions of attraction and desire are being played out within the group, and the 'masochistic', selfless female can be seen as one version which exists alongside more agentic versions, such as relationships with male teachers and the implications of this for approaches to curriculum subjects. Diary Group discussions point to the many ways in which girls try out different identities, projecting themselves into situations, including sexual relationships which may not be part of their experiences and which may not appear to be empowering. The structure and function of the Diary Group, however, provides the girls with a relatively 'safe' performance space for fantasising and articulating different forms of intimacy and connection in relation to young men. The collective articulation of desire and intimacy in the space of the Diary Group points to the importance of the female friendship group as a source of support and bonding. Liking the same bands, boys and teachers and spending so much time discussing the many facets of these desires may not appear to be an endorsement of the feminist project. However, in the face of the individualising culture of school and courtship that surrounds them, the Diary Group may be trying out different versions of desire and intimacy while drawing strength from the collective experience of female friendship.

One common image of girls' friendships, in particular, is that they are characterised by a capacity for sharing, caring and mutual support. This is exemplified by Christine, a 16-year-old girl living in Cape Town, South Africa who was interviewed, along with her female friends:

> I think friends are important, to be there for you, to comfort you in times of need. And sometimes they have to be there, like to fill that space, that need, that you are a person who's special, and you are wanted.
>
> (Quoted in The Open University, 2003a)

Christine's words indicate how those who rank as her friends have a special role and responsibilities to support her and to provide positive affirmation of her personal worth and of her actions. This is of particular significance during the adolescent period when young people are, typically, questioning and being questioned about their developing selves in more intensive ways, and when personal identities are being shaped. Although for many children and young people the family provides one important site for such work, friends offer a framework which has different properties.

Later in the conversation, Christine makes clear that she regards arguments between friends as a necessary part of developing these relationships:

> If you don't argue with your friends sometimes, there is something wrong. Then you know that, no, this person is just saying 'I'm your friend' but not really. If you recover from the argument and then they are still your friend, then you know that they are a true friend.
>
> (Quoted in The Open University, 2003a)

In this respect it is one of the hallmarks of 'true' friendships that within the relationship friends can criticise and challenge and disagree in ways which have a particular force and significance *because* they come from a friend: if this person, who is my friend, sees things differently from me then I need to take notice and work through the implications. The personal identity development function is fulfilled via other routes than the positively supportive.

But does even this recognition of the place of negative actions and emotions within friendships go far enough? The Canadian writer Margaret Atwood presents a telling account of remembered childhood in her novel *Cat's Eye*. The central character, Elaine, recounts the importance of friendships in her life in Toronto 40 years previously, and in particular her relationship with Cordelia. Though fictional, the power of such narratives resides in their almost certain origin in personal experience:

> On the way home from school I have to walk in front of them, or behind. In front is worse because they talk about how I'm walking, how I look from behind. 'Don't hunch over,' says Cordelia. 'Don't move your arms like that.'
>
> They don't say any of the things they say to me in front of others, even other children: whatever is going on is going on in secret, among the four of us only. Secrecy is important, I know that: to violate it would be the greatest, the irreparable sin. If I tell I will be cast out forever.
>
> But Cordelia doesn't do these things or have power over me because she's my enemy. Far from it. …
>
> With enemies you can feel hatred, and anger. But Cordelia is my friend. She likes me, she wants to help me, they all do. They are my friends, my girlfriends, my best friends. I have never had any before and I'm terrified of losing them. I want to please.
>
> (Atwood, 1990, p. 120)

Atwood's fictional depiction illustrates how power can be deployed within the confines of a friendship, where the very existence of the friendship is the prize. Equivalent real-life accounts are to be found in Valerie Hey's ethnographic study of girls, aged 11–18, in two secondary schools in a UK city (Hey, 1997). She documents the frequent interactions between the girls that centre on the less than supportive practices of 'bitching', falling-out and rituals of exclusion. This view challenges that of some feminist researchers who tend to romanticise girls' friendship and to celebrate their capacity for sharing, caring and mutual support. By contrast, the girls Hey (1997) observed were engaged in patterns and practices of friendship that were fuelled by tensions and conflict, as much as by support and care.

One closely knit group of 11-year-old girls included Erin, the acknowledged leader, Samantha, Saskia, Anna and Natalie. Hey observed that these girls participate in friendship in a constant and frenetic bout of activity, by talking and hanging out inside and outside school and by exchanging notes when they are in lessons. A particular social practice for this group was the issuing, accepting and rejecting of invitations in the form of notes that were passed between them. By these means they could include and exclude, and so negotiate their relations with each other. Saskia appeared particularly keen to identify herself as the main manager of the group's social life. At first sight this suggested that she was a central member of the group and this was an indication of her popularity. However, Hey's observations suggested that, despite her efforts, Saskia never achieved the status she so desperately wanted. She identified popularity with becoming Erin's best friend, but in desiring and not achieving this outcome she conceded rather than accumulated power within the group.

Activity 4   Passing notes

Allow about 10 minutes

Below is an extract from Hey's field notes of an episode concerning some members of this group of girls. Saskia, not for the first time, had excluded Anna from an arrangement by which the group would all meet at lunchtime at Samantha's house.

Read the subsequent exchange of written notes that took place in the classroom during a lesson and suggest an interpretation of what is going on.

Anna/ Natalie to Saskia:	Saskia we are not your friend because you are a snide and you are not very nice.
Saskia to Anna/ Natalie:	I did not [rest of this obliterated]
Natalie to Saskia:	because I am not OK GOT THE MESSAGE

Saskia to Natalie/ Anna:	Why did Anna write the first one. Anyway I don't care what you say because words don't hurt. But I still like you both. Can't you answer.
Natalie/ Anna to Saskia:	Don't you come cheeky to me girl.
Saskia to Natalie/ Anna:	I'm allowed to say what I want to, it's a free world
Natalie to Saskia:	Don't bubble up your mouth to me girl. Get it slag.
Saskia to Natalie/ Anna:	Why don't you try shutting up
Saskia to Anna:	Is Natalie my friend?
Natalie to Saskia:	NO!
Saskia to Natalie/ Anna:	If NO you don't like me then I don't have to do anything you say. If you were my friend then I would but you're not so I won't. [A naturalistic, relatively neutral drawing of Anna]
Anna to Saskia:	If you must draw my wonderful complexion draw it properly
Natalie to Saskia:	But shut your mouth cheeky
Saskia to Natalie/ Anna:	I know but I have never been good at art. PS. Is Nattie still my friend
Natalie to Saskia:	NO
Anna to Saskia:	[A drawing of Saskia with sticky up hair – teenage style – with arrows pointing to her chest with the phrase 'Saskia Stevens' and 'flat as a pancake']
Saskia to Anna/ Natalie:	I don't care if that's what I look like. I like the hair cut though.

(Hey, 1997, pp. 62–3)

Comment

At one level this exchange can be viewed as a written slanging match in which insults are traded back and forth. However, Hey applies further layers of interpretation. For example, she notes the references to 'slag' and the flat-chested depiction of Saskia in the picture as evidence of 'the capacity of girls to reposition other girls within the regime of the male gaze' (Hey, 1997, p. 63). In this way, too, the other girls effectively 'exclude her from the pleasures of girlhood and feminine approval' (Hey, 1997, p. 64). Nor was this some quickly forgotten exchange; Saskia was practically and effectively excluded from the group, she was ill for two weeks and never returned to the school.

Hey summarises these girls' friendship relations in the following fashion:

> The desire to become and the fear of being displaced as a girl's significant other appears to be what Erin, Samantha, Saskia and Anna bring to the negotiations. However, girls' tangible desires for power through friendship have to be reconciled with its ethical rules. These social rules are premised on the exact opposite of undisciplined individualism. ... The central premise of girls' friendship are: reliability, reciprocity, commitment, confidentiality, trust and sharing. The repertoire of emotions that are provoked if these rules are broken are as powerfully felt as those that have characteristically been claimed as the sole prerogative of sexualised relations. Girls' 'divorces' are messy, as we can see in what happened to Saskia.
>
> *(Hey, 1997, p. 65)*

5.2 Boys' friendships

While girls seem willing to talk – both to one another and to researchers – about friends and friendship, the same appears to be less true of boys. Though it may be more difficult to access the world of boys' friendships, it is, however, not impossible, as the studies described below demonstrate.

Christine Skelton (2001) investigated features of boys' friendship groups in north-east England primary schools, noting that the 6- to 7-year-old boys she observed tended to form large, loosely connected groups with a general absence of tight friendship groupings. However, these loose connections did not mean that the groups were without a structure.

Her observations of a group in one school identified one boy, Luke, as an obvious outsider and two others, Carl and Rick, as being marginalised on account of their physical appearance and personal habits. Rick was regarded as 'smelly' and Carl dribbled. As a consequence of being avoided by many of the children in the class, these two tended to seek each other out at 'choosing time'. Skelton observed that the relationships of the remaining eight boys were best understood in terms of their standing with John and Shane, the two boys who instigated the majority of competitive, challenging behaviours both to authority and among their peer group. Gary, Tommy and Matt were always the first to join in with John and Shane and, occasionally, they attempted to initiate and take the lead in various challenging actions. By contrast, Bobby, Adam, Dean, Sean and Martin always took part in group actions but were unlikely to lead.

Skelton drew an analogy between the relationships among these boys and a military hierarchy:

- John and Shane were the generals who organised the action and led the initial assault.

- Luke, Gary, Tommy and Matt were the regular soldiers who were quick to see what was required and proficient in supporting the action of the leaders.

- Bobby, Adam, Dean, Sean and Martin were the conscripts who realised they had to join in, but their involvement was minimal and they sought to position themselves on the periphery of the action.

- Rick and Carl might be regarded as conscientious objectors. Recognising their marginal position, they preferred to avoid contact with the rest of the group. Nevertheless, they always took some role in any action, possibly because the alternative was more personally threatening.

This example presents a further perspective on the patterns of friendship that can exist within groups – in this instance boys aged six and seven. Within the group, children themselves construct and organise friendships in a hierarchical fashion, often based on their own notions of power and status. These friendships operate in ways which produce both individual and collective identities, and in the particular example provided by Skelton's research the boys' collective identity was defined by their oppositional stance to authority.

The idea that it is more difficult to gain access to boys' friendships is supported by a study of boys aged 11–14, also in the UK (Frosh et al., 2002), which suggests that their relationships with each other are structured around the contradictions of masculine identities. Many of the boys the researchers spoke to saw masculinity and toughness as

Figure 8 A boy's best friend is his cat

inextricably linked, making it difficult for them to discuss feelings of emotional closeness and intimacy within male friendship groups. In individual interviews with researcher Rob Pattman, however, many of the boys did discuss their feelings of intimacy and vulnerability at school and within the family. A notable feature of this was the ways in which, in one-to-one interviews, they spoke with affection about their pets. They talked about the pleasure they derived from caring for them, being able to stroke them and cuddle up to them and being loved by them. In many instances this was not something they would talk about with other boys at school for fear of being seen as 'wimpish'. A few of the boys contrasted the sorts of relations they had with their pets with much less intimate relations they had with people. These findings point to the ways in which conforming to masculine norms may constrain boys.

In ethnographic research in north-east England, I spent time in and out of school speaking with and observing a group of 16- to 17-year-old young men who styled themselves as 'Real Geordies'. 'Geordie', amongst other definitions, had once loosely been a term associated with coal miners from the region, but this colloquial interpretation has all but been forgotten. For the Real Geordies, being a Geordie was less about labour and production and more about going out and consumption. As I got to know the Real Geordies, I was struck by the similarity of their backgrounds, coming to share as they did a familial legacy of manual labour. With few exceptions they spoke of fathers and grandfathers who were part of a specialist skilled working-class stratum that included sheet-metal workers, constructionists, offshore operators, glaziers, fitters and mechanics. The Real Geordies shared many values derived from a working-class background that values loyalty, camaraderie and a 'work hard, play hard' ethic. As I grew to know the Real Geordies it became apparent that they forged friendship bonds through collective activities such as football, clubbing and drinking. These practices affirmed their desire to belong, developing their masculinities, and also expressed their emotional attachments to the locality. They are also a celebration of working-class excess lived in and through the body and worked out upon the landscape.

Connell has described these actions as 'body-reflexive practices' in which 'more than individual lives are formed: a social world is formed' (Connell, 1995, p. 64). In this sense the activities of the Real Geordies are formative of a changing idea of local identity that has shifted from the 'hard graft' once epitomised by the post-industrial workers of the 1980s UK TV drama *Auf Wiedersehn Pet*, towards the hedonistic party antics of characters in *Geordie Shore* (a UK reality TV show broadcast from 2011). At the same time ideas from the past – such as Geordies as fun, honest, hard working, hard drinking and, well, just 'hard' – are not simply erased but recuperated and reworked in the present. Significantly, these embodied actions alone do not do the work of friendship. Rather, it was also the way in which particular events and happenings could be narrated that enabled affective bonds and attachments to transpire. Here 'funny stories' referring to passing out, throwing up or acting completely out of character when under the influence of alcohol were continually narrated – such as the time Filo insisted on urinating from the Tyne Bridge and ended up with 'p*ssed-streaked troowsers!'; the occasion when Fat Mal ruined his best silk shirt when he fell asleep on top of his kebab and chilli sauce after a heavy night out with the 'lads'; or the chip-throwing fight that occurred in a local take-away and resulted in them all being barred from the establishment (Nayak, 2006). Masculinities, social class identifications and local ties were produced and affirmed through such body-reflexive practices and their retelling. The Real Geordies derived great satisfaction from the relating of humorous events, sexual anecdotes and tales of cartoon violence. These stories served to bind them together, providing them with a sense of collective history reinforced through mutual experience. It served as a memorialisation of ritual that became the bedrock upon which male friendships could be built.

Figure 9   Masculinity, drinking and belonging

Summary of Section 5

Children's experiences of friendship play a part in the development of their identity.

Gender difference may have an impact on friendship groups in many minority-world cultures. Boys and girls commonly form single-sex friendship groups characterised by large informal networks for boys and more tightly bound structures for girls.

Friendship may involve the playing out of powerful negative emotions, such as jealousy, hatred and fear, as well as positive feelings of support and care.

Children may use friendship as a way of regulating and controlling each other.

---

6   Multicultural friendships and migrant communities

A popular misconception is that children do not 'see' race. That is, they are innocent beings 'colour blind' to the embodied markers of difference which adults have falsely used to divide up humanity. Comforting as this pastel-coloured vision of childhood might appear, it is overwhelmingly inaccurate. A key problem is that it absolves children of agency and in doing so sets them apart from being participants in a racialised world. This section will argue that we all participate in race relations and have a stake within them. To counter the notion of 'childhood innocence' we explore how children can draw up 'race lines' around friendship groups, before going on to show how these lines are transgressed, shored up and continually refigured in everyday activities.

6.1   Racism in children's lives

Van Ausdale and Feagin (2002) spent a year in a multi-ethnic American pre-school observing 58 children aged between three and five years. Surprisingly, they discovered that even small children were developing sophisticated understandings of how race operates in the world; they avoided mentioning it in front of adults, as adults did in front of them. But once away from grown-ups small children could nevertheless draw upon the idea of race to hurt, discriminate and exclude other children, revealing them to be skilled managers of race privilege. In a study of children in an urban multi-ethnic primary school, Paul Connolly also disclosed how 'at the ages of 5 and 6 children appear to be already actively involved in appropriating, reworking and reproducing racialised discourses' (Connolly, 1998, p. 192). Such studies dispel common myths about childhood innocence. But what are we to make of these troubling race encounters: are they just 'child's play' or something more pernicious?

To begin to grasp the meaning of racism in children's lives we need to turn to children themselves and the cultural worlds they inhabit. In a sophisticated study of racist name-calling, Barry Troyna and Richard Hatcher (1992) interviewed a number of primary school pupils in order to ascertain how racism is manifested in children's friendship groups. They found that:

> Expressions of racist views were generally partial and fragmented, and to a great extent context-bound and embedded in social interaction. They were often combined with expressions of racial egalitarianism. It is our view this accurately reflects children's consciousness.
>
> (Troyna and Hatcher, 1992, p. 79)

It is worth pausing to reflect upon these findings. Troyna and Hatcher discovered that one of the most common reasons why children would deploy racist terminology was to 'act tough' – an issue especially applicable to boys. Troyna and Hatcher usefully distinguish between 'hot' name-calling, where children hurl racist insults in the heat of an argument that may be later regretted, and 'cold' name-calling, where racism is deployed in a clinical fashion under the guise that being white means being superior. The complex manner in which racism can operate alongside anti-racism is seen where white children may espouse racist opinions at one moment and then maintain that their best friend is black the next. Here race lines are carefully redrawn through an act Troyna and Hatcher term 'refencing', wherein particular minority ethnic friends can be included in friendship circles and bracketed out from the racist abuse directed more generally at others.

The authors also found that many white children did not distinguish between words containing racist overtones and other insults such as 'fatty', 'ginger' or 'specky'. To this extent racist taunts could have equivalence with other forms of name-calling in children's peer groups, a position that ignores the power of race discourse in society and colonial histories of exploitation. In ethnographic research I conducted with children and young people in a predominantly white community in the north of England, there was little understanding of whiteness as a marker of privilege in peer-group interactions. Rather, an overriding perception held by many children was that school anti-racist policies provided ethnic minority children with special benefits and as such were 'anti-white' practices, as the following vignette reveals:

[11–12 years]

ANOOP: Are there any advantages to being white in this school?

NICOLA: Well, no.

MICHELLE: Cos coloured people can call us [names].

JAMES: It's not fair reely cos they can call us like 'milk-bottles' and that, but us can't call them.

SAM: The thing is in this school, is like if you're racist you get expelled or something, but they [black children] can call us names and the teachers don't tek any notice of it.

JAMES: They tek no notice.

(Nayak, 2003, p. 147)

There are a number of striking things about this extract. To begin with white children are seen to disavow their race privilege by claiming they hold no structural advantages over minority ethnic children. So, although whiteness is a position of privilege in most minority-world societies, this privilege goes unseen. Secondly, the children put forward a model of race equivalence that fails to distinguish racist insults from other name-calling, 'they can call us names' (Sam), 'but us can't call them' (James). Thirdly, there is a suggestion that anti-racism is 'not fair', it affords special treatment to ethnic minorities, and it is white children who are most likely to be expelled.

While research on the exclusion rates of black pupils paints a very different picture from that imagined above, the important thing to observe is the manner in which children 'do race': investing in the belief that it is ethnic minorities who are beneficiaries and whites who are victims of 'unfair' race relations. Despite the unspoken investment in whiteness, I would contend that none of the children I spoke with above should crudely be categorised as racist. Rather, children are *ambiguous* agents and racist discourse is itself deeply contradictory.

The slippery nature of race-making practices in children's lives is evident in Suki Ali's (2003) study of 7 to 11 year olds undertaken in three schools in London and south-east England. Ali focuses her account on children of 'mixed heritage' who tend to be ascribed the label 'mixed race'. She found that appearance and popularity could work to refigure race markers to the extent that at least some children could engage in a 'post-race' way of being. One might think of how popular figures such as President Obama, the singer Beyonce or the racing driver Lewis Hamilton have managed to transcend some of the weight of race. Similarly, Ali discovered that 'Children in all the schools rejected hegemonic ideals that privilege whiteness in discourses of beauty and attractiveness' (Ali, 2003, p. 173). This suggests that in an increasingly globalised society our understandings of being white, black, mixed and so forth are contingent and shifting. That forms of 'non-whiteness' can be deemed desirable and 'exotic' and to signal urban 'cool' is indicative of the ambiguity and incompleteness of any race signs – in this case colour – to effectively represent who we really are. As a number of studies described in this section have shown, we may live in an 'increasingly post-race world … [but] the irrational and corporeal ground of "race" can still be a powerful force in social relations' (Ali, 2003, p. 2). The contingent, context-bound and multiple inflections of race that figure within children's friendships are discussed in the next activity.

Figure 10   The shape of school

Activity 5   Segregated spaces

Allow about 25 minutes

Consider the statement below from Mayra, a 15-year-old Hispanic student. She was one of 26 girls interviewed by Mary Thomas in her study *Multicultural Girlhood* (2011), set in a Los Angeles high school in the USA.

> My school is shaped like a rectangle. There is a big piece of grass in the middle and surrounding the piece of lawn are four sides lined up with buildings. The Punks, Goths, and Rockers hang out on one side of the school. Most of them are Whites and Asians. [NB. In the US this latter term is used to designate those who either herald from or whose parents are from Far East Asia.] They hang out on the lawn or on the left side of school. One of my best friends [who is white] hangs out there and although she's my best friend, we don't hang out [there] together. On the opposite side of the punks, there's the place where the gangsters hang out. That building is where their main spot is. You will not see Armenians there because mainly Hispanics hang out there. On the up side of school is where the preps, 'pretty people' and populars hang out. The lower side of school, 'the forest', is where the Armenians hang out. You won't see Hispanics there because this is their [Armenian] territory. The gangster spot and the Armenian spot are divided ... the 'border line' that divides these two [is] ...

Where there are fights between the two, they meet up here and that's where it happens.

(Quoted in Thomas, 2011, p. 9)

Now read through the passage again, but this time get a piece of paper and some coloured pencils and draw a map of the geography of children's lives in this school. Begin by drawing a map of public space in the school, identifying the various cliques, subcultures and gangs you encounter. Having located multiple friendship groups, colour-code each of these areas using a different shade so that the territories they occupy are distinguishable from one another.

Comment

Having undertaken this exercise you have effectively mapped the geography of children's lives in a particular US high school. Reading the extract above alongside your personal map, reflect on the following points:

- Mayra's practice of not hanging out with her best friend during period break times
- the role of social class and whiteness in delineating space and friendship groups
- the idea of race as a performance enacted by students in school with consequences for social space and friendships
- the violent policing of border lines between groups
- the relationship between the micro-division of school space and the wider demarcation of urban space in Los Angeles, USA.

6.2   Friendship amongst child migrants

One of the most challenging aspects to friendship is the experience of migrant displacement. In particular, unaccompanied child asylum-seekers, refugee children and even some migrant youth may encounter friendship loss and find it difficult to make friends in their new homelands. Making friends in a new country where one has relatively few social ties, may face language barriers and is not attuned to cultural mores such as humour, fashion and popular customs presents enormous barriers. At the same time child migrants can be resilient and show great agility when it comes to adapting to the flux of changing circumstances.

Refugee and asylum-seeker children are amongst the most vulnerable when it comes to social networks, ties and belonging. Those who are unaccompanied asylum-seekers may be forced to place their trust in gang masters, lorry drivers, border patrol agents and state services as they make their journeys across continents and nation states. But even then friendships can still emerge and take on special meaning, as Karen Wells discovered in her qualitative interviews with young refugees and asylum-seekers in London:

INTERVIEWER: Who's this? Is this your friend?

MEKONNEN: Yes, he's from back home we studied together. He lives near my house. ... At home he lived far from my house but we studied together. In Eritrea it's not like in UK.

INTERVIEWER: Did you decide to come together to England?

MEKONNEN: No, no. I met him in Libya. I just saw him and said, 'Hi' [we were] together to Italy and from Italy they took him different place. ...

INTERVIEWER: Why did they take him there?

MEKONNEN: Because we were 10 people under 18, they took us different place. Then I met him there

(Wells, 2011, p. 324)

In this example we see how relatively weak ties can turn out to be transformative, where the shared experience of the migration journey seals a bond between the two. Mutual recognition means that the friendship is of the type of 'social convoy' Pahl (2000) described that carries us through life's hazardous journey. Like many migrants these children would regularly use the internet, email accounts and social networking sites such as Facebook to solidify the transient ties of friendship across time and space.

A number of studies on migration problematically assume that children are 'luggage' – adult appendages to a broader diasporic displacement. This assumption fails to recognise them as migrants in their own right. In the case of Irish return migrants, Ni Laoire (2011) found many children could initially feel like outsiders as they sought to adjust to new circumstances. Some would speak of being stared at in the classroom or marked out as different on the basis of their accent, dress and interests. Ni Laoire claims that gender differences emerge where many boys may find a place in local peer groups through football and other sporting activities, but girls may have to work harder at integration. Importantly, one of the ways to overcome these obstacles was through a process of mediation whereby cousins would be pivotal in helping facilitate integration in children's friendship circles. Of course, for returning child migrants the familial networks open to them are often absent for unaccompanied child asylum-seekers and many refugee children. This indicates that children's friendships are heavily structured by the state and its institutions where schools, detention centres, public housing and voluntary organisations play a role in governing the conditions under which friendship coheres. The displacement endured by many children across the world reveals that friendship, intimacy and trust are essential to their long-term emotional well-being.

Summary of Section 6

Children are not passive subjects who reflect ideas, but are active agents capable of producing, reproducing and contesting racism.

The privileges of whiteness tend go unseen and are rarely remarked upon.

Young children are often found to be ambiguous in their expressions of racism, drawing upon exclusionary and egalitarian ideas according to situation and context.

Children and young people may draw lines of race around friendship, though these can be partial and incomplete in their rendering.

The 'doing' of race through activities and practices can turn arbitrary space into territory.

Migrant, refugee and asylum-seeker children may face particular barriers when it comes to forming friendships.

---

7   Friendship, Facebook and social networking

An area that has spawned a great deal of media attention concerns the increasing influence that new technologies have upon the lives of children and young people. Exploring the emerging literature in the field, most authors fall into one of two camps. The first group comprises those who see new media as a positive influence in children's lives, extending their horizons and enabling them to become global citizens who can participate in an increasingly interconnected world. This liberal depiction of new media emphasises it as an empowering, democratic sphere in young lives. Against this, a more conservative position has been adopted by some commentators who regard new media technology as detrimental to children, epitomised in reports of cyber-bullying, pornography, paedophilia and the wider risks posed to those left unsupervised. Working between the lines of each of these perspectives, I argue instead that any understanding of new media needs to be placed squarely within children's cultural worlds – observing how they actually use technology, listening to what they have to say about it, and critically evaluating the meaning it has in their lives.

There can be little doubt that mobile phones, social networking sites, internet gaming and other electronic media have completely altered the experience of childhood in recent times. As this chapter is concerned with friendship we shall turn our attention specifically to practices of social networking. The explosion of social networking sites, such as Bebo, MySpace, Friendster and Facebook, and electronic forms of communication, including Twitter and YouTube, have created new platforms upon which children's identity and interactions can be staged. Many schoolchildren post carefully posed photographs of themselves and their friends on their 'wall' in what is often a deeply self-conscious act of self-presentation that speaks to a social world 'out there'. In the case of Facebook, which follows the format of the American high school graduation album, sites were originally set up to keep in touch with old school friends, enabling users to look at one another's profiles and in some cases add personal testimonials.

Children's social websites are often designed through a collage of profiles, photographs and comments left by the user which is made accessible to those enlisted to the friendship network and they in turn may evaluate these images to respond accordingly. Personal websites and 'walls' may contain photographs of a fun night out with friends, family holidays snaps or images of pop stars and celebrities. In this way children can act as editors of their lives, selecting images and information in a biographical narrating of who they are, or at least who they wish to be as they self-present to an 'imagined community' (Anderson, 1991). Such stylised acts are what the sociologist Anthony Giddens (1990) has referred to as the unfolding 'biographical project of the self' that is a familiar characteristic of the contemporary period –

concerned with the narrating and making of identity. His point is that identity is partly an act of self-creation that involves individuals narrating their past in order to make sense of who they are in the present as exemplified in social networking personal profiles.

What is further particular to social networking sites is that they exist as technologies for the 'doing of friendship'. In developing this argument we can see how they perform as arenas of sociality for children and young people. Children are often introduced to social networking sites through electronic messages from friends encouraging them to sign in. Once they have done so they may view a friend's profile, keep up with their latest postings and also post messages to the wider network. In doing this they are not only interacting with their friend, but with their friend's peers who may in turn be enlisted on to their 'wall' or website. The rapid relay of information in this way means an extraordinary amount of data can be speedily disseminated and discussed. Gossip, rumours and news take on heightened significance when children 'go viral' with information about others.

Bea Larby is 15 years old and attends an inner-city London school. She remarks how, 'At my school we hear three words, slut, sket and slag, everyday.' In an interview with journalist Sandra Laville, Bea explains how sexist abuse is a practice to which many young women fall victim. She recalls, 'One girl, her ex posted naked pictures of her and sent them around the school. She left school because everyone thought she was a sket, she used to get bullied in corridors. People would say, look there she goes that sket, but no one did anything to stop it' (Laville, 2011, p. 7). Rather than being straightforward, children's friendships must be formed alongside the types of peer surveillance, shaming, bullying and harassment described by Bea.

In steering a path between the positioning of social networking sites as either 'empowering' or 'risky' it can be helpful to look more closely at children's actual experiences. In doing so it is apparent that children's virtual peer groups are not dissimilar to other friendship circles which comprise cliques and hierarchies. Many social networking sites allow participants to mark out 'best friends', 'top friends', and so on, but this can create an intimate inner-circle where intense jealously and anxiety pervade, especially when a user does not find their status replicated on one of their 'top friends' walls. In a study of American teenage MySpace users, Boyd (2007) found some young people were overwhelmed with the emotional intensity of online friendships, as one respondent recounts in familiar youth 'text-speak':

> 'Myspace always seems to cause way too much drama and i am so dang sick of it. Im sick of the pain and the hurt and tears and the jealousy and the heartache and the truth and the lies … it just SUCKS! … im just so sick of the drama and i just cant take it anymore compared to all the love its supposed to make us feel. i get off just feeling worse. i have people complain to me that they are not my number one on my top 8. come on now. grow up. it's freaking myspace', Olivia, 17

(Quoted in Boyd, 2007, p. 14)

Figure 11 Children's online worlds can take on different meanings

What is interesting about Olivia's impassioned response is that it graphically demonstrates the emotional work of friendship. The popularity of social networking sites can mean young people are forever scrutinising themselves and one another in an endless loop of critical appraisal. Secondly, there is a powerful sense that these distant, disembodied, virtual relations are nevertheless marked with intensive affects and emotions, 'the pain and the hurt and the tears and the jealousy and the heartache'. Thirdly, while a number of reports have been conducted concerning the extent of young people's internet usage, exposure to pornography, risk of cyber-bullying and so forth, these studies largely omit the lived experience of young people themselves and how social networking sites figure in the broader compass of their lives.

To further illustrate the value of first-hand experiences we can turn to a small-scale study of 16 London undergraduate users of social networking sites (Lewis and West, 2009). For the majority of these students Facebook, the preferred medium for dialogue with peers, was simply a 'displacement activity'. Rather than being central to their lives it was something to turn to in idle moments and a means of keeping up with what was going on. As an informal mode of communication, a main appeal for students was that Facebook involved low-level commitment, enabling them to keep in contact with people they had met on the odd night out but would not necessarily feel a need to go for a coffee with. These 'hi and bye' friends (Lewis and West, 2009, p. 1219), as one respondent referred to them, could be easily integrated and managed through Facebook. Such accounts paint a more prosaic picture of social networking sites in the lives of children and young people, reminding us that many friendships in late modernity can be diverse, diffuse and transient in their composition. This is in part due to widespread social transformations creating more mobile, temporal and fragmented societies across parts of the minority world. It might be thought that in age of 'online identities' and 'virtual selves', children and young people may no longer yearn for face-to-face contact. Instead, the evidence of student Facebook users and others implies that meeting up, going out and the sharing of live experiences is still an essential ingredient of friendship.

Summary of Section 7

New media technologies such as mobile communications and social networking sites are transforming the experience of childhood.

Research into children and new media is predominantly split between positive or negative accounts of their impact on children's lives.

Examining how children actually use new media and what they have to say about it offers a more grounded approach for empirical analysis.

> Social networking sites are technologies that facilitate particular ways of 'doing' friendship in the contemporary moment.

8 Conclusion

This chapter began by documenting the significance of friendship in children's lives. I charted the manner in which friendship changes throughout the course of childhood from infancy through to early adulthood. What is noticeable is that friendship is one of the primary means through which children learn about self and others. In order to develop multiple perspectives on children's friendships, attention was drawn to the value of cross-disciplinary accounts, focusing on psychological, sociological and anthropological perspectives. There are of course many other ways of approaching children's friendships, for example historically or through literary depictions. The point of adopting a multidisciplinary perspective is to acknowledge different traditions, ideas and approaches whilst recognising that interpretations of childhood are diverse and contested.

A core aim of this chapter has been to emphasise the role that social contexts play in structuring friendship. It is argued that children's friendships are rarely a consequence of chance, but are mediated through a number of relations including parents and carers, siblings, school selection, neighbourhood districts and social status. An important dimension of children's friendship includes forms of play, shared experiences and, as children grow older, an ability to communicate with one another and develop bonds of trust. While it remains important to explore friendship as a social practice, this chapter also emphasises how it is infused with intensities of feeling – jealousy, anxiety, love, humiliation and a range of intangible unarticulated emotions.

As we have seen, friendship is a precarious social practice for many children that may be split across lines of gender, class or ethnicity. Indeed, participating in friendship can often be a way of performing and consolidating these divisions, marking out those who belong from those who do not. For example, while sex demarcation is a familiar divide segmenting children's friendships in many minority-world states, these splits may be less marked in other parts of the world. To this extent I have argued that children are active agents who participate in social relations and bring them to bear in everyday life through the making and breaking of friendship. I concluded by exploring some of the ways in which social networking and new media are changing ideas of friendship and relationship practices for children and young people and I described some evidence of transformation in terms of the immediacy of communication and possibilities for spanning geographical boundaries. However, celebratory reports of new media as empowering and the counter-posing view that they are risk-laden activities rarely capture how young people actually put to use technologies in the development of friendship and what this means to them – a focus we develop throughout this book.

References

Ali, S. (2003) *Mixed-Race, Post-Race, Gender, New Ethnicities, and Cultural Practices*, Oxford, Berg.

Anderson, B. (1991) *Imagined Communities: Reflections on the Origin and Spread of Nationalism*, London, Verso.

Atwood, M. (1990) *Cat's Eye*, London, Virago.

Beazley, H. (2002) 'Vagrants wearing make-up: negotiating spaces on the streets of Yogyakarta, Indonesia', *Urban Studies*, vol. 39, no. 9, pp. 1665–83.

Berg, M. and Medrich, E. A. (1980) 'Children in four neighborhoods: the physical environment and its effect on play and play patterns', *Environment and Behavior*, vol. 12, pp. 320–48.

Bigelow, B. J. and La Gaipa, J. J. (1980) 'The development of friendship values and choice', in Foot, H. C., Chapman, A. J. and Smith, J. R. (eds) *Friendship and Social Relations in Children*, Chichester, John Wiley.

Blazek, M. (2011) 'Place, children's friendships, and the formation of gender identities in a Slovak neighbourhood', *Children's Geographies*, vol. 9, no. 3–4, pp. 285–302.

Boyd, D. (2007) 'Why youth (heart) social network sites: the role of networked publics in teenage social life', in Buckingham, D. (ed) *MacArthur Foundation Series on Digital Learning: Youth, Identity, and Digital Media Volume*, Cambridge, MA, MIT Press.

Byrne, B. (2006) *White Lives: The Interplay of 'Race', Class and Gender in Everyday Life*, London, Routledge.

Campos, R., Raffaelli, W., Ude, W., Greco, M., Ruff, A., Rolf, J., Antunes, C. M., Halsey, N., Greco, D. and the Street Youth Study Group (1994) 'Social networks and daily activities of street youth in Belo Horizonte, Brazil', *Child Development*, vol. 65, pp. 319–30.

Connell, R. (1995) *Masculinities*, London, Polity.

Connolly, P. (1998) *Racism, Gender Identities and Young Children: Social Relations in a Multi-Ethnic Inner City Primary School*, London, Routledge.

Corsaro, W. (1985) *Friendship and Peer Culture in the Early Years*, Norwood, NJ, Ablex.

Damon, W. (1977) *The Social World of the Child*, San Francisco, CA, Jossey-Bass.

Frosh, S., Phoenix, A. and Pattman, R. (2002) *Young Masculinities*, Basingstoke, Palgrave Macmillan.

Giddens, A. (1990) *Modernity and Self Identity in the Late Modern Age*, Cambridge, Polity.

Hey, V. (1997) *The Company She Keeps*, Buckingham, Open University Press.

James, A. (1993) *Childhood Identities: Self and Social Relationships in the Experience of the Child*, Edinburgh, Edinburgh University Press.

Kehily, M. J., Mac an Ghaill, M., Epstein, D. and Redman, P. (2002) 'Private girls and public worlds: producing femininities in the primary school', *Discourse*, special issue on friendship, vol. 23 no. 2, pp. 167–78.

Konner, M. J. (1981) 'Evolution of human behaviour development', in Munroe R. H. and Whiting B. B. (eds) *Handbook of Cross-cultural Human Development*, New York, Garland STPM Press.

Laville, S. (2011) 'Teenage domestic violence: "no one did anything to stop it"', *Guardian*, 16 April, p. 7.

Lewis, J. and West, A. (2009) '"Friending": London-based undergraduates' experience of Facebook', *New Media and Society*, vol. 11, no. 7, pp. 1209–29.

Little, T. D., Brendgen, M., Wanner, B. and Krappman, L. (1999) 'Children's reciprocal perceptions of friendship quality in the sociocultural contexts of East and West Berlin', *International Journal of Behavioural Development*, vol. 23, pp. 63–89.

Nayak, A. (2003) *Race, Place and Globalisation: Youth Cultures in a Changing World*, Oxford, Berg.

Nayak, A. (2006) 'Displaced masculinities: chavs, youth and class in the post-industrial city', *Sociology*, vol. 14, no. 5, pp. 813–31.

Newson, J. and Newson, E. (1976) *Seven Years Old in the Home Environment*, London, George Allen & Unwin.

Ni Laoire, C. (2011) '"Girls just like to be friends with people": gendered experiences of migration among children and youth in returning Irish migrant families', *Children's Geographies*, vol. 9, no. 3–4, pp. 303–18.

Opie, I. and Opie, P. (1959) *The Lore and Language of Schoolchildren*, Oxford, Oxford University Press.

Pahl, R. (2000) *On Friendship*, Cambridge, Polity.

Punch, S. (2000) 'Children's strategies for creating playspaces: negotiating independence in rural Bolivia', in Holloway, S. and Valentine, G. (eds) *Children's Geographies: Playing, Living, Learning*, London, Routledge.

Rubin, Z. (1980) *Children's Friendships*, Glasgow, Fontana.

Selman, R. L. (1980) *The Growth of Interpersonal Understanding*, New York, Academic Press.

Shostak, M. (1983) *Nisa – The Life and Words of a !Kung Woman*, New York, Vintage Books.

Skelton, C. (2001) *Schooling the Boys: Masculinities and Primary Education*, Buckingham, Open University Press.

The Open University (2003a) U212 *Childhood*, Video 3 Band 4 'Friendship', Milton Keynes, The Open University.

The Open University (2003b) U212 *Childhood*, Video 2 Band 2 'Kinship', Milton Keynes, The Open University.

Thomas, M. (2011) *Multicultural Girlhood*, Philadelphia, Temple University Press.

Troyna, B. and Hatcher, R. (1992) *Racism in Children's Lives*, London, Routledge.

UNICEF (2005) *State of the World's Children: Excluded and Invisible*, New York, UNICEF.

Van Ausdale, D. and Feagin, J. R. (2002) *The First R: How Children Learn Race and Racism*, Lanham, MD, Rowman and Littlefield.

Wells, K. (2011) 'The strength of weak ties: the social networks of young separated asylum seekers and refugees in London', *Children's Geographies*, vol. 9, no. 3–4, pp. 319–29.

Reading A
Bad blood

Lorna Sage

Source: *Bad Blood*, 2000, London, Fourth Estate, pp. 105–8.

Try as I might to lose myself in the landscape, however, I was still only an apprentice misfit and self-conscious in the part. Other kids who hung about at all hours turned out to have errands – big brothers or sisters to fetch, a message to carry to someone working down the fields, or to Dad in the pub. You loiter with a lot more conviction if you've even the shadow of a purpose to neglect and that I lacked. And the truth was that often no amount of trudging would get me to the state of dreamy abstraction I craved. Then I was simply lonely. I wanted friends desperately and, as it happened, the move to The Arowry held out hope, for it gave me a second chance with two girls from school who'd had nothing to do with me when I'd lived in the vicarage – Janet Yates and Valerie Edge, who were now neighbours. Valerie, brown, rosy, curly-haired and tall for eight, lived at the first council house to be finished, which already had a proper garden with dahlias in the borders. Janet – slighter like me, but unlike me, neat and tidy – came from a smallholding down the lane, with a bush of pungent, grey 'Old Man' at the gate and a path made of red-and-blue bricks. Gates and gardens figured large in our friendship because we spent at lot of our time together leaning or swinging on one or other of our gates. With Valerie and Janet you didn't wander off, not because they weren't allowed to, exactly, but because they were too grown-up, they saw no point in it.

They were busy being big girls, practising for real life, which meant not so much mothering dolls or playing house or dressing up (although we must have done all these things), as whispering in a huddle, sharing secrets, giggling behind our hands and linking arms around each other's waists. It was like a dance, a dance of belonging with no private space in it, all inside-out intimacy, and I found it euphoric, intoxicating. And then we would quarrel, for the magic number three is a formula for dissension: two against one, two whispering together, turning away and giggling, the third shamed and outcast. It's obvious now that this was the real point of the whole elaborate dance, its climactic figure, but back then, of course, each quarrel seemed a disaster and I'd run home, tears streaming, and howl on my own back doorstep for hours. My mother, dismayed in the first place by my obsession with such ordinary (if not common) little girls and even more put out by the intensity of my grief when they turned their backs on me, would say, 'It's not the end of the world.' But she unwittingly provided me with exactly the right words. That's what it was, the end of the world, every time.

I cast myself as the odd one out, but in truth it wasn't always so at all. The real shame that sticks to this memory comes when I recall the pang of pleasure I felt when Valerie and I shut out Janet. Our emotional triangle was a very good rehearsal for the world, the mimic anticipation of group psychology was perfect, even down to the fact that Valerie was never excluded. She was more sure of herself to start with and she remained innocent of the needy jealousy the other two of us suffered, so became ever more blithely, unconsciously cruel, our unmoved mover. Valerie for her part adored her mum. …

It was Valerie's mum's example that inspired a game that was not – for once – part of the dance of rejection. True, it just involved Valerie and me, but Janet was away for the summer holidays, staying with some auntie or cousin, not a shadowy rival waiting in the wings. This game – *Doing the Flowers for the Dolls' Wedding* – developed a mimic reality and depth our other games lacked. *[note: Mrs Edge supplemented the family income by making wreaths and 'doing flowers for weddings']* It didn't seem like play at all, in fact, that was its charm. We planned for weeks, discussed exactly what the dolls wanted, made lists of the different bouquets and sprays we'd need for the bridesmaids and matron of honour, as well as the bride herself (who'd ordered flowers for her hair too) and priced them all, including buttonholes for the families, strictly graded in order of kinship and importance, with mothers top. We were confined to wild flowers mostly, and of course we had to miniaturise everything for the dolls, but these additional problems only enhanced the busy, anxious pleasure of the whole thing. In the days before the big day we picked our flowers and ferns, and put them in separate jam jars ready to be made up into bunches of different sizes and splendour, which was something you had to do at the last minute.

We even arranged to borrow a camera, to take a group picture of the happy event, in order to immortalise our handiwork, although I don't think we managed to take one, for I never remember seeing it. Perhaps it was an overcast day, or possibly no one would lend us a camera for they were expensive, temperamental, grown-up toys back in 1952. Nonetheless, although the wedding itself hasn't left much trace, it was a great success, for it was the background *Doing* of the flowers over all that time (we were only nine, it must have seemed an age) that counted. So much so that neither the dolls nor their clothes figured at all prominently in our professional calculations about how to get things exactly right – although the dolls were all the wrong sizes and baby-shaped (we were pre-Barbie, let alone Ken). This was fantasy at work, with the emphasis on work. And the other thing that made it idyllic was that we plotted and staged it all on my back doorstep, since Valerie's mum didn't want us under her feet.

Chapter 4

Youth cultures

Lesley Gallacher and Mary Jane Kehily

Contents

In this chapter, you will:

- gain an understanding of the concept of youth cultures and its usefulness for studying the cultural worlds of children and young people

- apply the concept of youth culture to young peoples' lives and the social practices in which they engage

- come to understand the distinction between youth cultures and subcultures and the different contributions they make to the study of young people

- critically evaluate the concept of subculture and its significance to the study of young peoples' lives

- discuss the emergence of subcultures in particular times and places and analyse how they have changed over time

- observe how globalisation and commercialisation affect youth cultures.

1   Introduction

Reflecting on being in London in 1988 just as the rave music scene exploded in what became known as the 'second summer of love', Spaceman says:

> It was brilliant. Brilliant. And then I met this gang of guys, and this is where my descent, my climb into the big league of p*ssheads and f***ing scammers and working-class yobbos *really* started. I started knocking round with them. They were f***ing tough guys and I used to go out thieving with them. I lost my job, because I couldn't be bothered working. I found that thieving with these guys was much more f***ing fun. You didn't have to get up in the morning, it was more um … lucrative. The money was f***ing great. The crime wasn't so serious: it was just shoplifting and we burgled a couple of hotels.
>
> (Quoted in Williamson, 2004, p. 58)

Williamson's serial ethnography of the Milltown Boys, a group of working-class young men he first met in the 1970s, presents an insider account of the dynamics of youth culture and how they feature in the broader context of a life being lived. Spaceman's biography is deeply inflected by a close affiliation with his first youth culture, the anti-school lads who lived on the same estate and attended the same school in the north of England. Biographically, the Boys shared a sense of themselves as outlaws and rebels, having fun bunking off school and notching up personal records for petty crime in pursuit of an alternative index of achievement. Generationally, the Boys were among the first young men to experience the shrinking labour market of post-industrialised times. Unlike their fathers' generation, the transition from school to work was troubled; growing up in Milltown entailed leaving to get a job. Revisiting the Boys in 2000, Williamson pieces together the stories of this class-cultural cohort that fragmented in adulthood but at other levels remained linked through the experience of being young together and being one of the Boys.

This chapter develops the idea that children and young people create their own distinct and significant cultures and that these can be observed and studied. However, the distinctive cultures of young children and of youth are often seen differently. Whereas the cultural worlds of children at play are usually regarded as a benign feature of childhood, youth cultures are often seen as dangerous and challenging. This chapter will explore the concept of youth culture and subculture by looking at specific examples of young people in action. In this chapter, 'youth culture' refers to the organic activity of young people at a general level, while 'subculture' refers to particular groups of young people identifiable by their distinctive *style*. Within the tradition of youth scholarship there is a rich vein of research that develops the idea that youth constitutes a distinct kaleidoscope of subcultural groupings. These studies frequently illustrate intra-group differences and many ways in which young people relate to and participate in society. It is through the concept of youth subculture that the activities of many young people have become visible.

2 Making sense of youth cultures

Cultural groupings are not necessarily the preserve of the teenage years and are not confined to the domain of leisure. Generations of school-based researchers have identified the presence of strong and abiding subgroups within the student body. *Learning to Labour*, Willis's (1977) study of a UK secondary school, provides a generative example of boys defined by their approach to learning as either 'lads' or 'ear'oles'. As the unfolding ethnography reveals, the two groups were formed in relation to each other as conformist pupils who listened to teachers ('ear'oles') or non-conformist lads, preoccupied with 'having a laff' as part of an expanding repertoire of resistance to authority. In an Australian study, Connell (1989) elaborated on Willis's approach by identifying further divisions within a school-based male peer group: 'cool guys, swots and wimps'. Generally inspired by ethnographic observation, such characterisations of life in school suggest that students position themselves within groups that can be recognised by their different responses to teachers, discipline, sport, academic achievement and play. There is a suggestion that the cultural groupings to which young people affiliate in school may be significant in shaping their lives and futures. Willis relates school experience to opportunities after school most strongly by arguing that the trickery and subversion of the lads act as preparatory work for the working-class occupations they will inherit. Clearly an analysis rooted in industrial times, the study's subtitle, *How Working Class Kids Get Working Class Jobs*, loses its explanatory power in the post-industrial landscape, leaving other researchers to explore links between laughter, lads and masculinity (Kehily and Nayak, 1997; Woods, 1983).

Mac an Ghaill (1994) and Shain (2003) offer more recent accounts of student culture, reflecting some of the changes in gender relations, work and patterns of migration. Mac an Ghaill's typology of the student population in a metropolitan sixth-form college in the UK placed young men within the following groups:

- the Macho Lads – a working-class group, antagonistic towards school and middle-class school culture, who formed their own values in opposition to school

- the Academic Achievers – recognised and shared school values, mutually affirming their relationship with school

- the New Entrepreneurs – invested in the emergent high-status technical and vocational subjects of the digital age

- the Real Englishmen – middle-class students who rejected school but were not hostile to it and who prized individuality and honesty.

Shain's (2003) study of Asian girls in school focused on the differences between separate groups of young women often characterised as one group due to a shared ethnic minority heritage. Based in two

Figure 1 An influential early study documenting the culture of 'the lads', a group of working-class boys at a West Midlands comprehensive school

contrasting UK locations, Shain draws on the categories of Gang Girls, Faith Girls, Survivors and Rebels to describe the diverse identities of Asian girls in ways that challenge many Western misconceptions.

Activity 1   In my youth
Allow about 10 minutes

Look back on your own youth and identify any youth cultures of which you were a part. Did they have a distinctive name or label? What were their particular characteristics: dress, hairstyle, music, behaviour? How old were you at the time of your involvement? If you weren't yourself a member of such a culture, what do you remember of those that were? What do you see as the equivalent cultures that attract young people today?

Comment

The youth cultures available to you as a young person depend on the period you grew up in and other factors such as location, socio-economic background and ideas that you identified with at the time. We describe our own experiences:

Lesley

I grew up in Glasgow and, as a teenager in the mid-1990s, my musical tastes centred around Britpop. Some of my friends and I all wore jeans, t-shirts, parkas and Adidas trainers and argued over important issues like whether Blur or Oasis were better. Many of my friends preferred to listen to heavier rock or metal music and identified themselves as moshers. They wore heavy boots, combat trousers and camouflage colours, had their noses, tongues and eyebrows pierced and dyed their hair all manner of improbable colours. Others, my sister included, identified as goths and dressed all in black with pale foundation and heavy dark eye make-up, lipstick and nail polish. I have never been able to play any musical instruments or sing, but lots of my friends were in bands who put on sporadic gigs in church halls where the boys all played the same Nirvana and Foo Fighters covers, while the girls covered Hole songs. Together we didn't make up or identify as a coherent subculture in our own right, but we identified collectively against those we referred to as 'trendies' in their designer clothes or 'neds' in their Kappa tracksuits.

As my friends and I grew older we could increasingly go to gigs, or just hang out in pubs and clubs associated with the indie music scene in Glasgow (even if we were not yet old enough to drink legally); we were able to identify more strongly as 'indie kids'. My friends remained in bands but they became more musically diverse, influenced by local indie bands (some of whom went on to become moderately famous), and often quite pretentious with it. I grew up and moved on from this scene fairly early (largely due to becoming a mother at 19), but many of my friends never did and still frequent the same pubs and clubs they have been for the last 15 years. Some of them have even gone on to find work within the music industry as sound engineers or independent record company managers.

Mary Jane

The two youth cultures that were prominent in the mid-1970s during my teenage years in a small town in Warwickshire, England, were 'mods' and 'rockers', neither of which appealed; I saw them as a choice between obsessively neat but ugly clothes or an excess of leather and grease. I was more influenced by the legacy of the hippy culture than by youth cultures that offered the possibility of membership in Leamington Spa. The idea of being a hippy was on the wane but the hippy ethos was much in evidence. Me and my friends were against wars, governments and 'selling out' and for all things 'mind expanding'. We wore long hair, long dresses, lots of velvet and patchouli oil – and having a purple bedroom wall was compulsory. Despite smelling like cat's wee, intimacy was very much in vogue and I recall many tender moments huddled up with friends listening to the Velvet Underground. While I am tempted to make fun of this time in my life and see it as a resource for humour, I also recognise that identification with a youth culture is formative and can linger well into middle age (the Velvet Underground are still my favourite band).

But what about youth cultures today? If I were young now, would I be part of a cultural group and if so which one? Well, the playful appeal of retro fashions like 'boho chic' is an obvious one for me. It may exist only in the pages of women's magazines but reality shouldn't be the problem it was in my youth. Indulging in lots of floaty material, rose bud tattoos and accessories the size of a sailing dinghy, perhaps I could be the consumer-happy princess that second-wave feminism would never allow me to be. For the days when I'm not shopping till my nose bleeds, there are the environmental protest movements, animal rights activism and the global anti-capitalist demonstrations that owe a great deal to the hippy era and can be seen as a reworking of earlier themes and issues.

Talking about my generation?

The following extracts are intended to introduce you to the idea of looking at young people as participants in self-defining cultural groups and to considering some contrasting approaches to the study and analysis of young people in society.

The Grubbies

I was a Ted, not in the hard core. I was only a follower, part of a wave, but I was a believer. I was also in a group of working-class grammar school boys christened the 'Grubbies' or 'arty farties'. We were interested in things of the mind. It was a rather elite set. One of these Grubbies lived in a flat which was unusual with a front room overlooking a main road. The room had a high ceiling. There was a record player with speakers and his collection was classical. We used to sit there on the floor, sometimes in darkness, three or four of us grammar grubs and we'd play as loud as we could doom-laden Stravinsky and Vaughan Williams and read Thom Gunn and loving all the big boom. And a feeling that something was going to happen, the same feeling – that we were capable of changing the whole way the world was. Of changing our own life. A new world … And we would just sit there, holding ourselves, posing to ourselves, some of us smoking, and let this huge sound sink into us. Doing nothing else … but you had the sense that something was … going to happen.

(Gosling, 1980, pp. 45–6)

Shooming

Shooming is the state of ecstasy that dancers aspire to, losing themselves in Bam Bam's rhythms in order to leave the real world behind.

(John Godfey, quoted in Redhead, 1993, p. 62)

Untitled Emo poem

two shots of hate from a mouth as loud as a gun,

like an assasin … who does it for fun.

two deafening blows in a war that has just begun,

life gone away … i'm done.

> two red roses sitting on my coffin, the wind blows, leaving only one
>
> the world i know disappears ... like the setting sun.
>
> ('Alone', no date)

It is commonplace for adults to suggest that young people in the minority world have a difficult time making the transition to adulthood. The stereotype of the teenager as moody, difficult and estranged from adults is ubiquitous in soap operas, comedy and other media representations. Young people themselves may offer a different and more diverse account.

Gosling's description of growing up in Nottingham in the 1960s provides us with another layer of understanding to add to the comments about being a teenager in Leamington Spa. Interestingly, Gosling indicates that it was possible to be a member of more than one different youth culture at the same time. He had allegiances to being a Teddy boy and a 'Grubbie'. These two groups in themselves were not entirely congruent – Teds were associated with the working class, popular culture and living in the moment, while the Grubbies appeared to be forging a more elitist sensibility based around classical music and the anticipation of personal and political change. Dual membership for the young Ray Gosling, however, made sense for him as a working-class grammar school boy. He also suggests, very touchingly, that the important points of connection were *conviction* and *feeling*; you had to be a 'believer' and this produced a shared sense of emotional togetherness between you and your peers.

Successive generations of youth researchers have pointed to the relationship between youth cultures and wider society. In the context of Thatcherism in the UK, rave culture of the late 1980s and early 1990s created a chemically enhanced bubble in which the pleasures of the drug ecstasy and dancing all night provided an escape from the real world. Redhead (1993, p. 4) refers to this phenomenon as 'hedonism in hard times'. Set against the legislative measures of a government that appeared to attack the poor and the young, the 'second summer of love' promoted smiley-faced egalitarianism, peace and love, on the level dance floor of reclaimed buildings and agricultural land.

More recently, young people in the minority world have been referred to as 'Generation X', 'Millennials' and 'digital natives'. These names conjure up different characterisations of youth to be branded as a generational cohort, from the nihilistic, gloom-stricken with more than a passing interest in despair, hatred and self-destruction to the narcissistic attention seekers of new technological times. The negativity of contemporary youth has a history that finds points of resonance in the Romantic poets of the nineteenth century and in twentieth-century 'confessional poetry', but is more commonly seen as a reflection of late modernity. Interestingly, Emo, the group most associated with heightened sensitivity and the anxious introspection of being young finds expression in music *and* poetry. A much visited website, Emo Corner, describes the function of Emo poetry as:

> emotionally provocative poetry. … Some of these themes include suicidal thoughts, painful experiences, anger inspiring events, or any other kind of emotion. …
>
> The important thing … is that it is serving a purpose for the writer. The art that is produced from Emo poetry is only a byproduct of the process of creating it: through this process, the writer is able to exorcise the feelings that torment him or her and produce the poem
>
> (Emo Corner, 2008)

In contrast to rave and the Grubbies, a self-conscious irony can be found among Emos, who are more likely to communicate through new technology:

> How to be emo: 'Attitude is everything. Typically you will be expected to be depressed and insecure. But it's more important to be sensitive and quiet. Avoid confrontation; you have to be introverted and too wrapped up in your own emotions to care about the opinions of others. But you can defend your opinions via the internet provided you get very emotional about doing so.'
>
> ('Alone', no date)

Summary of Section 2

Young people may be seen as a distinct cultural group within society, often defined in terms of life stage and maturity.

Youth cultures are an important way in which young people create cross-generational and intra-generational differences, express their individual identities and respond to wider social relations.

Youth cultures are often associated with distinctive styles of dress and behaviour.

3 Subcultures

In the last section we discussed the concept of youth culture as a space in which young people exist as a distinct group defined by their age, their activities and their position within society. This section further explores youth culture while paying attention to the differences between young people, which are often inflected through social categories such as class, ethnicity and gender. Sometimes these differences may be marked by a set of different interests, values and aspirations. Researchers who have studied the activities and behaviour of young people in minority-world societies developed the concept of subculture as part of an attempt to understand youth culture from the perspective of young people themselves. Participants in a subculture usually have things in common with one another that serve to distinguish them from other social groups and from other young people. Tim O'Sullivan et al. (1994) and Sarah Thornton (1997) offer the following ways of defining subculture:

> As the prefix implies, *sub*cultures are significant and distinctive negotiations located within wider cultures ... The term and its supporting theory has developed almost exclusively in the study and explanation of youth ... youth negotiate and advance 'their own' distinctive and especially symbolic subcultural responses to the problems posed not only by age or generational status, subordination and control, but also by class position and inequality,

particularly as they are experienced and combined in the spheres of education, work and leisure.

(O'Sullivan et al., 1994, pp. 307–8)

Subcultures have generally been seen to be informal and organic … The defining attribute of 'subcultures' lies with the way the accent is put upon the distinction between a particular cultural/social group and the larger culture/society. The emphasis is on variance from a larger collectivity who are invariably, but not unproblematically, positioned as normal, average and dominant.

(Thornton, 1997, pp. 4–5)

These definitions make it clear that subcultures exist in relationship to the society from which they emerge and that their existence may provide an insight into the experiences of young people, especially in the areas of education, work and leisure.

The prefix 'sub' in the word 'subculture' signals that these groups have a position which is set apart from or even subordinate to the broader culture. It also captures the sense in which participants in subcultures often see themselves, and are seen by others, as different or oppositional in some way. The sociologist Albert K. Cohen was one of the first to explore the concept of subculture and the ways in which it can aid an understanding of the social world (Cohen, 1955). For Cohen, subcultures arise when people with similar problems get together to look for solutions. Through their interactions with one another the members of a subculture come to share a similar outlook on life and evolve collective solutions to the problems they experience. In the process a distance is created between the subculture and the dominant culture. Indeed, achieving status within a subculture may entail a loss of status in the wider culture.

As you will see in the following section, youth subcultures frequently seek to define themselves as being against the culture that exists around them and particularly against the values they associate with the parental home. It could be argued that there is a tendency in studies of subcultures to emphasise the unconventional, deviant and non-conformist aspects of subcultural groups. However, within the context of non-conformity, participation in subcultures also demands a considerable amount of conformity. Subcultural groups are commonly marked by distinctive modes of appearance, a particular style, forms of dress and adornment that make the participants look different, sometimes even spectacular and shocking. In the context of youth cultures, style takes on a particular meaning as 'the means by which cultural identity and social location are negotiated and expressed' (O'Sullivan et al., 1994, p. 305). Membership of a subculture may also bring with it a certain emotional experience. It is important to stress that being a member of a subculture is not about being a victim. Individuals involved in subcultural activity often speak of the highs and lows of life as part of a subculture, the mundane inertia of 'doing nothing' (Corrigan, 1979) and the moments of risk and excitement described by Spaceman as 'brilliant'.

A final point of definition rests on the understanding that many contemporary subcultures are involved in acts of self-definition dependent on social context. The visibility of young people in the minority world can be seen as a post-World-War-2 phenomenon associated with growing affluence and young people's participation in the workplace as economic subjects with the ability to develop particular interests. The 'birth' of the 'teenager' remains part of the mythology of the post-war years, existing as a well-worn cultural narrative of modern times. Green (1999) locates the primal scream of the modern teenager as a 1950s event. For the first time, so the story goes, young people found themselves with free time and a disposable income. In the past, young people moved from school to work and from the family home to the marital home with little time or money for carefree pleasure. But the optimism and relative affluence of the post-war years provided the space for something else to emerge. Increased employment opportunities and greater financial independence provided young people with some resources for the pursuit of cultural 'play'. The mass production of everyday items such as food, clothes, music and literature provided further resources for cultural groups and subcultural formations.

Summary of Section 3

The term 'subculture' can help us to understand differences between young people as well as offering some insight into the views of young people themselves.

Some subcultural groups may have underground or marginal status within society that may challenge the conventions of the wider society.

Subcultural activities and practices may be exciting and pleasurable.

4   Youth cultures in action

So far we have discussed youth cultures and the notion of subculture in general terms. In this section we will explore further the concept of youth cultures as developed by researchers in different global locations. In particular, we will look in detail at examples of three different youth subcultures offering expressive and stylised commentaries on their environment: skinheads, hip hop and Lolita. In each case there is a need to read and analyse these cultures in the context of the societies in which they take shape. There's a story to be told about young people's presence within particular communities – where subcultures emerge and how they are shaped by a sense of place. While it is important to account for the sociocultural conditions from which subcultures emerge and in which they are nourished, it is equally important to consider how they are affected by processes of globalisation as they are exported for global consumption and subsequently adapted to the needs of young people in a range of different locations and contexts.

4.1   Skinheads

Skinhead style emerged in 1970s Britain at a time of social and economic change. Phil Cohen (1972) described the breakdown of traditional working-class communities in the East End of London as old, rundown and cramped terraces were demolished and replaced by new housing developments. Long-established communities were uprooted, dispersed and finally rehoused in new environments which, although brighter and more hygienic, were often considered to be unfriendly and even alien. Workplaces and traditional forms of employment were also disrupted and many young men had no choice but to find work outside the area. The disruption of family life, kinship patterns and working relations has been well documented. In this literature, the focus on the East End before redevelopment often conjures up an imaginary past, the 'classic white slum' as Hebdige (1979) describes it. At the same time, the structure of British society

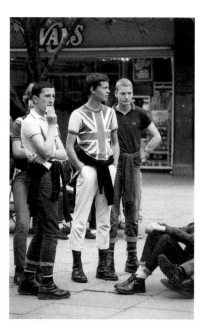

Figure 2   Skinhead style and nationalist sentiment

was changing due to the impact of post-war immigration from former colonies in the Asian subcontinent and the Caribbean. Changes in social relations were also taking shape. The emergence of a new sexual agenda posed questions concerning the position of women in society and their rights in relation to men. Such questions inevitably challenged the dominance of the white heterosexual male. Within the context of widespread change, the skinhead appears to have represented the concerns of the present couched in the myth of the past. Skinheads were associated with nationalism, fighting, racial violence and a recognisably 'hard' look: shaven head, jeans and builder's boots. Cohen (1972) describes the skinhead style of dress as 'a kind of photostream caricature of the model worker', ready for manual work but actually taking up leisure time.

John Clarke's (1975) study of 'skinhead mobs' in the West Midlands area of England further explores skinhead youth culture to suggest that they emerge as a response to the decline of traditional working-class communities in the UK in the post-war period. For Clarke, skinhead groups defining themselves as 'mobs' represent an attempt not just to mourn the loss of working-class community but actually to recreate it. The term 'mob' and its associations with revolutionary zeal and criminal activity capture a sense of proletariat energy and protest that is forceful and purposeful. Skins had things to be angry about and this anger provided them with a collective cause or 'solidarity' as Clarke puts it. Hall and Jefferson (1976) suggest that youth subcultures can be understood symbolically as acts of 'articulation' that speak to the concerns of participants.

As a subculture, skins were involved in a protest of 'double articulation': firstly with the values of their parents' culture and secondly with the state, which appeared to have neglected or betrayed the white working class. To view youth subcultures as adolescent rebellion is to underestimate the extent to which young people seek to comment on generational change and social structures. Clarke and Cohen document the many ways in which the skinheads felt constrained by the environment they found themselves in and the people around them: the police and the legal system; schools and youth clubs; social workers, middle-class 'do-gooders' and the aspiring working class; hippies, ethnic minority groups and gays. Such a wide-ranging hit list is indicative of the extent of their anger and suggests that skinheads as a group felt alienated and besieged. They had a sense of belonging to a community that was, from their perspective, becoming fragmented and in decline. Their feelings of marginalisation led to feelings of frustration and aggression. The skinheads' concern over territory, the marking and regulation of their neighbourhood by their presence and their graffiti also points to a constant need to defend what is theirs – to say, 'This part of the city/estate/street is our space, we rule here.' This assertion of authority in certain localities also brings into sharp focus the skinheads' feelings of dispossession and dislocation at a more general level which could be interpreted as, 'We rule here 'cos we don't rule anywhere else.'

So far the portrait emerging is that skins hate everything and everybody. Is there anything they do enjoy? Clarke's account suggests that the skinheads enjoyed the rituals of football and fighting. Within these spheres of activity skins can display a style of masculine prowess premised upon being physically tough and being together. Clarke describes the skins' uncompromising stance in the face of violence and the highly prized feelings of group loyalty which made it important to support friends when 'trouble' erupted. Violent acts of bigotry, such as 'paki-bashing' and 'queer bashing', provided an arena for the values of the skinhead group to be displayed and consolidated. Clarke suggests that these practices can be understood as defensive reactions to the breakdown of cultural homogeneity and simultaneously a search for 'magical resolutions' to powerful and contradictory feelings. Ethnic and sexual minorities became the locus of disgust for skinheads' sense of loss and powerlessness in the face of social change. Many of the themes discussed by Cohen and Clarke are developed in the following reading.

Activity 2   Reading A

Allow about 20 minutes

Read the extract in Reading A by Anoop Nayak, from '"Pale warriors": skinhead culture and the embodiment of white masculinities'. As you do so, make some notes on the following questions:

- What reasons does the author give for the emergence of the subculture?

- What are the defining features of the subculture? It may be helpful to include details of how the participants look, behave and feel.

- As far as you can tell, what source material and research methods does the author draw on to develop his analysis?

Comment

Anoop Nayak's study of skinheads in the Kempton Dene area of Birmingham, UK in the 1990s offers different ways of understanding skinhead style. Nayak's study is an illustration of the ways in which youth cultures develop and change over time. The skinheads of Kempton Dene shared features in common with skinheads of earlier periods, but there were also significant differences. Nayak points to the variations in haircut, clothes and musical influences to indicate the diversity and fluidity within the subculture. Furthermore, Nayak makes visible an account of white ethnicity that has not been central to earlier studies. Seeing skinheads through the lens of white ethnicity highlights the many points of engagement between black and white cultures and reveals the contradictions inherent in skinhead identity. Nayak suggests that although ethnicity remains a much studied aspect of black minority groups, little is known about the ethnicity of white youth and the way in which racism may feature in their lives. In the light of this omission, his study explores the process whereby explicitly racist young men evoke whiteness within their suburban neighbourhoods in relation to their two obsessions – being authentic and being British. Contemporary research on skinhead youth indicates that skinhead style can be appropriated and interpreted in different ways.

Since the first wave of skinhead culture in the 1970s, successive generations of young people have taken on the identity of skin in ways that change or even subvert the earlier version. In the context of 1980s Britain, anti-racist activists sought to challenge and invert the stereotypical image of the skinhead by appropriating the skinhead 'look'. A notable rebranding of the skinhead image can be found in the band The Redskins. As members of the Socialist Workers Party and the Anti-Nazi League, the band took up the skinhead look to promote anti-racism through grass-roots political activism and popular social movements such as Rock Against Racism. Rock Against Racism was promoted by rock bands through gigs, rallies and mass demonstrations and achieved success and widespread support as an energetic campaign to promote racial equality and celebrate diversity.

A further reworking of the skinhead image can be seen in a study referred to by Nayak: Murray Healy's (1996) analysis of working-class gay men in Europe and the USA. Healy documents the ways in which his respondents adopted the signature skinhead haircut and mode of dress to assert their working-class homosexual masculinity. The gay skins in Healy's study were keen to demonstrate that being gay did not necessarily involve a compromise with white class-coded masculinity and its associations with fighting and resilience. They sought to establish themselves as a subculture within a subculture, distancing themselves from middle-class homosexuals who they felt all too frequently adopted an effeminate 'camp' style that could be regarded as embodying the stereotype of the limp-wristed queen.

Nick, one of Healy's respondents, illustrates the way subcultural membership intersects with class, gender and sexuality. Dropping out of school and leaving home at 16, becoming a skinhead made Nick a somebody, 'the most angry, most aggressive, most violent image I could think of was the skinhead. … Being a skinhead gave me an identity, values, self-worth, all the things I was lacking in myself' (Healy, 1996, p. 152). Moving from a social housing estate in Coventry to the gay scene in London he recalls, 'Tripping up queens, intimidating them, that sort of thing, especially the really camp ones' (p. 153). Shaving the head, getting facial tattoos done and adopting an antagonistic posture became a means of authenticating this rough masculinity. Using the body as a canvas upon which competing masculinities – camp or hardness – could be situated, Nick's skinhead style was his calling card. Moving in and out of sexual encounters from rent boy to lover, pretending to be racist or straight depending on the nature of the transaction, his physical resources generated the funds to sustain living in the capital. Nick's sexual biography is also revealing of the important role that subculture plays in young lives. It shows us how subcultures tend to be seen as the preserve of deviant youth groups that operate with their own styles, values and repertoire of beliefs. The gay skin, however, moves beyond the subcultural milieu to call all forms of masculinity into question, making any claims to an authentic skinhead identity thoroughly counterfeit.

Figure 3   Russian skinheads marching with orthodox nationalists in Moscow in 2006

Looking at skinheads in the UK over time, from the 1960s to the 1990s, it is important to note the dynamism of youth cultural forms as they evolve and develop in different locations. The study by Pilkington et al. (2010) of Russian skinheads considers a further incarnation of this spectacular subculture. Based on an ethnographic study of skinheads in Russia in the 1990s, Pilkington et al. illustrate the shifting character of skinhead style that changes over time for individuals and groups. Having no fixed meaning, skinhead identity is made anew through repeated performances – acts, practices and embodied communication – that constitute the meaning of skin. Located in the northern region of Vorkuta, the emergence of skinheads in the 1990s is steeped in the significance of place: the bitter legacy of a gulag outpost, remote prison camps, post-Soviet social change and subsequent industrial decline. In the 1930s, Vorkuta's prison population was used to drill for oil and natural resources. The city developed a reputation for high levels of deviance, especially among young people. The physical environment contributes to the extreme and suffocating 'aura' of the place documented by the research team. Vorkuta is snowbound for eight months of the year, leaving its residents isolated and frost bitten in a land where in the words of a local saying, 'nothing grows except gangsters and criminals'. In the post-industrial landscape of the 1990s, skinhead subculture emerged in response to local conditions as a defensive expression of white supremacy premised upon the 'action' of protest, particularly fighting and racial violence. While commonalities with skins in the UK can be found, the authors point out that the meaning of skin is uniquely configured to address conditions in Vorduka and cannot be seen as a pale imitation of Western versions.

Unlike first-wave skins in the UK, Vorduka's skinheads were not engaged in a class-based protest. Rather, their identity prioritises forms of togetherness and group bonding that unite them as loyal friends with shared values. Same-sex friendships and embodied practices, such as piercing and tattooing, characterise the 'action' of the group as more intimate practices are preferred to the public display of their Western counterparts.

A final point lies in the cultural context shaping contemporary subcultures. Pilkington et al. recognise subcultures as being affected by their representation in the media and in public discourse, making subcultural identity a cultural resource available to all. Within this expanding 'blizzard of signs', individuals are required to reflect in order to understand the skin through repeated performance.

4.2   Hip hop

Like the skinhead subculture, hip hop emerged in the early 1970s and was a reaction to great social and economic change. Historians usually trace the roots of hip hop back to The Bronx in New York and situate it within the experience of young black men in urban areas. Hip hop originated from large, outdoor block parties where local youths would set up powerful sound systems and dance through the night. Musically, hip hop was a hybrid art form from the outset. Paul Gilroy (1993) explains that hip hop music was a variation of Jamaican sound system culture that was transplanted to the South Bronx where it combined with other popular musical traditions to form something unique. Hip hop culture is composed of four core elements: graffiti, breakdancing (or b-boying), DJ-ing and MC-ing (or rapping). These core elements coalesce with styles of verbal language, attitude and fashion to produce a distinctive subcultural identity.

By the end of the 1970s, hip hop began to emerge from this very local scene through the release of recorded hip hop. Craig Watkins argues that this marked both the beginning and the end of the hip hop movement in the sense that leaving behind its very localised origins and face-to-face dynamic enabled hip hop to expand to become 'a cultural and economic juggernaut' (Watkins, 2006, p. 10). From the release of 'Rapper's Delight' by The Sugarhill Gang in 1979, hip hop grew in popularity throughout the 1980s and 1990s to the extent that it is now almost ubiquitous in early twenty-first-century US culture, and internationally.

Figure 4 A breakdancing battle

As hip hop has grown in popularity over the years, and become increasingly commercialised to the extent that it can almost be considered as an industry in its own right, it has become the subject of much controversy in US society. Tricia Rose (2008) argues that the massive commercial success of hip hop in the contemporary USA has been based on the promotion of highly negative and one-dimensional stereotypes of inner-city life for black Americans. Early hip hop did tell stories around the problems of ghetto life, such as the way that gang life functions as a trap or the need to take up street crime as 'work' in the face of chronic black unemployment. However, the massive commercialisation of hip hop has foregrounded far more simplistic, absurdly celebratory and outright destructive renderings of the lifestyle, centred around what Rose refers to as, 'the trinity of commercial hip hop – the black gangsta, pimp and ho' (Rose, 2008, p. 4). This has resulted in a set of increasingly bitter and polarised debates about hip hop.

Top ten arguments in public debates about hip hop

Hip hop's critics

    1 Hip hop causes violence

> 2   Hip hop reflects black dysfunctional ghetto culture
>
> 3   Hip hop hurts black people
>
> 4   Hip hop is destroying America's values
>
> 5   Hip hop demeans women
>
> Hip hop's defenders
>
> 1   Just keeping it real
>
> 2   Hip hop is not responsible for sexism
>
> 3   'There are bitches and hoes'
>
> 4   We're not role models
>
> 5   Nobody talks about the positive in hip hop
>
> (Rose, 2008, pp. 25–6)

Rose does not seek to take a position within these debates, which she describes as both staggering and destructive. She argues that debates about hip hop matter a great deal because they stand in for larger debates about race, class and the value of black culture in the USA. Rose contends that discussion about hip hop has become a means for defining poor, black young people and for interpreting the contexts in which they live their lives. By blaming hip hop for all social ills in the USA, critics are able to obscure and ignore larger social, economic and political contexts. Indeed, they are able to turn the results of deeply ingrained institutional racism and long-term disempowerment into 'proof' that ghetto conditions are the result of black people's behaviour. The defenders of hip hop are just as guilty of ignoring this broader context. By arguing that hip hop simply reflects the reality of life in the ghetto, and making excuses about violence, sexism and homophobia, the defenders of hip hop are sidestepping the issues that really matter. Far from defending poor, black young people, they are contributing to their problems. Rose wants to expose the underlying attitudes that are shared by both sides in these debates. In doing so she intervenes in the debates by redirecting attention to the real issues and the possible solutions that could improve the lives of black young people.

Like Rose, Bakari Kitwana (2002) uses the phrase 'hip hop culture' as equivalent to 'black youth culture', and even refers to young black people as 'the hip hop generation' because the spectrum of black youth has come to identify with it. However, there is some debate as to how useful it is to think of hip hop culture as an essentially 'black culture', particularly given its growing popularity with young people from a wide range of ethnic backgrounds.

Activity 3   Hip hop and 'black culture'
Allow about 20 minutes

> For anyone to even try to insinuate that Hip Hop is not of complete and unique African/American tradition is an insult to the art. ... Understand that no matter what you THINK, Hip Hop is of solely African origin. And that no matter how you FEEL, it will never stop the fact that Hip Hop is Black.
>
> *(Adissa the Bishop of Hip Hop, no date)*

In this quotation, Adissa the Bishop of Hip Hop unequivocally states that hip hop is and must be thought of as an essentially black culture. Do you agree with him? What about non-black people who embrace hip hop culture?

Comment

Adissa the Bishop of Hip Hop is not alone in insisting that hip hop is an essentially black culture. Indeed, as we noted above, hip hop is often used as a proxy for 'black culture'. Many academics and cultural critics argue that hip hop cannot be understood in isolation from the context from which it emerged. As a result, the growing market for hip hop among the white middle classes has often been understood in terms of 'the Afro-Americanisation of white youth' (Cornel West, quoted in Kitwana, 2002, p. 10). Ian Condry (2006) explains that this process is sometimes cast in a positive light and sometimes viewed negatively. It can be viewed as uniting Americans whatever their race under the banner of a unified popular culture, or it can be viewed as a superficial appropriation which obscures and commodifies the experiences of the urban, black poor. Craig Watkins comments that hip hop may provide 'a strange form of ghetto tourism' for white, middle-class youth, which allows them to experience the resilience of black youth vicariously without having to share any of their problems (Watkins, 2006, p. 97). For this reason, Condry commends the work of scholars who emphasise the connections between hip hop and the sociopolitical struggles of African Americans.

However, Watkins describes the alignment of hip hop with an essential 'black culture' as a 'false premise', which actually serves to undermine attempts to mobilise the culture politically. He argues that hip hop has always been multiracial, multicultural and multilingual. Versions of the history of hip hop which stress its essential African American character do so at the expense of the many white, Latino and Asian youths who have contributed to its development. Similarly, Paul Gilroy (1993) warns that it is as dangerous to define hip hop as a fundamentally 'black culture' as it is to gloss over the racial politics from which it emerged. He notes some irony in the fact that the inherent hybrid nature of hip hop as a transnational and purposefully malleable form has been translated into an expression of essential racial authenticity.

Tony Mitchell (2001) argues that hip hop cannot possibly be viewed as a singular and authentic expression of African American culture because it has become a tool for young people reworking their local identities all around the world. In the twenty-first century, hip hop has become a significant force in global popular culture, which has been taken up within and adapted to suit the needs and interests of young people in a range of international locations. The spread of hip hop culture has not resulted in a homogenisation of youth culture on a global scale, however. Instead, the globalisation of hip hop has been accompanied by a diverse range of local variants, as those aspects of hip hop culture that resonate with young people in particular locations are taken up and reworked in often highly specific ways.

Often, young people outside the USA turn towards hip hop as a means of distinguishing themselves from older generations. Young people in post-socialist Mongolia separate themselves from socialist-era generations through the adoption and adaptation of hip hop culture (Marsh, 2010), while young people in South Korea combine hip hop elements with a range of other musical styles in order to express their disillusionment with the intensive schooling practices preferred by their parents. For example, Seo Taiji (the most popular Korean hip hop star of the 1990s) released a song critiquing the Korean system of education, called 'Kyo-shil idaeyo' (classroom ideology). On stage, and dressed in a 'quasi-military' school uniform, he would introduce the song as follows:

> All students have to think of only one thing – getting into a good university. All this studying is like slavery: why should we memorise so much? We have the right to learn what we want. Why

do the schools force us to have the same goals, though we all have differing abilities?

(Quoted in Morelli, 2001, p. 251)

Sarah Morelli (2001) explains that hip hop has also become a vehicle for the dreams of working-class Koreans, who set up dance practice studios in the hope that their sons will be able to develop high-profile careers as breakdancers and lift their families out of poverty.

Young hip hoppers outside the USA do worry about how their appropriation of the culture affects its 'authenticity'. Indeed, they are often as concerned about the cultural politics of race within hip hop as the academic scholars and cultural critics discussed above. Ian Condry (2006) discusses the tensions between the need to respect hip hop's roots, the urge towards 'authenticity' and attempts at innovation within Japanese hip hop. However, he explains that debates about race within Japanese hip hop need to be contextualised within Japanese society. The cultural politics of race in Japan do not centre around notions of 'black' and 'white', so practices of skin darkening (known as 'blackface') or hair kinking do not necessarily carry the same connotations that they do in the USA.

Similarly, Andy Bennett (1999) argues that young, white hip hop fans in north-east England choose to adopt a subcultural identity that is riddled with tensions and contradictions. In the absence of a significant black population within Newcastle, white working-class youth use hip hop as a means of collective expression. Although many of these young people argue that their preference for hip hop music and cultural activities has little to do with race, they are subject to criticism from other young white Geordies who view them as 'race traitors' (Nayak, 2003).

4.3   Lolita

So far we have concentrated on subcultures that have been associated with young men. Early studies of youth cultures tended to focus on young men's dominance of public space and viewed the street as a backdrop for the unfolding of male subcultural activity. Girls and young women were often invisible in these studies and were positioned within the domestic sphere – the home and the bedroom. This was, at least in part, a reflection of gendered social relations in the 1970s, which have been challenged and altered through processes of feminist struggle and social change in the intervening decades. Contemporary research in girlhood indicates that there are different ways of being a girl and that femininity is no longer so rigidly defined. This has allowed young women more freedom to shape their own identities and to create interesting new subcultural spaces (as well as participating in established subcultures).

In twenty-first century Japan, youth cultures often revolve around a constantly evolving set of very distinctive 'street fashions'. Yuniya Kawamura (2006) explains that these fashions are not produced or controlled by professional fashion designers, but by teenage girls who rely on their distinctive appearance to produce a subcultural identity. Lolita or 'Loli' is a particular subcultural aesthetic, which is often associated with the Harajuku area of Tokyo where many Lolis gather to socialise and to pose for photographs. Although the subculture is not exclusively female, there are far more female Lolis than male.

In the minority world, the term 'Lolita' is likely to evoke images of the sexually precocious title character from Vladimir Nabokov's 1955 novel. Yet, while the subculture does reference this character in its name, Lolita takes on a completely different meaning in the context of Japanese youth culture. The roots of the Loli subculture can be traced back to the *kawaii* or cute trend in 1970s and 1980s Japan. In the 1980s, band members within the newly emerging visual-*kei* (or visual style) music scene began to wear elaborate costumes and make-up which explored what has become known as the Lolita aesthetic. This very distinctive style of dress draws on and adapts a wide range of influences, including British Victoriana, particularly porcelain dolls and Lewis Carroll's *Alice in Wonderland* books, and Japanese popular cultural forms. In addition to visual-*kei* bands and celebrities, the style is influenced by characters from anime and manga (Japanese animation and comics).

By the beginning of the twenty-first century, the Lolita subculture had grown exponentially in popularity both within Japan and internationally. A wide variety of Lolita-style clothes and accessories can be bought in specialist boutiques and, increasingly, in mainstream shops. The Lolita aesthetic centres around an idealised image of Victorian childhood. Lolis wear clothes designed to de-emphasise the features of an adult female body: they use flattened bodices, high waists and full skirts with voluminous underskirts in order to conceal their bust and hips. They often wear their hair in ringlets with a bonnet, and make use of a range of accessories, including aprons, small bags, stuffed animals or parasols.

Figure 5 Sweet Lolita posing for a photograph

This style of dress is complemented by striking poses intended to evoke the illusion of a very young girl or of a porcelain doll. When posing for photographs, Lolis often stand with their knees together and toes pointed inwards and their head inclined to one side.

This 'classic' or 'traditional' Lolita aesthetic has diversified into a wide range of different subgenres. 'Sweet Lolitas' emphasise the *kawaii* (or cute) aspects of the style and incorporate overtly Romantic or Rococo elements, and 'Gothic Lolitas' incorporate influences from Victorian mourning dress into the overall aesthetic and make use of a range of cute yet macabre accessories (like coffin-shaped bags or injured teddy bears). Indeed, the Gothic Lolita look is so popular that it is often said to have produced its own subgenres, such as Elegant Gothic Lolita or Elegant Gothic Aristocrat Lolita, who wear longer dresses and use different accessories.

Kawamura (2006) argues that Lolita identities are resolutely not political or ideological; Lolita is primarily an aesthetic and the subculture is concerned with the production and display of innovative fashion. Despite this claim, she argues that Japanese street fashions are a way for young people to express shifting cultural values in contemporary Japanese society. Like the Japanese hip hoppers discussed previously, the Lolita subculture challenges traditional Japanese values. For Osmud

Figure 6   Gothic Lolita posing for a photograph

Rahman and colleagues (2011), the Lolita subculture in Japan, and in east Asia more generally, is as much a way of reacting to societal pressures as it is an expression of their dreams and fantasies. The subculture provides young Lolitas with a way to escape from their immediate realities and to express their feelings about their lives and experiences as young women. Far from being resolutely apolitical, then, the Lolita subculture is intricately interwoven with contemporary Japanese sexual and gender politics. These politics are explored in more detail in Reading B.

Activity 4   Reading B

Read the extract in Reading B, 'Lolita aesthetic and identity', by Theresa Winge. As you do so, make some notes on the following questions:

- What does Winge mean when she describes the performance of Lolita subcultural identifty as carnivalesque?

- How does Winge explain the relationship between Lolita subculture and female sexuality in Japan?

Comment

Theresa Winge argues that the Lolita subculture in Japan is a combination of both distinctive dress and what she calls 'ritualised performance' in particular public spaces. She describes the experience of these performances in terms of the 'carnivalesque' insofar as they allow Lolitas some release from the usual norms of Japanese society. By performing as part of this subcultural community, Lolitas are able to assert their difference from mainstream society without entirely abandoning the collectivism privileged in Japanese culture.

Winge explains that Lolitas attempt to prolong childhood through the use of extensive use of *kawaii* or cuteness. As a result, the Lolita subculture may appear to be anti-feminist because it portrays an ideal of feminine passivity by valorising the image of virginal youth. However, Winge argues that the doll-like Lolita aesthetic creates a safe space for young women to perform their sexuality.

The Lolita subculture has caused controversy both within Japan and internationally. Much of this controversy centres around issues of female sexuality and sexualisation, particularly surrounding *lolicon* (a Japanese portmanteau of 'Lolita complex') or sexual attraction to prepubescent girls. Winge argues that the Lolita subculture is entirely separate from *lolicon* as a sexual fetish. She explains that although Lolitas attempt to prolong childhood through the use of *kawaii*, they are striving to create the appearance of living dolls, rather than young girls. In contrast, Vera Mackie (2009) argues that the Lolita aesthetic and *lolicon* are different manifestations of the same anxiety about female sexuality: Lolitas are attempting to escape from the pressures within Japanese society by prolonging their girlhood, while adult men choose to focus on the image of young girls which they find less threatening than adult women.

Since its emergence as a subculture some decades ago, the Lolita subculture has grown in popularity and influenced popular culture both within Japan and internationally. A range of dedicated fashion labels and accessory boutiques have emerged to supply the subculture, although many Lolitas continue to adapt these items or make their own. The subculture has also been commodified for consumption within Japanese popular culture more generally, particularly in manga, anime and video game franchises. As a result, the Lolita aesthetic has been embraced outside the subculture, particularly among 'cosplayers' (fans who choose to dress up as characters from their favourite anime, manga or video game). Theresa Winge explains that cosplayers are not really considered to be part of the Lolita subculture: even though they share the same aesethic, Lolitas feel that cosplayers do not really understand Lolita culture.

Aided by export of Japanese media products, the Lolita subculture has begun to circulate globally and dedicated boutiques and fashion labels have emerged in Australia and the UK. Vera Mackie (2009) explains that Lolita brands aren't designed for export; they are intricately linked with the dreams and frustrations of young women in Japan, and with rebellion against Japanese society. This means that the Lolita aesthetic rarely reflects the Japanese subculture when it is adopted for global consumption. For example, the American singer, Gwen Stefani, incorporated a group of female dancers known as the 'Harajuku Girls' into her act. In doing so, she removed the subculture from its original performative context, and adapted it to the norms of minority-world music videos. The overt sexualisation of the aesthetic in the Harajuku Girls was the source of much discontent within the Japanese subculture (Winge, 2008).

Figure 7   Characters from the Rōzen Maiden anime

Stefani has also further commodified the Lolita subculture through a range of perfumes called 'Harajuku Lovers'. Stefani's engagement with the Lolita subculture has brought accusations of Orientalism – the exoticisation and fetishisation of majority-world cultures. Yet, Vera Mackie reminds us that the Lolita subculture is itself a bricolage of different international factors, which have been redefined into something uniquely Japanese. In this sense, 'the exoticisation of the European past in the adoption of the Gothic Lolita style in Japan is paralleled by the Orientalist exoticisation of the "Harajuku Girls" in the United States' (Mackie, 2009).

Summary of Section 4

Youth cultures exist in relationship to the context of the societies in which they take shape.

Subcultures may be a response to changing social and economic relations.

Subcultural activity may be understood as an attempt to resolve some of the contradictions faced by young people in particular social and economic circumstances.

Youth cultures change and develop over time, and are adapted to the needs of young people in different places.

5 Young people as a distinct cultural group

In the previous section, we traced the development of three very different subcultural groups – skinheads, hip hoppers and Lolis – and considered some of the way in which these subcultures have changed and developed over time. Approaching subcultures in this way allows us to uncover a range of different issues that have arisen as particular subcultures have been popularised, mediated, commercialised and globalised. It also raises questions about what happens to subcultures when the young people involved grow up.

Activity 5   Growing up on hip hop
Allow about 15 minutes

Bakari Kitwana (2002) refers to African Americans born in the period between 1965 and 1984 as the 'hip hop generation'. This cohort would have been aged between 28 and 47 at the time of publication, far older than the age range of 0–18 for 'childhood' as defined within the United Nations Convention on the Rights of the Child and even older than more generous definitions of 'youth' and 'young people' as aged up to 26 or even 30.

Do you think that it is useful to define this generation in this way? To what extent do you think that adults can or should be defined by the subcultural affiliations of their youth?

Comment

Kitwana defines this generation of African Americans in this way because he believes that hip hop has played an extremely important role in shaping and defining their lives, culturally, socially, politically and economically. In this way, he is defining a generation as a cohort of people born within a specified age range who have shared similar cultural experiences. However, the identification of this particular cohort as 'the hip hop generation' is somewhat problematic insofar as it does not include a large number of people who have been, and currently are, actively involved in hip hop culture. Kitwana's 'hip hop generation' does not include those who originated the movement in New York in the 1970s (who would be a decade older than the generation Kitwana identifies). Instead, he refers to this cohort as a 'bridge generation' between those whose identities had been defined by the civil rights movement in the USA and the 'hip hop generation' proper who came after them.

Nor does the 'hip hop generation' include those born after 1984, including the enormous numbers of young people for whom hip hop culture has been, and continues to be, an important cultural reference point and experience. Similarly, defining this group as a singular 'hip hop generation' ignores the differences within this cohort (and particularly any African Americans who have never been involved in hip hop culture at all). Kitwana indicates that those born in 1965 may interpret hip hop in a very different way from those born in 1984, and will identify different events as having been significant within the culture. Indeed, he explains that each subgroup within this 'generation' believes that they were the first to really have 'grown up on hip hop'. As you have seen, hip hop also has different resonances for young people involved in the culture today, influenced by factors such as their cultural background and international location.

Even though our adult lives and preferences are often profoundly influenced by our experiences as young people, moving on from youth cultures is very often seen as part of the transition to adulthood. Indeed, older people who refuse to leave their subcultural identities behind them and 'grow up' are often viewed as 'culturally cringeworthy' and can be subject to considerable mockery. Likewise, returning to the subcultural style of your youth is often described as a symptom of a 'midlife crisis', and viewed as somewhat embarrassing.

While subcultures are an important part of many young people's lives, this is not the case for all young people. For many, and particularly for young women, leisure time is characterised less by the display of subcultural identity in public space and more by a 'culture of the bedroom' in which they can express themselves through interior decoration and spend time with their friends (McRobbie and Garber, 1976; Harris, 2001; Lincoln, 2004).

Deindustrialisation and the regeneration of city centres in the UK have produced new ways of inhabiting space for young people. A key shift in the late twentieth century (which has continued into the early twenty-first) was identified by Robert Hollands (1995): the shift from production to consumption. Young people are less likely to define themselves through work and the labour market. Rather, their identities are increasingly organised round the night-time economy of 'going out', heavy spending and excessive drinking. Going to pubs and clubs on Friday and Saturday night has become the cornerstone of weekly experience for many young people (many of whom are not old enough to do so legally). This new way of relating to public space embraces the participation of young women, most visibly in the emergence of 'ladette' culture in the 1990s, in which young women increasingly emulated the long-established behaviour and practices of young men by getting drunk, being loud, having one night stands and boasting to their friends afterwards. The redeveloped city centre appears populated by a mundane youth culture: large, undifferentiated and seemingly happy to sink their financial resources into the uniformly contrived leisure spaces of multinational corporations. Muggleton and Weinzier (2004) frame this development as a mainstreaming of youth cultural practice, pointing to the demise of subcultural space and subcultural formations in the face of global capitalism.

The increased commodification and commercialisation of all areas of social life limits the possibilities for young people to find their own subcultural space. Indeed, the notion of a dominant culture is also changing and fragmenting, creating multiple cultures rather than a singular mainstream and various subcultural groupings. Steve Redhead (1993) argues that subcultures in the UK have been replaced by 'clubcultures', signalling the impact of globalisation on youth culture. Redhead defines clubcultures as global and fluid youth formations that are based around the media and the niche marketing of dance music as a youth-culture-for-all. Sarah Thornton (1995) provides a complementary approach to Redhead's in her study of clubcultures. Thornton suggests that through engagement with different styles of dance music, young people define themselves in relation to their peers.

Drawing on the work of Bourdieu (1984), Thornton develops the idea of 'subcultural capital' to analyse the forms of taste and distinction that characterise the club scene.

Further studies have critiqued the concept of subculture and tried to find other terms to express young people's relationship to culture, self-activity and self-expression. Contenders for the new, reconfigured subcultural crown include 'scenes', 'tribes' and 'neo-tribes'. 'Scenes' is a term used widely in studies of popular music to explore musical collectivities. 'Tribes' and 'neo-tribes' draw on the work of Maffesoli (1995) to describe loose groups of young people whose stylised tastes and lifestyles come together during moments of shared interest. Recent studies of youth formations indicate that definitions of subculture cannot be fixed in terms of earlier studies or sociocultural moments. Like other sociological concepts, it is subject to change and redefinition.

Summary of Section 5

Recent studies have suggested that contemporary youth cultures are becoming ever more homogeneous and 'mainstream'.

Scholars have experimented with new concepts to understand young people's cultural activities beyond traditional notions of subcultures.

Although youth cultures can have long-term effects on their participants, moving on from them is often seen as an important part of the process of 'growing up'.

---

6   Conclusion

In this chapter, you have explored the role that youth cultures and subcultures play in young people's everyday lives. Youth cultures are often a way for young people to respond to, and often to react against, the world around them. In doing so, they are able to assert their sense of individual identity and to distinguish themselves from their parents and other adults in society. By participating in particular subcultures, young people also set out to differentiate themselves from other groups of young people. Youth cultures are, therefore, an important aspect of young people's lives. They are also important because youth cultures are often used as an indicator for wider issues in society. As Christine Griffin (1993) points out, the values, behaviour and attitudes of young people can be read as a comment on the society at present and can also be seen to hold the key to the nation's future. Viewed in these terms, youth as a social category always represents something bigger than itself.

References

Adissa the Bishop of Hip Hop (n.d.) *A Response: Hip Hop is Indeed Black Culture, Davey D's Hip Hop Corner* [online], http://www.daveyd.com/addissablackart.html (Accessed 27 June 2011).

'Alone', *Untitled Emo Poem* [online], http://www.emo-corner.com/emo-poems-quotes/ (Accessed 13 June 2011).

Bennett, A. (1999) 'Rappin' on the Tyne: white hip hop culture in northeast England – an ethnographic study', *The Sociological Review*, vol. 47, no. 1, pp. 1–24.

Bourdieu, P. (1984) *Distinction: A Social Critique of the Judgement of Taste*, Cambridge, MA, Harvard University Press.

Clarke, J. (1975) 'The skinheads and the magical recovery of community', in Hall, S. and Jefferson, T. (eds) *Resistance Through Rituals: Youth Subcultures in Postwar Britain*, London, Hutchinson.

Cohen, A. K. (1955) *Delinquent Boys: The Culture of the Gang*, New York, Free Press.

Cohen, P. (1972) 'Subcultural conflict and working class community', *Working Papers in Cultural Studies 2*, University of Birmingham, Centre for Contemporary Cultural Studies.

Condry, I. (2006) *Hip-hop Japan: Rap and the Paths of Globalisation*, Durham, NC, Duke University Press.

Connell, R. W. (1989) 'Cool guys, swots and wimps: the interplay of masculinity and education', *Oxford Review of Education*, vol. 15, no. 3, pp. 291–303.

Corrigan, P. (1979) *Schooling the Smash Street Kids*, London, Macmillan.

Emo Corner (2008) 'Emo poems & quotes', www.emo-corner.com (Accessed 19 October 2012).

Gilroy, P. (1993) *The Black Atlantic: Modernity and Double-Consciousness*, Cambridge, MA, Harvard University Press.

Gosling, R. (1980) *Personal Copy: A Memoir of the Sixties*, London, Faber and Faber.

Green, J. (1999) *All Dressed Up: The Sixties and the Counterculture*, London, Pimlico.

Griffin, C. (1993) *Representations of Youth*, Cambridge, Polity.

Hall, S. and Jefferson, T. (eds) (1976) *Resistance Through Rituals: Youth Subcultures in Postwar Britain*, London, Hutchinson.

Harris, A. (2001) 'Revisiting bedroom culture: spaces for young women's politics', *Hecate*, vol. 27, no. 1, pp. 128–38.

Healy, M. (1996) *Gay Skins: Class, Masculinity and Queer Appropriation*, London, Cassell.

Hebdige, D. (1979) *Subculture: The Meaning of Style*, London, Routledge.

Hollands, R. (1995) *Friday Night, Saturday Night: Youth Cultural Identification in the Post-industrial City*, Newcastle, University of Newcastle.

Kawamura, Y. (2006) 'Japanese teens as producers of street fashion', *Current Sociology*, vol. 54, no. 5, pp. 784–801.

Kehily, M. J. and Nayak, A. (1997) 'Lads and laughter: humour and the production of heterosexual hierarchies', *Gender and Education*, vol. 8, no. 1, pp. 69–88.

Kitwana, B. (2002) *The Hip Hop Generation: Young Blacks and the Crisis in African American Culture*, New York, Basic Civitas Books.

Lincoln, S. (2004) 'Teenage girls' "bedroom culture": codes versus zones', in Bennett, A. and Kahn-Harris, K. (eds) *After Subculture: Critical Studies in Contemporary Youth Culture*, Basingstoke, Palgrave Macmillan.

Mac an Ghaill, M. (1994) *The Making of Men*, Buckingham, Open University Press.

Mackie, V. (2009) 'Transnational bricolage: gothic Lolita and the political economy of fashion', *Intersections: Gender and Sexuality in Asia and the Pacific*, no. 20 [online], http://intersections.anu.edu.au/issue20/mackie.htm#n47 (Accessed 1 August 2012).

Maffesoli, M. (1995) *The Time of the Tribes: The Decline of Individualism in Mass Society*, London, Sage.

Marsh, P. K. (2010) 'Our generation is opening its eyes: hip-hop and youth identity in contemporary Mongolia', *Central Asian Survey*, vol. 29, no. 3, pp. 345–58.

McRobbie, A. and Garber, J. (1976) 'Girls and subcultures', in Hall, S. and Jefferson, T. (eds) *Resistance Through Rituals: Youth Subcultures in Post-war Britain*, Essex, Hutchinson.

Mitchell, T. (ed) (2001) *Global Noise: Rap and Hip-Hop Outside the USA*, Middletown, CT, Wesleyan University Press.

Morelli, S. (2001) '"Who is a dancing hero?": rap, hip-hop and dance in Korean popular culture', in Mitchell, T. (ed) *Global Noise: Rap and Hip-Hop Outside the USA*, Middletown, CT, Wesleyan University Press.

Muggleton, D. and Weinzier, L. (2004) *The Post-Subcultural Reader*, New York, Berg.

Nayak, A. (2003) *Race, Place and Globalization: Youth Cultures in a Changing World*, Oxford, Berg.

O'Sullivan, T., Hartley, J., Saunders, D., Montgomery, M. and Fiske, J. (1994) *Key Concepts in Communications and Cultural Studies*, London, Routledge.

Pilkington, H., Omel'chenko, E. and Garifzianova, A. (2010) *Russia's Skinheads: Exploring and Rethinking Subcultural Lives*, London, Routledge.

Rahman, O., Wing-sun, L., Lam, E. and Mong-tai, C. (2011) '"Lolita": imaginative self and elusive consumption', *Fashion Theory*, vol. 15, no. 1, pp. 7–28.

Redhead, S. (ed) (1993) *Rave Off: Politics and Deviance in Contemporary Youth Culture*, Aldershot, Avebury.

Rose, T. (2008) *The Hip Hop Wars: What We Talk About When We Talk About Hip Hop – and Why It Matters*, New York, Basic Civitas Books.

Shain, F. (2003) *Schooling and Identity of Asian Girls*, Stoke on Trent, Trentham.

Thornton, S. (1995) *Club Cultures: Music, Media and Subcultural Capital*, Cambridge, Polity Press.

Thornton, S. (1997) 'Introduction to subcultures', in Gelder, K. and Thornton, S. (eds) *The Subcultures Reader*, London, Routledge.

Watkins, S. C. (2006) *Hip Hop Matters: Politics, Pop Culture, and the Struggle for the Soul of a Movement*, Boston, MA, Beacon Press.

Williamson, H. (2004) *Milltown Boys Revisited*, Oxford, Berg.

Willis, P. E. (1977) *Learning to Labour: How Working Class Kids Get Working Class Jobs*, Farnborough, Saxon House.

Winge, T. (2008) 'Undressing and dressing loli: a search for the identity of the Japanese Lolita', *Mechademia*, vol. 3, pp. 47–63.

Woods, P. (1983) 'Coping at school through humour', *British Journal of Sociology of Education*, vol. 4, no. 2. pp. 111–24.

Reading A
'Pale warriors': skinhead culture and the embodiment of white masculinities

Anoop Nayak

Source: '"Pale warriors": skinhead culture and the embodiment of white masculinities', in Brah, A., Hickman, M. J. and Mac an Ghaill, M. M. (eds), 1999, *Thinking Identities: Ethnicity, Racism and Culture*, Basingstoke, Macmillan, pp. 71–99.

Introduction – hybrid histories

The Skinhead movement in post-war Britain grew out of, and elaborated upon, a number of competing youth influences. As a symbol of working-class pride the Skinhead look came to epitomise certain aspects of labouring culture as witnessed in the early penchant for braces, denim and Doc Marten boots. Inspired by working-class Mods, life on the football terraces and a hatred of 60s Hippy peace culture, Skinheads have been seen to embody an exclusive white nationalism. But as we shall find, contemporary Skinhead subcultures are dynamic, strikingly diverse and even contradictory in terms of their formation and ritualised activities. At an international level Skinhead subcultures have been found to include feather-cut girls, young women, as well as working-class people from various ethnic backgrounds.

Indeed, the first wave of Skinheads from the late-60s sought to emulate and appropriate the signs, symbols and meanings familiar in the protest music of Jamaican Rude Boys. Throughout the 70s Skins popularised dancehalls moving in rhythm to the music of soul, blue-beat, motown and reggae. By the 80s they continued to dance to ska and two-tone – the shaggy, hybrid offspring that had emerged from the cultural promiscuity of youthful black–white interaction. Moreover, this multi-ethnic mixing of cultural styles was embodied in the clothing and mannerisms of Skinhead youth. As Dick Hebdige explains the cropped hair, boots, turn-ups and trilby hats form part of a wider 'dialectical interplay of black and white languages' (1979, p. 57). This has led Kobena Mercer to compare Skinhead style to a 'photographic negative' in which white youth adopt and adapt the meanings of blackness to enact a 'post-imperial mode of mimicry' (1994, p. 123). Paradoxically, while the popular representation of Skinhead youth is synonymous with white racism, the indications are that behind the dazzling dance of the Paleface may lurk the smudged shadow outline of black history.

Recognisably Skinhead style has changed over time and place, taking on new meanings and inflections appropriate to the lived context and situation. This semiotic struggle for the sign was evident during the 1980s when the Skinhead look was appropriated both by ultra-Right youth and supporters of the Socialist Workers Party Anti-Nazi League. Indeed, anti-racist bands such as the Redskins and organisations like SHARP (Skinheads Against Racial Prejudice), reveal the political fragmentation and variation within Skinhead youth cultures. At a global level the 'butch' image has also become popularised by Queer subcultures, in a figurative transgression that now 'short circuits accepted beliefs about real masculinity' (Healy, 1996, p. 5). The stylised appropriation of the look by a new metropolitan gay scene represents a symbolic re-coding of white masculinity that at once transgresses and resituates the meaning of Skinheadism. Diasporic movement and settlement has also led to the scattering of youth cultures, as witnessed in Moore's (1994) study of Perth Skinheads. Here, members were seen to continue to construct a 'traditional' sense of English ethnicity in the context of urban, multicultural Western Australia through rituals of football, fighting and drinking. Moreover, where Skinhead youth were once representative of the neighbourhood 'gang', new media technologies have given rise to 'virtual youth communities' and enabled meetings to occur that cross time and space, nations and continents. At the same time, there has been a world-wide branding of Skinheadism through the marketing of clothes, records, books, nostalgia and accessories. Within the global market place affluent youth consumers can now fashion a particular 'lifestyle' identity by purchasing subcultural styles over the counter. But as the ethnography will show globalisation and youth consumption have yet to render the meaning of place redundant.

Placing youth

Despite the enormous economic, political and cultural transformations that have shaped Skinhead style over the years, place and neighbourhood continue to have marked significance in young lives. Recent work has shown how in 'new' global times locality and place-bound identities are ... important influence[s] shaping the actions of young people (Skelton and Valentine, 1998). For example the Kempton Dene Skins reside in a working-class estate situated on the outskirts of Birmingham, Britain's second largest city. In contrast to the region's principal city, Kempton Dene is an ostensibly white neighbourhood and has relatively few material resources compared with the affluent suburbs that surround the estate. The ethnography illustrates how adolescent males deploy the shaven-headed look in a performance of local 'hardness'.

Darren: That's what everyone has down the Dene: a Skinhead. Don't they?

Robbie: It's the trademark. [...]

[Interviewer:] What's it a trademark for?

Robbie: Don't mess with the Dene.

Darren: Don't mess with the Skinheads!

Robbie: [chanting] Skiiiiiin – 'eads!

The Skins continue to position their identities not only against the multicultural inner-city of Birmingham (which they perceived as 'black') but also in opposition to the white middle-class suburban districts nearby. For these young men the haircut can be read as a cultural register for 'hard times' that reveals a certain naked vulnerability: the bald truth of a bleak future. Instead of playing down the image of Kempton Dene as a dodgy 'no-go' area, the Skins chose to celebrate this popular representation, turning it into a source of local pride. When asked if they liked living on the estate the responses were unequivocal.

Robbie: Yeah, I love it. Got a name, that's what I like.

[Interviewer:] What kinda name?

Darren: Born on the Dene, and I'll live on the Dene all my life.

Robbie: Ruff 'n' tuff. That's what we are. We stick together.

By adopting similar haircuts, dress codes and wider subcultural practices the Kempton Dene Skins could magically evoke a sense of community based on shared values and experiences (Clarke, 1975). This imaginative re-working commemorates masculine loyalty ('We stick together'), working-class conformity (the 'trademark' Skinhead) and local toughness ('Don't mess with the Dene'). The Skins portray themselves as 'Pale Warriors', romantic defenders of an ever retreating English way of life now felt to be threatened by immigrants, outsiders and bourgeois gentrification. The 'Pale Warrior' stance was further in evidence during conversations concerning immigration and employment. Here, the Skins discuss the plight of two local Asian shopkeepers who have set up trade in the area.

Daniel: It's our country, not theirs.

Leonard: Yeah, they don't belong in our country.

Daniel: Fuck 'em off. They've got all the jobs. Like me and Mark could be working now but fucking two pakis have jumped in our place haven' they?

This sense of ownership over nationhood ('our country') and the labour market ('our place') shows how a 'rights for whites' discourse could be utilised and enacted at the level of the local. The Kempton Dene Skins used racist language, graffiti and violence to further produce their neighbourhood as a white place. They asserted that parents and elder family members were also prejudiced against the prospect of immigrant families moving into the neighbourhood, and changing their 'way of life'. For the Skinheads the streets, shops and surrounding houses were also seen through a racial cartography. As Robbie revealed, 'The English fight for their territory … That's why we want them out of our country'. The perpetual harassment of Asian shopkeepers on the estate and the occasional rituals of 'paki-bashing', were violent reminders of how the local area could be constructed as a white space in which minority ethnic groups did not belong.

Contradictory cultural worlds: race, sexuality and gender

Despite this blanket expression of white hostility, the practices of the Kempton Dene Skins were highly contradictory with regard to the politics of race and ethnicity. Where early Skinheads favoured a 'braces-'n'-bovver-boots' appearance the Kempton Dene Skins re-worked black cultural style in an altogether different manner. Participants frequently wore loose checked shirts, training shoes, baggy jeans and hooded anoraks; apparel that was familiar to many black youth in the city of Birmingham. Although the Skins enjoyed smoking marijuana, listening to black music and occasionally using inner-city language (eg. 'wicked'), they were prone to 'bleach' these black cultural roots through white chauvinism. Where former Skinhead cultures looked to reggae, blue-beat and ska for inspiration, the Kempton Dene Skins looked to the equally contradictory influences of 'rave', ragga and hip-hop. This suggests that Skinhead style has developed, while continuing to be in 'dialogue' with and against black culture. The loose and fragile identifications made by the Skins with elements of black culture provided for a partial and contingent acceptance of certain forms of blackness and the rejection of other styles.

Robbie:	Blacks ain't as bad as pakis.
Mark:	We smoke their draw.
Robbie:	I'd rather hang around with a black than a paki.
Leonard:	Pakis smell.

Here, Asian youth are constructed as misshapen Others in the incomplete jig-saw of multi-ethnic dialogue. In contrast the Skins had established friendships with Calvin and Leonard who each had a black father and a white mother. By modifying their behaviour with the Skins, these young men managed to forge a significant, though precarious relationship with the subculture. As Calvin remarked, 'When I first come round here I used to dress like the blacks do, and when I hang around with them lot I just [copied] their clothes dress'. By 'whitening' their identities in the presence of the Skins Calvin and Leonard could deflect some aspects of racism from their lives. This in part was also a strategy of survival. 'I've mixed in with half of the crowd that are NF [National Front supporters]', recalled Calvin, 'And they know I'm alright … It's like if I didn't mix in with them they'd give me 'assel.'

If ethnicity was an issue that was subject to group- and self-regulation then gender was also an arena in which whiteness was carefully governed through the techniques of verbal and physical abuse.

Calvin:	If a white bloke sees a white girl with a black guy they might get jealous.
Robbie:	No they say, 'Oh look at that dirty bitch with a black man'.
Mark:	That's what I'd say if I saw a white girl with a black man, I'd call her a bitch.
[Interviewer:]	What about a white bloke with a black girl?
Robbie:	Batter 'em.

Although on the surface the Skinheads were violently condemnatory towards the idea of mixed relationships their discussions of sexuality were tinged with a high degree of ambiguity. Daniel had been expelled from school for 'paki-bashing' and held pronounced views on 'mixed' relationships. However, Calvin reminded the group that Daniel had once professed sexual desire towards the black pop artists Tina Turner and Janet Jackson. This comment was met with much jeering from the group and acute embarrassment from Daniel who was now unable to square the circle of blatant contradiction. At this point the group rounded on him and Robbie emphatically denounced Daniel as a 'nigger-lover'. Such illustrations reveal how the performance of whiteness through Skinhead style is always cross-cut by the circulating currents of contradiction. These ambiguities can be traced in the black cultural roots of Skinhead style including music, language, dress and marijuana-use. In the case of the Kempton Dene Skins the discussions disclose how the dark zones of race and sexuality were tightly interlaced with fear and desire (Fanon, 1952). Here, it was quite possible for young people to draw upon the codes of black culture but still maintain a more general hostility towards black people. At the same time this explicit hatred could be underscored by token black–white friendships, a covert admiration for street-based black masculinities, or black female sexual icons. These contradictions reveal that the potential of cultural hybridity to break down youth boundaries may be rudely curtailed by racist activity.

Concluding remarks

In these 'new times' of global change, labour insecurity and gender restructuring Skinhead culture may have international appeal for particular isolated white youth. The resurgence of Fascist Skins in Germany who oppose North African and Turkish *Gastarbeiter* (temporary guest-workers) is testimony to the revival of nationalism in a period when the power of nation states is felt to be receding. At the same time however, the effects of globalisation can be seen on even this most stalwart of British youth cultures. Steeped in the vibrant gloss of the black diaspora, before being hung out to dry on newly mown English lawns throughout the country, Skinhead culture has always proffered a thoroughly inauthentic mode of whiteness. The transnational geographies of Skinhead style vividly illustrate how the culture is emblematic of what Dick Hebdige describes as an oblique 'phantom history of race relations' (1979 p. 45). In the contemporary urban metropolis the Skinhead look remains a sign in perpetual motion, unstable and discursively replayed through multiple signifiers that fail to truly settle the question of whether this is a celebration of gay, straight, black, white, national or international identities. Unsettling the dominant meanings ascribed to Skinhead culture offers at least one way for understanding youth cultures at different scales and in different places within what is a rapidly changing world.

References

Clarke, J. (1975) 'The skinheads and the magical recovery of community', in Hall, S. and Jefferson T. (eds) *Resistance Through Rituals: Youth Subcultures in Postwar Britain*, London, Hutchinson.

Fanon, F. (1952) *Black Skin, White Masks*, New York, Grove Books.

Healy, M. (1996) *Gay Skins: Class, Masculinity and Queer Appropriation*, London, Cassell.

Hebdige, D. (1979) *Subculture: The Meaning of Style*, London, Routledge.

Mercer, K. (1994) *Welcome to the Jungle: New Positions in Black Cultural Studies*, London, Routledge.

Moore, D. (1994) *The Lads in Action: Social Processes in Urban Youth Subculture*, Aldershot, Arena.

Skelton, T. and Valentine, G. (1998) *Cool Places: Geographies of Youth Cultures*, London, Routledge.

Reading B
Lolita aesthetic and identity

Theresa Winge

Source: 'Undressing and dressing loli: a search for the identity of the Japanese Lolita', 2008, *Mechademia 3*, pp. 47–63.

Performance as ritualised identity

The Lolita presents her aesthetic for display in public spaces, in order to define and redefine her identity within Japanese culture. … Loli is a surreal amalgam of influences: anime or manga characters, Victorian-era porcelain dolls, the Nabokov Lolita character, visual-*kei* bands, and *kawaii*. But while the aesthetic is achieved through the use of clothing … the Lolita identity is accomplished through a ritualised performance – poses and mannerisms – in combination with the designated dress. …

While a Lolita has ritualised the aesthetic of dress and performance, she also has the freedom to select, acquire, and combine specific items of dress, ornamentation, and details to create individual meaning and identity. In this way, she draws from a range of influences to create an amalgam that expresses the Lolita aesthetic (Hebdige, 1979). Perhaps the best demonstration of this bricolage is the Gothic Lolita, who selects and borrows from Goth subculture (e.g., coffin-shaped backpacks and Ankhs), Japanese culture (e.g., *kawaii* objects – teddy bears in black dress and lace), and Victorian-era culture (e.g., the porcelain-doll aesthetic and mourning dress) to create new and meaning-laden fashions specific to the Gothic Lolita's identity. For example, the black patent leather Mary Jane platform shoes with lace details worn by Gothic Lolitas represent a combination of Victorian children's shoe style, lace details from Western children's dress, and the Gothic subcultural penchant for black platform shoes. Early in the history of the Lolita subculture, Lolitas would buy Goth Mary Jane platform shoes and attach lace and embellishments that they re-moved from second-hand children's clothing, in order to create the desired Lolita aesthetic; but today many stores carry ready-made shoes of this kind. In this way, Lolitas use bricolage to create fashions that remain within the Lolita aesthetic, yet express an individual identity.

Once the Lolita presents herself to the subculture and the dominant culture in a public setting, she acknowledges and confirms her membership in the Lolita subculture as a Loli. Here it is important to recognise the performance spaces where she displays and visually communicates her aesthetic and identity, such as urban streets, stages, televisions, Web sites, films, and magazines.

In these spaces Lolitas experience a sense of the carnivalesque – a celebration or space where there is temporary release from expected and established order and norms, time, and space (Bakhtin, 1965). The carnivalesque is commonly divided into three types: comic presentations, abusive language, and ritual performances. It is the last that best describes the spaces where Lolitas dress, gather, and display their aesthetic for insiders and outsiders. Within this carnival, an individual is part of the subcultural collective. She ceases to be herself; she is a Lolita. In these carnivalesque spaces Lolitas are free from the constraints of the dominant culture and free to display the Lolita aesthetic. They are also free to pose for photographs, which provides them with agency by making them objects of desire.

In addition to the agency gained from these carnivalesque presentations, the Lolita subculture also produces agency from the presentation of the Lolita aesthetic as a visual resistance. In Japanese culture, it is generally understood that it is better to dress according to dominant norms than suffer the disapproving gaze of the group (McVeigh, 2000; Reischauer and Jansen, 1995). Since the Lolita aesthetic exists outside these norms, its members often suffer public social rejection. Despite this rejection, or perhaps because of it, presenting the Lolita aesthetic provides subculture members with a way to visually and socially express their dissatisfaction with the dominant culture and their place within it.

The Lolita aesthetic visually communicates membership and identity in the Lolita subcultural community. At the same time, Lolitas also visually express their individuality, most commonly through their unique accessory choices. For example, young women dress as Gothic Lolitas, and because of their similar dress, they are visually grouped as members of the Lolita subculture. Still, each of these Gothic Lolitas displays individual and personal accessories: one wears a small black coffin backpack; another carries a black velvet purse; and yet another has a white and black teddy bear dressed in black lace. So within the constraints of the Lolita aesthetic (which creates and supports a sense of community and belonging through visual similarity), the Lolita subculture also allows for individualism and self-expression, creating a space for both the Lolita subcultural community and the individual member. The subcultural community is associated with a consistent recognised aesthetic, but it is also dynamic and rich with texture and variation created by the individual interpretations of that aesthetic. Maintaining individuality within the Lolita subcultural community is a delicate balance, but necessary to give the Loli a sense of agency.

The Lolita subculture functions not just as a visually recognisable community but also as a safe space for communal and individual resistance. Lolitas use this communal space for exploration of a subcultural identity and of the Lolita aesthetic. This adherence to the subcultural community and Lolita aesthetic demonstrates that Lolitas are not willing to completely surrender the ideals of uniformity and community established by their parent culture. Sweet Lolitas, for example, draw attention to themselves with their anachronistic dress, childlike mannerisms, and doll-like poses. But subsequently these stereotypes become objects of visual resistance against acceptable norms of dress and all that these norms stand for. Within the Lolita subcultural community, the Sweet Lolita is provided with the safety to present her individual Lolita aesthetic, and by maintaining her resistance and agency, she in turn empowers the subculture itself (Kinsella, 1995).

Kawaii

The concept of *kawaii* seems ubiquitous in Japanese culture, and it is a significant part of the Lolita aesthetic and identity. By exploring the relationship between Lolita and *kawaii*, it is possible to understand aspects of Lolita that go beyond the Nabokov character, living doll, sexual fetish, or transnational object. Japan seems obsessed with all things *kawaii*, and Lolitas reconnect to childhood through the use of *kawaii* objects (Aoyama and Cahill, 2003; Hasegawa, 2002; Kinsella, 1995), which embody and visually communicate much more than 'cute' or 'feminine/cute'; they also represent a desire for empathy, infantilism, compassion, and (dis)approval within the understood and hierarchical power structure (Kinsella, 1995; McVeigh, 2000). Therefore, carrying or wearing *kawaii* objects allows the Lolitas to hold on to and nonverbally communicate their childlike perspective toward the outside dominant culture, a culture that could be interpreted as playing the parental role. In this way, Lolitas also garner compassion and interest when they present *kawaii* objects, characteristics, and images, which indicate nostalgia for a past era and a desire to escape adult responsibilities for the carefree days of youth. In essence, Lolitas are attempting to prolong childhood with the Lolita aesthetic via the use of *kawaii*.

Kawaii serves an additional purpose within the Lolita aesthetic: it also creates a hyperfeminine and hypercute visual identity for Lolitas. From dress to mannerisms, the way Lolitas employ *kawaii* is said to give the viewer a feeling of 'moe' – a sense of intense attraction and contentment for things that have youthful, feminine attributes. A Sweet Lolita, for example, presents *kawaii* in excess and is often compared to sugary, sweet objects, such as candy (e.g., a lollipop or loli) and desserts. Moreover, the Sweet Lolita also exhibits stereotypical feminine characteristics (wearing lacy dresses, hair ribbons, and shoes with bows) in excess. From the standpoint of Japanese women's struggle for equality, this anachronistic portrayal of females as living dolls would seem to undermine the feminist position. For the outsider, Lolita is a representation of a woman as an object to be played with, an ideal girl to be loved or possessed, who manifests the culture's desire for virginal youth.

For a Lolita, though, this aesthetic creates a safe space to be sexy and strong behind the protection of the childhood patina, and a way to be different while having subcultural sameness (Miller and Bardsely, 2005).

Kawaii also satisfies Japan's nostalgia for previous eras, both Eastern and Western (Hasegawa, 2002; Nosco, 1990), by innocently incorporating aspects of these 'simpler times' into contemporary life. The use of *kawaii* within Japanese culture is intrinsically tied to 'neo-romantic notions of childhood,' (Kinsella, 1995, pp. 240–1) a childhood that is further removed from contemporary trappings and responsibilities by being located in another time period. The Lolita subculture's use of the Lolita aesthetic is an extreme example of seeking to experience the simplicity of the Victorian era by creating and wearing anachronistic fashions. But the Lolita subculture has not only borrowed from this historic era but also redefined it in a way that suits its own needs, as something that exists outside space and time – a 'neo-Victorian' era. Applied to the fashions, poses, and mannerism that created the Lolita aesthetic, this neo-Victorian perspective helps the Lolita achieve a type of escape from dominant Japanese ideology, culture, and society.

Objects of desire have power; moreover, desire and power are interdependent in the same way that sameness and otherness are interdependent (Foucault, 1980). This helps explain the power and agency that Lolitas have acquired by incorporating the sameness of the dominant culture – for example, *kawaii* characteristics – into the subcultural otherness of the Lolita identity, an identity that simultaneously also resists and subverts the dominant culture's power structures and the way they disadvantage Japanese women. This is how Lolita performs and achieves power and agency through her appearance.

References

Aoyama, T. and Cahill, J. (2003) *Cosplay Girls: Japan's Live Animation Heroines*, Tokyo, DH Publishing.

Bakhtin, M. (1965) *Rabelais and His World*, Cambridge, MA, MIT Press.

Foucault, M. (1980) *Power/Knowledge: Selected Interviews and Other Writings 1972–1977*, New York, Pantheon.

Hasegawa, Y. (2002) 'Post-identity kawaii: commerce, gender, and contemporary Japanese art', in Lloyd, F. (ed) *Consuming Bodies: Sex and Contemporary Japanese Art*, London, Reaktion Books.

Hebdige, D. (1979) *Sub-culture: The Meaning of Style*, London, Routledge.

Kinsella, S. (1995) 'Cuties in Japan', in Skov, L. and Moeran, B. (eds) *Women, Media, and Consumption in Japan*, Honolulu, University of Hawai'i Press.

McVeigh, B. J. (2000) *Wearing Ideology: State, Schooling, and Self-Presentation in Japan*, New York, Berg.

Miller, L. and Bardsely, J. (2005) *Bad Girls in Japan*, New York, Palgrave Macmillan.

Nosco, P. (1990) *Remembering Paradise: Nativism and Nostalgia in Eighteenth-Century Japan*, Cambridge, MA, Harvard University Press.

Reischauer, E. O. and Jansen, M. B. (1995) *The Japanese Today: Change and Continuity*, Cambridge, MA, Harvard University Press.

Chapter 5

New media and participatory cultures

James Ash

Contents

In this chapter, you will:

- examine the concept of 'new media' and some key features of new media technologies, particularly how they blur distinctions between the 'production' and 'consumption' of culture

- critically discuss the roles that new media technologies play in children and young people's lives

- examine how children and young people are targeted and constructed by new media, and how they engage with cultural products

- discuss the informal learning, knowledge and skills children and young people acquire through using new media technologies, and how these relate to the learning and skills valued in schools.

1 Introduction

This chapter explores children and young people as active audiences for both old and new media. Children and young people's relationships with media have often been viewed negatively, partly because 'consumption' tends to be defined as the passive, less significant end point of a more active process of 'production'. Instead, we suggest, production and consumption should both be seen as dynamic, interrelated circuits, which continuously generate 'things' that are both symbolic and material. According to this perspective, children and young people have always been active meaning makers in relation to media, because interpreting culture is a creative act. However, key aspects or 'affordances' of new media technologies blur the distinctions between cultural production and consumption in striking and visible ways, and you will explore some of these through examples of games and online worlds, and the forms of knowledge and community they build. Finally, you will look at young people contributing to, and being recognised for, cultural production in respect of the Harry Potter books and computer games, and at some of the controversies surrounding 'fan' productions, piracy and issues of copyright.

2 From media consumption to 'convergence cultures'

Television, video games, mobile phones, the internet and other electronic media play a significant role in contemporary children's lives, all around the world; many children spend more time – and often more willingly – with these technologies than they do at school. This situation is rarely viewed in a positive light, however. Children are often assumed to be particularly uncritical or passive media consumers who, because of their youth and inexperience, are vulnerable to being sucked into relationships with the media that use up all their time and replace useful knowledge with trivia, or the worthy values their parents wish to instil in them with antisocial and materialistic ones, all with dire consequences for the kind of adults they will become.

These arguments relate to particular ideas about media consumption, as well as about children. As Celia Lury (2011, p. 10) notes, everyday notions of consuming as 'using up', 'devouring', 'finishing off', and expressions like 'being consumed by envy/greed/desire', reveal the deep-rooted anxieties that circulate around the notion in our society. More broadly, consumption tends to be opposed to 'production': the latter is conceived of as an active process of manufacturing, marketing and selling, which *causes* a subsequent stage involving purchase or 'consumption', generally seen negatively as derivative, passive, and so on, and as merely the effect of the first (Lury, 2011, p. 11).

In this chapter, we follow Lury's emphasis on the *'appropriation* and *transformation'* (p. 11) – rather than 'using up' – involved in consumption, and on the dynamic, continuous circuits of making and remaking involved in what have previously been seen as separate processes of production and consumption. What get appropriated and transformed are not just tangible goods but also symbolic meanings, as you will see in the discussion of young people's engagement with media. Children do not passively 'receive' messages, but interpret and use media in many different, creative and sometimes surprising ways – in other words, they are the co-producers of culture, and active participants in it.

These arguments are primarily conceptual, in that they concern how we should think about consumption and about the relationships between audiences and cultural texts. There is also a long history of children and young people's creativity in modifying and generating new material related to books, films, television, music and poetry that they love.

However, changes in technology over recent years have emphasised the need for such rethinking: by permitting young people to become producers of their own cultural artefacts through 'remixing' existing texts and objects, new media blur and complicate the boundaries between producer and consumer – especially, although not only, when some of these artefacts rival the quality of the media they remix.

Defining new media

The term 'new media' assumes a comparison to something that might be called 'old media'. However, as Lisa Gitelman and Geoffrey Pingree (2003) observe, all media were once 'new'; objects like the telephone or television that are now a familiar backdrop of many people's lives were once alien, strange and even threatening. You may have grown up playing video games, but they are still described as 'new media' by many commentators. Similarly, many children and young people will not consider technologies like the internet and mobile phones to be unusual or 'new' at all, whilst currently 'new' devices like tablet PCs or smart phones may be considered 'old' and familiar in the future – or indeed, by the time you are reading this.

The idea of new media, then, is not just about how old or well established particular technologies are, but about their 'digital' or computational nature and their particular 'affordances' or kinds of engagement they invite or permit. The internet (particularly those technologies described as 'Web 2.0') and video games are therefore considered to be new media because of their interactive nature. Lev Manovich (2001) suggests that key features of new media include programmability and openness to be changed by users. Old media like film offer audiences only one path from beginning to end, while video games may allow multiple different ways to solve the same puzzle or to navigate a level. Grouping a disparate collection of technologies under the heading 'new media' can obscure the difference between different forms of new media as well as the commonalities between digital and other media. For example, basic websites allow some degree of interactivity insofar as users can choose which links to follow and which to ignore, while Web 2.0 technologies, like social networking sites and video-sharing websites, allow users to upload their own content as well as commenting on content supplied by other users.

Despite these problems, the term 'new media' is often employed as part of marketing discourses by companies who want to emphasise the novelty of their products in comparison with existing technologies. The term 'new' is used to conjure feelings of excitement and the sense that the product can open new ways of interacting with the world. Advertisements for the Apple iPad, for example, repeatedly use words like 'magical' and 'revolutionary' to emphasise the way in which this particular product differs from 'older' computer products.

The term 'new media', then, is complex and quite problematic. It is often unclear what is actually meant by new media, or whether it is useful to talk about new media at all. In this chapter, the term is used quite loosely as a combination of these three different understandings to refer to any contemporary technology that generates new, or modifies existing, media practices. That is to say, new media is less an object than a means of describing how media objects emerge, are used by people and become embroiled in circuits of production and consumption.

2.1 Participation, creativity and production

A broad variety of media objects, platforms, services and systems – such as the internet, mobile phones and video games – referred to as new media technologies, have changed how children and young people are able to engage with consumer products, and each other, in various ways. Yet we should be careful of overstating the extent of this change. Children and young people were creatively responding to, participating in and producing the cultural worlds around them long before the advent of new media technologies. William Corsaro (1993, 2005) uses the term 'interpretive reproduction' to describe how children and young people creatively appropriate the resources of the adult world around them, and use them to address their own concerns and to produce distinctive peer cultures. He shows this through examples from his ethnographic studies of preschool classrooms in Italy and the USA. Similarly, Vivian Paley's (1984) study of American kindergarten classrooms in the early 1980s argued that children regularly retold and altered aspects of the *Star Wars* films and other media texts in ways that helped them make sense of their lives.

Henry Jenkins argues that new media technologies differ from older cultural practices because they enable content to be translated and shared within a broad, international peer group, thus drawing on and broadening the potential of children and young people's productive energies. Jenkins explains this in terms of what he calls 'convergence': 'the flow of content across multiple media platforms, the cooperation between multiple media industries, and the migratory behaviour of media audiences who will go almost anywhere in search of the kinds of entertainment experience they want' (Jenkins, 2006, p. 2). Convergence describes a mixture of technological, industrial, cultural and social change. New media technologies allow consumers and producers to form new relationships through the kinds of content they create and consume, and media can now travel more easily between various devices and objects. This does not mean that old media (such as cinema or television) will simply disappear; these different forms of media coexist and interact with one another (as when television programmes are increasingly accompanied by a range of interactive content on official websites).

This process of convergence helps generate what Jenkins terms a 'participatory culture', in which children and young people develop their voices and identities through the media they create and interact with. As Jenkins puts it:

> Convergence doesn't just involve commercially produced materials and services travelling along well-regulated and predictable circuits. It doesn't just involve mobile companies getting together with the film companies to decide when and where we watch a newly released film. It also occurs when people take media in their own hands.
>
> (Jenkins, 2006, p. 17)

Participatory culture is supported and enabled by a whole range of associated technologies and services that have become available to children and young people. It is increasingly easy for children and young people to access digital media production tools, such as video-editing or image-processing programs on their computers, to create their own videos and blogs, and upload them to websites. However, the claims often made about how 'empowering' or how radically different from earlier (presumably 'non-participatory') cultures this is, are unduly inflated and should be treated with considerable caution. Creating content requires money or access to technologies and the confidence and expertise to use them (all of which tend to be provided by parents in one way or another, although this is generally overlooked). Businesses have also taken advantage of new media technologies to develop covert marketing strategies, of which their target groups of children and young people are unaware, and which have been criticised as insidious and exploitative.

Activity 1   Cyberpets and immersive advertising

Allow about 15 minutes

Use the information below to make some notes about how children and young people are socialised as consumers through their use of the interactive website Neopets.

Figure 1   Neopets being drawn in the Nickelodeon booth during an international comic convention held in San Diego in 2010

Neopets is an online community in which users can adopt and nurture a virtual pet. Two British university students created Neopets in 1999 and sold it the same year to an American market researcher, who then sold it to Viacom Inc (a large media company with a prominent children's entertainment division which includes the Nickelodeon television network) in 2005. The site is extremely popular with children and young people internationally (Robinson and Horst, 2010), and is often described as one of the 'stickiest' sites on the internet because it has an extremely high rate of repeat visits (Ito, 2010, p. 241).

The site offers a premium subscription service and a free membership giving access to a limited range of features. Users can distinguish between subscribed and free users by the items to which they have access. Members adopt their own Neopet and play games in order to win 'Neopoints', the Neopian currency. They can use their Neopoints to buy food for their Neopet and other items in the game. The currency can be traded and exchanged on the 'Neodaq Index' (a simplified version of the Nasdaq international stock market). Another way that members can earn Neopoints is by participating in market research surveys, which allow market research companies to find out detailed information about the 'tween' and 'teen' markets, which can, in turn, be used to market products to children and young people more effectively.

Although Neopets does generate some income through its subscription option, most of its revenue is generated through a strategy known as Immersive Advertising (the term has been trademarked). Immersive Advertising is similar to product placement in television and film, where branded goods are shown on screen either being used by characters or forming part of the set. For example, members can buy McDonald's food for their Neopets and they can play sponsored games, such as the 'Pepperidge Farm Goldfish Sandwich Snackers Game' (which is based on an American snack biscuit). Companies can also provide offers through the site. The toy company Mattel made virtual versions of their Diva Starz dolls available to Neopets members. According to Courtney Lane, the director of Mattel's girls' interactive division, this time-limited offer allowed Mattel to 'create a strong brand impression and generate real excitement around the characters ... that's very hard to do in a 15-second TV commercial' (quoted in Grimes and Shade, 2005, p. 187). In this way, Immersive Advertising on Neopets can act as an effective strategy for building brand identification and loyalty.

Now consider these questions:

- How do you feel about the idea of Immersive Advertising and the kinds of market research carried out on Neopets?

- Is Neopets is an example of 'convergence'? If so, what do you think are its advantages and disadvantages for children and young people?

Comment

Neopets can be understood as both an enjoyable children's media practice and a shrewd way of advertising and collecting information about children's consumer preferences. Playing games and nurturing Neopets are undeniably activities that many children and young people (as well as the site's adult members) enjoy. However, it is precisely this enjoyment that makes it a popular and effective form of marketing.

It can also be argued that the whole structure of Neopets acts to socialise its members as consumers. The website provides its users with a range of income-generating activities (games, surveys and speculative activities) and ways to spend this income. Indeed, the site tasks them with nurturing their Neopets by buying them food, shelter and other items. The logic of the site is such that members' actions are judged by the amount of Neopoints they are able to generate and the goods that they own. In this way, Neopets teaches children that their activities can (and should) have some economic value and defines their success in terms of the accrual of material goods and objects.

Laura Robinson (2010) discusses Eddie, a teenage boy from California whose story points to how websites such as Neopets can create and reinforce an idea of children as economic subjects and teach values that carry over into adulthood. Eddie continued to play Neopets in high school, long after it had stopped being 'cool' within his peer group. He explained that his enjoyment of the game derived almost entirely from his economic ventures on the Neodaq index, rather than from nurturing his Neopets. As he explained: 'I just wanted to hoard my cash to make more. I wouldn't waste points feeding my pets. I didn't want to buy them anything – just to play the market' (quoted in Robinson, 2010, pp. 331–2). Eddie explained that he 'knew' that Neopets was teaching him about capitalist practices, but he saw this as training for his future adult life: 'You know I want to make money someday and playing all the time like that made me feel that it was all real. That everything had real consequences' (p. 333). However, Eddie also recognised that the structure of the site's market created an unrealistic expectation about how money could be made on the stock market. Speculating on the Neodaq generally results in financial gain; all Neopets stock increases in value over time. This is in sharp contrast to the real stock market, which of course regularly involves drops in value of individual companies and sometimes crashes in the market as a whole. By exaggerating the value of market speculation, or at least by ignoring the risks, Neopets might be argued to socialise children and young people into contemporary capitalist processes and practices in a completely uncritical way.

However, this is not to say that all young people experienced Neopets in the same way, as Robinson and Horst's (2010) study of children's different understandings and uses of Neopets makes clear. Research into other online virtual communities, including Webkinz (Wohlwend et al., 2011), Club Penguin and Barbie Girls (Marsh, 2010) shows children and young people interacting with online worlds in many different ways. For instance, Lisa Jackson and colleagues (2008) identified eight different roles that were adopted by children using the BBC Adventure Rock website:

- explorer-investigators, children who were principally involved in following quests or solving mysteries
- self-stampers, often older children who were most concerned with how they presented themselves within the online world
- social climbers, who were predominantly interested in their social position within the world
- fighters, most often boys who were interested in violence, destruction and superpowers
- consumer-collectors, older children who wanted to accumulate items of value within the system
- power users, who sought to share their knowledge of and experience in the game with other users
- life-system builders, who were preoccupied with building new worlds or populating them
- nurturers, who concentrated on looking after their pets or avatars.

Figure 2   Girl playing on Club Penguin website

Similarly, in her study of working-class children (aged 5–11) in England, Jackie Marsh (2010) differentiated between different classes of play behaviour in both Club Penguin and Barbie Girls, including fantasy play, sociodramatic play, games with rules, and a kind of 'rough and tumble' play without physical contact between children's bodies.

These three examples suggest that online immersive worlds like Neopets are not singularly about the creation of economically minded subjects; they are flexible sites in which different users can choose between activities, engage in ways that suit a range of needs and interests and take different things from the experience. However, this is not to say that the Immersive Advertising and the consumerist aspects of Neopets and other online communities are unimportant or should be ignored. The ability to customise these worlds, to socialise with friends, and to direct your own activities in an open-ended way is indicative of how marketing to children has become more complex and in order to be effective actively draws on and encourages children and young people's participation.

Summary of Section 2

Participation, creativity and production are an integral part of children and young people's cultural worlds.

'New media' technologies alter the relationships between consumers and producers through the kinds of content and relationships they make possible.

There is controversy over businesses that use new media technologies for (sometimes covert) marketing strategies and information-gathering activities.

---

3 Active engagement

Children and young people are now a substantial and coveted consumer market. Debates about how children (and their parents) are targeted and constructed as consumers, however, sometimes present them as manipulated by designers or manufacturers into doing and thinking exactly what they want, as if products and services have fixed meanings and effects on consumers. The approach we take here, however, argues that objects and processes do not have a fixed or stable meaning, but instead are open, with meaning emerging from contexts of use and interpretation. As the examples in the section above demonstrated, what children and young people actually do with the products and services they buy and use cannot always be predicted in advance. In this section we will explore this issue further, and also discuss how new media technologies increasingly anticipate and invite creative modifications and adaptations.

Figure 3   Pokémon

3.1   Pokémon and interactive media cultures

The role of interactivity in children and young people's consumer cultures has been well documented through the phenomenon of Pokémon. Pokémon was originally launched as a video game in which players capture and collect small animals (also known as Pokémon) and use them to battle one another. The franchise was created by the Japanese video game company, Nintendo, and has since gone on to become a global phenomenon. Since the successful release of the first Pokémon video game in Japan 1995, the series has expanded to include a long-running cartoon series, a number of feature-length movies and a collectible card game, along with an enormous range of other licensed merchandise. The international Pokémon craze was the subject of much media coverage in the late 1990s. Although this media interest has now waned, the franchise has remained very popular. In 2011, Pokémon Black and Pokémon White became the fastest selling Pokémon video games of all time, selling 1.08 million units in North America on launch day alone (BusinessWire, 2011).

As a brand and franchise, Pokémon forms part of a transmedia marketing campaign. The video games, toys, card games and other merchandise combine to create a set of texts and objects that are to be consumed together. While individual consumers are not compelled to engage with all of these, knowledge about the card game translates into understandings about the television show and video game, which encourages children to engage with and consume Pokémon in its many forms (Tobin, 2004). David Buckingham and Julian Sefton-Green (2003) explain Pokémon's global success in terms of how easily it can be integrated into children's daily lives and how it can reflect aspects of childhood in many different cultures. The plots of the television series, video games and feature films revolve around themes of competition and friendship, which are nearly universal in children's media. Yet, Pokémon can mobilise these familiar narrative themes in distinctive ways by aligning a range of old and new media technologies that encourage users actively to engage with the products. Indeed, the success of the series is premised on encouraging this kind of active participation in the phenomenon.

The Pokémon video games and card games require players to develop considerable knowledge and information about the different species of Pokémon, supported by a range of official and unofficial merchandise, including guide books, posters, online Pokédex (electronic catalogues of data about Pokémon) and smart phone applications. As Buckingham and Sefton-Green explain:

> The successful Pokémon player will need to build up a detailed taxonomy of the various species and their unique characteristics and powers. The Pokémon belong to different categories (Water, Fire, Psychic, etc.), whose different strengths and weaknesses must be assessed when they come to compete. The knowledge that is at stake here is that of quasi-scientific classification ... Indeed, the posters that display all the 151 Pokémon resemble nothing so much as a periodic table.
>
> (Buckingham and Sefton-Green, 2003, p. 388)

Unsurprisingly, but unfortunately, parents and other non-participants – including schools – often fail to appreciate the complexity and volume of knowledge acquired by audiences as a consequence.

The phenomenon also encourages cultural practices of meeting and sharing. For instance, Pokémon video games encourage social interaction between players by being released in two complementary versions – such as Pokémon FireRed and Pokémon LeafGreen (released in 2004) or Pokémon Diamond and Pokémon Pearl (released in 2006 in Japan and internationally in 2007) – each of which contains a small number of Pokémon that are exclusive to it. In order to 'catch them all', players have to meet up with others who have different versions of the game and agree to exchange Pokémon using a special link cable or wireless connection. Exchanging cards also fosters social bonds and connections, and the immense amount of knowledge generated around the video and card games offers the potential for rich conversation between players.

These practices are not a happy, coincidental side effect, but a central part of why the series is so successful. As Buckingham and Sefton-Green put it:

> Activity of various kinds is not just essential for the production of meaning and pleasure; it is also the primary mechanism through which the phenomenon is sustained, and through which commercial profit is generated. It is in this sense that the notion of 'audience' seems quite inadequate.
>
> (Buckingham and Sefton-Green, 2003, p. 389)

Pokémon complicates the idea of an 'audience' that simply 'receives' messages, and of a framework which opposes consumption to production. Pokémon products are not produced and then consumed; the phenomenon is produced and sustained *through* the practices of its consumers.

Reading A expands on the active processes of consumption through the example of another Japanese media mix, Yu-Gi-Oh!, which, like Pokémon, has been adapted and exported to consumers around the world. It peaked in popularity at around the same time as Pokémon, but remains popular internationally at the time of writing.

Activity 2   Reading A
Allow about 20 minutes

Mizuko Ito reports the results of a study she carried out in Tokyo between 1998 and 2002 exploring Japanese schoolchildren's engagement with the Yu-Gi-Oh! media mix. Read through an extract from the study – Reading A, 'Yu-Gi-Oh!, media mixes and everyday cultural production' – and try to answer the following questions:

- What makes 'hypersocial exchange' among Yu-Gi-Oh! players different from other forms of social interaction?

- How do the children's 'microeconomics' of exchange and bartering differ from adult 'otaku' forms of card purchasing and trading?

- Is it fair that the card manufacturers actively create a series of cards that are rare and difficult to obtain? What effect does the existence of rare cards have on the Yu-Gi-Oh! community?

Figure 4   Some of the Yu-Gi-Oh! cards

Comment

Mizuko Ito argues that the practices of personalising games and engaging with the sophisticated 'viral' knowledge exchanges surrounding them are key sites of learning and sociality. Players do not occupy a generic position of spectatorship, but acquire unique, esoteric knowledge tailored to their interests, and develop their own custom content as part of this engagement. This kind of relationship to media content has been present among fans of more traditional media for a long time, but it is much more pervasive in interactive media formats.

The role of cross-media marketing is also important here. In the Yu-Gi-Oh! anime (televised cartoon series) and manga (comic book), the characters are often shown visiting hobby shops and buying the trading cards. By doing the same, children can come to identify more closely with the characters from the series. The card game also contains a number of rare and ultra-rare cards. As Buckingham and Sefton-Green (2003) argue, this is a shrewd move on the part of the franchise owners, as it allows them to make huge profits from selling what is in fact a factory-produced card. However, in addition this has given rise to fan practices attempting to identify which packs might contain rare cards and considerable mythology and rumours about the process of tracking them down. The latter are particularly important to the children involved, who have neither the money nor the freedom to engage in the practices themselves. Rare cards take on an almost fantastical quality within children's cultures of engagement with Yu-Gi-Oh!, which elevates the activity beyond a simple television show, comic or card game. The production of enchantment is a key part of what sustains and even produces interest in the Yu-Gi-Oh! phenomenon.

Pokémon and Yu-Gi-Oh! draw on long-established practices of collecting and trading. In the 1920s, M. T. Whitley demonstrated the enduring popularity of collecting behaviour among North American children in order to counteract claims that it had been dying out from the end of the nineteenth century. He argued that children's collecting behaviour revolved around a series of 'trivial things' (Whitley, 1929, p. 261) such as stamps, marbles, autographs and ribbons, but could help give children a sense of identity and individuality. Stacey Baker and James Gentry (1996) studied American six- and 11 year olds' collections and found that while all the children collected similar objects (sports cards, dolls and rocks, for example) they had different reasons for doing so. Six year olds collected in order to get more than their friends, whereas 11 year olds did it as a way of making them feel unique. As one 11-year-old child put it: 'It makes me feel good about myself that I've got some baseball cards that some other people don't have' (Baker and Gentry, 1996, p. 136). It is important to keep in mind that differences such as age and gender can play an important role in how these products are taken up and used.

However, the kinds of collecting behaviour surrounding Pokémon and Yu-Gi-Oh! differ somewhat from this more 'traditional' form. Someone can collect an almost limitless number of ribbons or rocks, and there is no point at which the collection will necessarily or automatically be considered 'complete' – although this is less true of stamps, perhaps. Pokémon, by contrast, stimulates the desire for completion, whether by collecting all the Pokémon in the video games or all the cards in the card series. Such active engagement also, then, constitutes a form of consumer socialisation as well as consumer 'empowerment'.

Some health educators and activists have attempted to use these channels to carry 'alternative' messages. Alan Blum (1995) discusses an initiative by DOC (Doctors Ought to Care) in the USA, which issued a 'Deck-O-Butts' series of cards for teenagers. This was successful, according to Blum, because it built on the popular practice of cigarette card trading whilst allowing young people to mock cigarette advertisers. He concludes that influencing young people's behaviour needs to observe and build on their cultural practices:

> All too many efforts to educate young people about tobacco have relied on pamphlets, posters, and preaching on the dangers of nicotine. In the future, strategies must increasingly focus on observing and listening to teenagers in their natural mass media saturated habitat and learning from them about the important issues and images in their world.
>
> (Blum, 1995, p. 221)

Similar arguments suggesting that youth may be 'reached' using the strategies adopted by global brands, but in order to convert them to more pro-social purposes or causes, are no doubt tantalising to health educators, politicians and many others. However, the market research agencies that specialise in studying youth in what Blum calls their 'natural habitat' suggest that developing such knowledge is complicated, expensive and does not necessarily guarantee results – and so warn against assuming that the success of media phenomena like Pokémon or Yu-Gi-Oh! stems only from a corporate conspiracy to manipulate their young consumers.

Summary of Section 3

Products like Pokémon and Yu-Gi-Oh! invite and require children's active participation to sustain the phenomenon, generating practices and 'enchantment' that go beyond what producers might anticipate or predict.

This active engagement is controversial; it is sometimes seen as more creative than consuming mass-market products, but it is also argued to make children and young people complicit in their ongoing socialisation as particular kinds of consumers.

Outsiders – including schools – often fail to understand the complexity of knowledge acquired by players.

4   Productive engagement: remix culture

This section moves on to look at examples of children and young people's creative media production that is often described as 'remix'. For Knobel and Lankshear (2008, p. 22), to remix is 'to take cultural artifacts and combine and manipulate them into new kinds of creative blends'. The act of simply commenting on a book, film or video game and discussing it with others involves remixing the original text, and its author's creativity, into our own lives, evaluating these cultural materials and using them to extend our own ideas. This process of remixing culture is not new, nor is it limited to recent developments in digital technology. Knobel and Lankshear suggest that 'at the broadest level … remix is the general condition of cultures: no remix, no culture' (p. 23). However, it is enabled in particular ways by new media.

Activity 3   Reading B
Allow about 20 minutes

In Reading B, 'Creative production in the digital age', Patricia Lange and Mizuko Ito discuss how new media technologies encourage, enable and even require children and young people to become creative producers. Once you have read through the extract try to answer the following questions:

- What kinds of learning do young people acquire through using new media technologies? What are the possible effects on those who are not able to use them?

- Do you think that modifying existing material such as photos or movies is as creative as producing all materials from scratch? Why or why not?

Comment

Lange and Ito argue that shifts in digital technology have allowed a new category of 'creative producers' to emerge, which disturbs traditional distinctions between consumers and producers, as well as between old and new media. They suggest that this is largely a positive development, on the grounds that social networking and media-sharing sites enable children and young people to socialise and interact with one another while gaining and creating new literacy, knowledge and skills that may be useful to them in later life. However, we should be cautious about accepting their claims uncritically. Young people without access to a computer or the internet may feel left out or isolated from their peers. If commercial media provide the common story material for contemporary childhood, children who cannot access these sites and services may be excluded from that shared culture. The material in the box below discusses the problem of what is often referred to as the 'digital divide' in more detail.

The question of creativity in relation to children's use of media in the digital age is a complex one. For example, is creating a new background that fits within a MySpace profile a process of creation or modification, or both? The background has to fit the existing regulations of the MySpace site, but young people can create new logos and designs for that background using image-processing software. This background could incorporate elements of existing photos that young people have retrieved from another source and modified, but which they did not take themselves. In this case, the line between creation and modification is a difficult one to draw. We will start to think about the ways in which these lines are drawn in the remainder of this section and in Section 5.

The digital divide

The term 'the digital divide' is often used to distinguish between those who do and those who do not have access to information and communication technologies (ICTs). It sometimes distinguishes broadly between countries in the minority world (where access to ICTs is widespread) and the majority world (where access is patchier), but also when discussing inequalities within countries. However, as Mark Warschauer (2002) explains, there is no binary division between a group of 'haves' and a group of 'have-nots'; we need instead to think of degrees of access to ICT on a continuum. Additionally, Warschauer argues that inequalities will not be resolved simply by providing computers and internet connectivity, since a wide range of social and cultural resources are required for people to use technology effectively.

To explain this, Warschauer discusses the 'Hole-in-the-Wall' experiment to provide computer and internet access to street children in the poorest areas of New Delhi, India in 1999. Researcher Sugatra Mitra set up an outdoor computer kiosk which provided dial-up internet access 24 hours a day. Five computer stations were housed inside a booth. Holes were cut in the walls of the booth to allow access to the monitors, as well as to specially designed joysticks and buttons in lieu of a more traditional keyboard and mouse set-up. Volunteers helped to keep the computers and internet connection working, but no teachers were provided to teach the children and young people how to use the technology. The idea was to provide 'minimally invasive education', in which children and young people would learn at their own pace and speed.

Official reports claimed the project was a great success and a model for bringing ICT to the world's poor, which has subsequently received considerable funding from the World Bank and national governments. It may have been persuasive in part because it played on existing images of children as 'digital natives' with a natural affinity for new technologies. However, Warschauer – a relatively rare voice in this debate – explains that the computers rarely had functioning internet access; none of the software had been made available in Hindi, the only language the users could speak; the design of the kiosk made it difficult for children and young people to work together in learning how to use the technology; local parents complained about the lack of organised instruction and even that it had a detrimental effect on children who spent spare time playing computer games at the Hole-in-the-Wall rather than doing their homework. Warschauer claims that as a result 'the community came to realise that "minimally invasive education" was, in practice, minimally effective education.'

Livingstone and Helsper (2007) also argue that near-universal access to ICT among children and young people aged between nine and 19 in the UK has not resolved the 'digital divide', because social and cultural factors contribute to inequalities in both the nature and quality of access. Age and gender inequalities persist, even where children and young people have access at home: boys and older teens use the internet more than girls and younger children, and non-users are more likely to be poorer. The 'digital divide' can also manifest as a generational gap that separates children from their parents or teachers: Eszter Hargittai argues, 'There are clear generational differences in people's ability to use the Web ... People in their teens and people in their 20s are quicker than people in their 30s and 40s who are quicker than older respondents' (Hargittai, 2002, pp. 12–13).

However, Pål Aarsand (2007) argues in his study of practices of family video game use that the 'generational divide' was an interactional resource allowing children to feel empowered and in control as they taught their parents and grandparents how to play the games. New media technology in this instance served as a medium to help children and adults meet and exchange knowledge productively, rather than creating distance and separation between these groups.

In the remainder of this section, we will work through two examples – Harry Potter fan activities and video games – in order to think about the possibilities for and consequences of youth creative production.

Figure 5   Harry Potter fan art produced by children

4.1   Harry Potter: fan fiction and Wizard Rock

Popular culture audiences have always taken and altered existing texts to create new narratives, images and experiences. Henry Jenkins (1992) claims a long and distinguished lineage for fan fiction and fan art (stories or images that are written or drawn by fans based on their favourite franchises and characters) by locating them within the storytelling traditions of ancient civilisations. He therefore links oral cultures of the past that retold stories many times to fit with particular situations or contexts, with the many hours some children spend acting out, writing or drawing stories from books or media texts.

Ernest Bond and Nancy Michelson (2009) explore children and young people's creative responses to the Harry Potter series of books by J.K. Rowling (and the media mix that accompanies it). By 2009, the book series had finished but was still inspiring many young people to respond creatively to it by writing fan fiction and producing all manner of fan art, music and music videos (often using images from the films, alongside popular songs in a range of genres). In these fan productions, readers (and viewers) were able to expand on the material found in the source texts, by extending the histories set out in the book, or developing the characters or plots, or even imagining their own stories and characters within the Harry Potter world.

Figure 6   The Hungarian Horntails performing

Harry Potter has spawned, amongst other responses, a whole musical genre of 'Wizard Rock' or 'Wrock'. Wizard Rock bands sing about scenarios from the books, as well as inventing their own narratives in their song lyrics, such as two high school girls from New Jersey who formed 'The Moaning Myrtles' to sing about being trapped in a toilet and having a hopeless crush on Harry. Some bands have members of all ages, such as the 'Hungarian Horntails' formed by a seven-year-old boy, his four-year-old brother and one of his classmates. The Wizard Rock scene is even the topic of a documentary, entitled *We Are Wizards* (Koury, 2008).

These forms of productive consumption extend into the use and creation of numerous websites and blogs where Harry Potter fans can upload, read and discuss their fan fiction stories and other fan productions. One such site is *The Daily Prophet*, a fan-fictional online newspaper for Hogwarts created in January 2000 by Heather Lawver, a 14-year-old North American girl (Jenkins, 2006; Bond and Michelson, 2009). By 2006, the site had amassed a contributing 'staff' of 102 children and young people from around the world. Although the site has been inactive for a number of years now due to Lawver's health, it was an educational venture through which Lawver tutored other children and young people through the process of editing their fan fiction writing. Lawver describes the site as:

> An organisation dedicated to bringing the world of literature to life … By creating an online 'newspaper' with articles that lead the readers to believe this fanciful world of Harry Potter to be real, this opens the mind to exploring books, diving into the characters, and analyzing great literature. By developing the mental ability to analyze the written word at a young age, children will find a love for reading unlike any other. By creating this faux world we are learning, creating, and enjoying ourselves in a friendly utopian society.
>
> (Quoted in Jenkins, 2006, p. 172)

The site had an explicit educational purpose, which mirrored the kinds of educational activities that are usually undertaken in school but that was centred around children and young people's interests.

Bond and Michelson (2009) argue that the literature authored by, and for, children and young people and made available as a result of developments in internet browsing and publishing software, has made it possible to rethink what we mean by 'children's literature'. They even suggest that before this, very little 'real' children's literature existed at all, because it was written for them by adults. This, however, seems to be a rather romantic argument, implying that child-authored texts are radically new and different. For Reading B, you thought about the positive potentials of new media as a means of educating children about digital technologies. *The Daily Prophet* is entirely led by children and young people, who teach each other the necessary skills associated with reading, writing and web authoring. But what makes *The Daily Prophet* site any different from an English or IT lesson in school? James Paul Gee (2004) argues that new media ventures like it differ from traditional sites of learning such as schools, because they operate as 'affinity spaces'.

Affinity spaces are informal spaces in which children can help each other to learn and engage with material because they are emotionally invested in the topic. Their collaborations often take the form of peer evaluation: fan producers discuss, critique and offer suggestions on how to improve each other's work. This is a well-established practice within fan fiction communities, in which fan fiction writers can form strong and long-lasting bonds through their shared interests. For example, Lange and Ito (2010) discuss a 13-year-old Asian American fan fiction writer known as 'orangefizzy', who explains that the enjoyment of writing fan fiction comes from the active reading fan community that provides feedback, comment and critique.

Some fan fiction writers subject their stories to a 'beta reading' process before publishing them online. The term itself is drawn from the process of 'beta testing' computer software before release. Pairs or groups of beta readers work together to improve each other's writing and offer suggestions for improvement before publication. Henry Jenkins (2006) argues that this two-way process of peer review differs from a classroom process because writers have a shared interest in the subject and a desire to have their work read by other fans online, and thus they are more highly motivated to improve their writing than may be the case in schools (although the evaluative criteria applied may also be quite different).

However, one can exaggerate the value of the feedback given to fan fiction stories, especially after publication on websites, as this 17-year-old Chinese girl living in Canada explains:

> No, the thing with reviews on fanfiction ... people don't usually do constructive criticism. Mostly, it's encouragement/expressing desire for the author to hurry up with the next chapter.
>
> (Quoted in Lange and Ito, 2010, p. 277)

The fan practices associated with Harry Potter show how popular cultural forms offer more than enjoyment and attachment to the texts themselves; they also enable even young audiences to explore and develop skills and competencies in perhaps unexpected areas.

4.2 Video games: gamers, walkthroughs and machinima

Video games are now an established part of children and young people's entertainment experiences, with a variety of video game genres (such as role playing and shoot-em-ups) and video game consoles. Ito and Bittani (2010) identified three broad types of video game use across this diversity, involving:

- killing time – solitary and time-filling practices of video gaming

- hanging out – video games provide a context for children and young people to spend time together and develop shared interests
- geeking out – video gaming becomes the central aspect of the activity and video gamers increasingly compete with one another online.

These 'organising' and 'mobilising' practices of video gaming (Ito and Bittanti, 2010) have also contributed to the development of professional gaming or 'e-sports' ('electronic sports', playing games in tournaments). The creation of regular circuits of large tournaments, with high stakes (cash or other prizes), has led to increasing corporate sponsorship and the emergence of a group of 'professional gamers' who make a living by competing at tournaments and through sponsorship and licensing deals. E-sports are most popular in South Korea, which has three network television channels dedicated to gaming and the top players can earn up to $US 1 million per year (Hjorth, 2011). While less known outside of South Korea, e-sports are gaining ground around the world and annual tournaments are now held in a number of countries, including the USA, the UK and Germany.

Activity 4   The world's youngest professional gamer
Allow about 20 minutes

Victor De Leon or 'LiL Poison' holds the *Guinness Book of World Records* title as the 'Youngest Pro Gamer in the World'. His website explains that he started video gaming aged two and competing aged four at a local New York Halo Tournament. At six, MLG recruiters signed him as a Pro Gamer and officially made him the youngest signed professional gamer in the world.

Since going professional, LiL Poison has gone on to compete in over 250 events in the USA for the first person shooting games Halo CE, Halo 2 and Halo 3. He is managed by his father. In 2011, aged 12, he appeared in a documentary entitled *LiL Poison: The Story of the World's Youngest Professional Video Gamer* (Massive Productions, 2011). The press release for the documentary describes its content:

> The father and son travel cross country to play Halo, with the hope of winning prize money and scoring sponsorship deals. When little Victor's parents divorce amidst tumultuous circumstances, LiL Poison's game begins to suffer and his sponsorship deals decline. Vic Snr finds himself in tough times. LiL Poison's potential success becomes a possible way

out of the family's financial predicament. Torn between fulfilling his father's dreams of fame and fortune and his own desire to be a kid, little Victor must face the most important tournament of his career.

(Massive Productions, 2011)

The trailer for the documentary shows the parents' divorce and Victor Jnr crying under the pressure of competition at a tournament. Other moments show Victor Jnr enjoying playing Halo and his father's admiration and love for his son.

Figure 7   LiL Poison, 'the world's youngest professional gamer'

Based on this information, reflect on the following questions:

- How do you feel about LiL Poison's status as a professional gamer?
- When LiL Poison competes at tournaments is he working or playing?
- Should playing video games competitively be defined as a 'sport'?

Comment

For LiL Poison, the boundaries between 'work' and 'play', 'consumption' and 'production' have become very blurred indeed. The games he plays have the potential to be the main source of financial income for his whole family. In the trailer for the documentary, his father explains that he encourages his son to compete so that he will grow up to be in a completely different financial position. LiL Poison's video gaming skill offers a way to create a secure and stable family home. However, the pressures of playing video games professionally have a deep impact on LiL Poison's childhood. The majority of competitive gamers are adults, who play between five and eight hours a day to hone their skills. To keep up, LiL Poison must balance these demands with his homework, and even prioritise his video gaming above everything else. He has to spend much of his time in very adult environments, both in his online play at home and at tournaments. The British Board of Film Classification rated Halo 3 (one of the games he plays) as suitable for players aged 15 years and older. The other games in the Halo series are also rated as 'mature' (for players aged 16 or 18 and over). Yet, aged 12, LiL Poison has been playing the series for many years. Many aspects of this example may make you feel uncomfortable, but it illustrates how leisure or entertainment practices can become redefined as work and tied into circuits of production, even for very young children.

As with the Harry Potter series, video gaming is accompanied by a diverse range of practices and user-generated texts and materials. The design and structure of video games, which can create experiences that last many hundreds of hours, encourage video gamers to create all manner of 'cheats, fan sites, modifications, hacks, walk-throughs, game guides, and various websites, blogs, and wikis' (Ito and Bittanti, 2010, p. 220) to help them to navigate the complexity of video games. In doing so, they form what Ito and Bittanti term a broader 'knowledge network' around specific games.

Mia Consalvo (2007) argues that these networks should be understood as a form of 'gaming capital'. Knowledge about games is created and shared among young people, and can yield prestige and recognition. For example, many video gamers write detailed 'walkthroughs' explaining how to play individual video games, which they upload to sites like Gamefaqs.com for other video gamers to download and help them to play the games more effectively. Popular walkthroughs can be downloaded hundreds of thousands of times and the site carries a constantly updated chart of the most popular walkthroughs currently available. Video-sharing websites like YouTube allow many young people to produce commented video walkthroughs of games. However, those who produce walkthroughs and video guides are still very much in the minority, compared with the majority who access them.

Game publishers and designers have recognised video gamers' desire to actively create and produce content that is associated with their games and now build video games which allow high levels of customisation or 'authoring'. As Ito and Bittanti put it:

> In the early years of gaming, the ability to do player-level modifications was minimal for most games, unless one were a gamer hacker and coder, or it was a simulation game that was specifically designed for user authoring. Today, many games come with the ability to create a custom avatar and customize the game experience, and some players see these capabilities as one of the primary attractions of the game. Games such as Pokémon or Neopets are designed specifically to allow user authoring and customization of the player experience in the form of personal collections of unique pets.
>
> (Ito and Bittanti, 2010, p. 222)

One could argue that the only reason games companies build customisation tools into their games is to police what users do with them. Perhaps they hope that by enabling a surface level of customisation they can discourage young people from actively trying to 'hack' the game, modifying their intellectual property in ways that they see as unsuitable.

More specialised practices of gaming capital include the production of 'machinima' videos. The term 'machinima' comes from a loose combination of the words 'machine' and 'cinema'. It is used to describe the process of creating real-time animation by manipulating a video game's engine and assets (Machinima, 2012). Young people use video games like Halo as a kind of studio in which to act out their own dramas and stories and to dub voices on top of their in-game characters. In order to create machinima, young people need a variety of skills in different specialist computing applications, including professional movie editing and post-production software such as Final Cut Pro or Adobe Premiere. These practices also work to place young people into broader, cross-generational communities of expertise, as they log-on to forums and share or seek advice.

Figure 8 A still from a Machinima production made in July 2009, using a digital animation software package called *Moviestorm* developed for the 'amateur' and movie enthusiast market

Aaron is a 14-year-old Armenian machinima maker. He makes stunt videos from the game Battlefield (Lange and Ito, 2010). Aaron explains that machinima are both time and labour-intensive to produce, and often draw on the expertise of a number of different people. Like films and television, machinima are usually collaborative productions. Aaron's machinima videos often involve around 20 people, who are increasingly chosen because they have demonstrated some talent for video editing or image processing using particular software. As machinima has become more established as a practice, it has become more difficult for potential producers to become involved in projects, as they must first have acquired and demonstrated the right talents.

For many young people, creating machinima is a window into the world of digital media production. Although they may be largely self-taught, these producers are often highly skilled. Social networking sites and other fan community web pages provide outlets where their skill can be recognised through comments and ratings from other users. A single positive comment from a peer group member on an online message board or YouTube video can be enough to validate a young person's effort in creating such artefacts.

In her study of video-sharing practices, Patricia Lange (2010) found that young people worry about mean-spirited, discriminatory and hurtful comments from people they refer to as 'haters', who use their anonymity to attack others' work with little risk of reprisal. However, even though they disliked these comments, many of the young people she talked to did not think they should be restricted or removed, but wanted to show their support for 'free speech' online by leaving them in place. Questions of free speech and originality are very important to children and young people: young people involved in making machinima often view their work as completely original texts, rather than 'remixed' versions of existing ones. Nonetheless, the fact that they are modifying copyrighted texts means that 'ownership' and 'authorship' are becoming increasingly contested issues, as we will see in the next section.

4.3   Participation or piracy? The Potter wars

Companies have responded to young people's cultural practices by creating objects that encourage, or at least enable, 'remix' as a cultural practice. For many children and young people, processes of remix, in which they use a whole range of technologies, involving images and sound as well as text, are becoming integral to how they make meaning and express ideas and share them with others.

However, as we have observed, corporations have a vested interest in encouraging creative and productive forms of consumption that extend longevity and the range of products or brands. As Jenkins puts it:

> Convergence ... is both a top-down corporate-driven process and a bottom-up consumer-driven process. Corporate convergence coexists with grassroots convergence. Media companies are learning how to accelerate the flow of media content across delivery channels to expand revenue opportunities, broaden markets, and reinforce viewer commitments. Consumers are learning how to use these different media technologies to bring the flow of media more fully under their control and to interact with other consumers. The promises of this new media environment raise expectations of a freer flow of ideas and content. Inspired by those ideals, consumers are fighting for the right to participate more fully in their culture. Sometimes, corporate and grassroots convergence reinforce each other, creating closer, more rewarding relations between media producers and consumers. Sometimes, these two forces are at war and those struggles will redefine the face of ... popular culture.
>
> (Jenkins, 2006, p. 18)

In this sense, convergence is both a risk and an opportunity for media producers and young people. If content is tightly controlled by media producers, they risk alienating the very groups of people they wish to engage as audiences or in the future as creative artists. Yet producing new media texts is a costly and risky process that has to be funded (mostly) by consumers who pay for it; this in turn requires enforceable systems (such as the law of copyright) to make sure that they do. There are some problematic issues here, such as how to encourage children and young people to engage fully with existing cultural material without, at the same time, creating audiences of the future who think that all culture should be free and have no respect for the legitimate needs of artists to make a living.

You read before about Heather Lawver, a young girl who had started a fan website for the Harry Potter series of books called *The Daily Prophet*. Shortly after creating the site, she became involved in what was dubbed 'the Potter wars'. This began when Warner Bros, the owners of the rights to the Harry Potter movie franchise, began sending 'cease and desist' letters to owners of Harry Potter fan web pages that they viewed as infringing their intellectual property rights. In response to the Warner Bros actions, Heather set up the organisation Defense against Dark Arts. Using the language of the Harry Potter books, she argued that Warner Bros were destroying the magic and imagination that made the books so appealing to readers (Jenkins, 2006). The media (both old and new) quickly picked up on the story and in the face of negative media exposure, Warner Bros backed down and apologised to the young people running the fan sites.

This example shows how new forms of productive consumption in fan cultures call into question traditional understandings of relationships between producers and consumers of texts, and of intellectual property law and copyright. A key issue here is what counts as a 'fair use' of other people's creative works. As Jenkins explains, 'Nobody is sure whether fan fiction falls under current fair-use protections. Current copyright law simply doesn't have a category for dealing with amateur creative expression' (Jenkins, 2006, p. 189). Without clear legal precedent, and a considerable degree of co-dependency, fans and media producers have had to negotiate in different ways. Harry Potter fans argue that media producers cannot stop fans reinterpreting existing material. While it is in Warner Bros commercial interest to retain control over the characters and words of Harry Potter, they also recognise that children and young people want to write fan fiction because they are emotionally invested in the Harry Potter universe – making them the key target audience for Warner Bros products.

Activity 5   Attributing authorship

Allow about 15 minutes

The following 'disclaimers' are taken from Harry Potter fan fiction stories shared online.

> Disclaimer: I don't own these characters, but I do own their personalities? [grin] ... kind of? I dunno. But anyway, JK Rowling is amazing.
>
> Disclaimer: i do not own harry potter this is purely a fan written story.
>
> Disclaimer: Harry Potter Universe is not mine, just Dana Cresswell is :)
>
> Disclaimer: I do not own Harry Potter or any of the other characters ... I am just borrowing them!
>
> (Shirky, 2011, p. 91)

- Why do you think fan fiction writers might choose to preface their stories with a disclaimer of this sort?
- What does this suggest about their understanding of the ethical norms in these communities?

Comment

Fan fiction writers commonly begin their stories with a disclaimer explaining that they do not own the source text on which their stories are based. Clay Shirky argues that they show some awareness of intellectual property law, recognise that they do not own J. K. Rowling's (or any other author's) work, and express respect and love for the texts that have inspired them.

These disclaimers carry no legal weight, but they tell us much about the ethical norms within fan fiction communities. For instance, a key principle is that one must always give credit where credit is due; plagiarism is not tolerated. Similarly, fan fiction writers – according to Shirky – distinguish between two different realms of creative acts: a 'world of money' in which creators are paid for their work – which they do not aim to damage or to join – and a 'world of love' and affection in which they themselves operate. They seek recognition from other fans for their creative achievements within a given fictional world, rather than profit: within their communities, the 'purity' of their own motivation matters more than the absolute legality of their activities in the eyes of others.

Different media industries, and individual corporations within those industries, have responded to 'remix culture', and its increasing profile, in different ways that reflect how far they perceive it as a threat or an opportunity. For instance, the music and film industries have tended to take a hard line approach to the use of their materials in any 'remixed' form (as in the Potter wars) because of the threat posed to their business model by cultures of downloading; yet they have thereby often lost the goodwill of (potential) consumers. Other industries have taken a more ambivalent, and even encouraging, approach on remixes as a form of free publicity. For example, Tatsuo Tanaka (2011) found that illegal distribution of anime (Japanese animation) on YouTube does not negatively affect DVD rentals in Japan and even appears to increase DVD sales. In this way, remixes like 'anime music video' or 'fansubs'* can be an excellent, and very well targeted, promotion tool for their products, which young people undertake of their own accord.

* **Anime music videos** are made by editing together clips of anime accompanied by a music soundtrack.

Fansubs are anime videos which have been translated into English and subtitled by fans.

Despite this, media corporations often want to retain some degree of control over their products, so that they cannot be used in ways that damage their brand. Microsoft allows video gamers to produce machinima so long as they abide by a set of 'Game Content Usage Rules', such as 'You can't use Game Content to create pornographic or obscene Items, or anything that contains vulgar, racist, hateful, or otherwise objectionable content' and 'you can't sell or otherwise earn any compensation from your Item, including through advertisements in the Item. We will let you have advertising or optional donation requests on the page hosting the Item, but that's it' (Microsoft, 2012). In this way, Microsoft hopes to benefit from the positive aspects of remix culture while retaining some control over their brand image and the goodwill of video gamers.

Summary of Section 4

The term 'remix' is often used to describe how young people use new media technologies in engaging with popular cultural texts, although it is a general condition of cultures, rather than a development unique to new media technologies.

As the term suggests, remix blurs the boundaries between source material and new product, and may require different criteria for evaluation than traditional ones of 'originality'.

Children and young people can develop impressive skills through practices of creative production, but these cannot easily be recognised or reproduced within the formal learning environments of schools.

Consumers and producers can clash over issues of ownership and authorship of the texts and products they create, work with and remix.

Corporations have responded to remix practices differently depending on whether they view them as an opportunity or a threat.

5 Conclusion

In this chapter we have examined how new media technologies are shifting the ways in which children and young people can engage with culture and share the results with each other. However, these kinds of 'participatory cultures' are deeply ambivalent. Children and young people can learn and develop new skills such as video editing or writing fiction, but these are not necessarily reflected or valued in the more traditional forms of classroom learning they encounter at school. Along with learning skills, young people may be enlisted into advertising and marketing products, or providing information about themselves as a market in ways that generate profit for others. Similarly, new media technologies can increase generational divides between adults and children, but they can also bring them together in new ways across hierarchical expectations. New media technologies have created spaces where children and young people become more deeply implicated in existing circuits of production and consumption, as a direct consequence of the opportunities these forms provide for them to become actively involved in producing their own remixed media content.

References

Aarsand, P. (2007) 'Computer and video games in family life', *Childhood*, vol. 14, no. 2, pp. 235–56.

Baker, S. M. and Gentry, J. W. (1996) 'Kids as collectors: a phenomenological study of first and fifth graders', *Advances in Consumer Research*, vol. 23, no. 1, pp. 132–7.

Blum, A. (1995) 'DOC's Deck-O-Butts trading cards: using humour to change youth attitudes about tobacco', *Tobacco Control*, vol. 4, no. 3, pp. 219–21.

Bond, E. L. and Michelson, N. J. (2009) 'Writing Harry's world: children co-authoring Hogwarts', in Heilman, E.E. (ed) *Critical Perspectives on Harry Potter*, 2nd edn, London, Taylor and Francis.

Buckingham, D. and Sefton-Green, J. (2003) 'Gotta catch 'em all: structure, agency and pedagogy in children's media culture', *Media, Culture and Society*, vol. 25, no. 3, pp. 379–99.

BusinessWire (2011) *New Pokémon Video Games Shatter U.S. Sales Records* [online], http://www.businesswire.com/news/home/20110308006797/en/Pok%C3%A9mon-Video-Games-Shatter-U.S.-Sales-Records (Accessed 4 March 2012).

Consalvo, M. (2007) *Cheating: Gaining Advantage in Videogames*, Cambridge, MA, MIT Press.

Corsaro, W. A. (2005) *The Sociology of Childhood*, 2nd edn, Thousand Oaks, CA, Pine Forge Press.

Corsaro, W. (1993) 'Interpretive reproduction in children's role play', *Childhood*, vol. 1, no. 2, pp. 64–74.

Gee, J. P. (2004) *Situated Language and Learning: A Critique of Traditional Schooling*, New York, Routledge.

Gitelman, L. and Pingree, G. B. (eds) (2003) *New Media 1740–1915*, Cambridge, MA, MIT Press.

Grimes, S. M. and Shade, L. R. (2005) 'Neopian economics of play: children's cyberpets and online communities as immersive advertising in Neopets.com', *International Journal of Media and Cultural Politics*, vol. 1, no. 2, pp. 181–98.

Hargittai, E. (2002) 'Second level digital divide', *First Monday*, no. 7 [online], http://www.firstmonday.org/issues/issue7_4/hargittai/ (Accessed 4 March 2012).

Hjorth, L. (2011) *Games and Gaming: An Introduction to New Media*, Oxford, Berg.

Ito, M. (ed) (2010) *Hanging Out, Messing Around, and Geeking Out*, Cambridge, MA, MIT Press.

Ito, M. and Bittanti, M. (2010) 'Gaming', in Ito, M. (ed) *Hanging Out, Messing Around, and Geeking Out*, Cambridge, MA, MIT Press.

Jackson, L., Gauntlett, D. and Steemers, J. (2008) *Children in Virtual Worlds: Adventure Rock Users and Producers Study* [online], London, BBC and University of Westminster, http://www.bbc.co.uk/blogs/knowledgeexchange/westminsterone.pdf (Accessed 28 June 2012).

Jenkins, H. (1992) *Textual Poachers: Television Fans and Participatory Culture*, London, Routledge.

Jenkins, H. (2006) *Convergence Culture: Where Old and New Media Collide*, New York, New York University Press.

Knobel, M. and Lankshear, C. (2008) 'Remix: the art and craft of endless hybridization', *Journal of Adolescent and Adult Literacy*, vol. 52, no. 1, pp. 22–33.

Koury, J. (2008) *We Are Wizards*, New York, Brooklyn Underground Films.

Lange, P. G. (2010) 'Achieving creative integrity on YouTube: reciprocities and tensions', *Enculturaltion*, no. 8 [online], http://enculturation.gmu.edu/achieving-creative-integrity (Accessed 28 June 2012).

Lange, P. G. and Ito, M. (2010) 'Creative production', in Ito, M. (ed) *Hanging Out, Messing Around, and Geeking Out*, Cambridge, MA, MIT Press.

Livingstone, S. and Helsper, E. (2007) 'Gradation in digital inclusion: children, young people and the digital divide', *New Media and Society*, vol. 9, no. 4, pp. 671–96.

Lury, C. (2011) *Consumer Culture*, 2nd edn, Cambridge and Malden, Polity Press.

Machinima (2012) *About Us* [online], http://www.machinima.com/about (Accessed 14 May 2012).

Manovich, L. (2001) *The Language of New Media*, Cambridge, MA, MIT Press.

Marsh, J. (2010) 'Young children's play in online virtual worlds', *Journal of Early Childhood Research*, vol. 8, no. 1, pp. 23–39.

Massive Productions (2011) *LiL Posion: The Story of the World's Youngest Professional Video Gamer*, Massive Productions.

Microsoft (2012) *Xbox: Game Content Usage Rules* [online], http://www.xbox.com/en-US/Community/Developer/Rules (Accessed 4 March 2012).

Paley, V. G. (1984) *Boys and Girls: Superheroes in the Doll Corner*, Chicago, IL, University of Chicago Press.

Robinson, L. (2010) 'Box 7.5 Eddie: Neopets, Neocapital, and making a virtual buck', in Ito, M. (ed) *Hanging Out, Messing Around, and Geeking Out*, Cambridge, MA, MIT Press.

Robinson, L. and Horst, H. A. (2010) 'Box 5.1 Neopets: same game, different meanings', in Ito, M. (ed) *Hanging Out, Messing Around, and Geeking Out*, Cambridge, MA, MIT Press.

Shirky, C. (2011) *Cognitive Surplus: Creativity and Generosity in a Connected Age*, London and New York, Penguin.

Tanaka, T. (2011) 'Do illegal copies of movies reduce the revenue of legal products? The case of TV animation in Japan', *Research Institute of Economy, Trade & Industry, IAA Discussion Paper*, 11 January [online], http://www.rieti.go.jp/en/publications/summary/11010021.html (Accessed 15 August 2011).

Tobin, J. (ed) (2004) *Pikachu's Global Adventure: The Rise and Fall of Pokémon*, Durham, NC and London, Duke University Press.

Warschauer, M. (2002) 'Reconceptualising the digital divide', *First Monday*, vol. 7, no. 7 [online], http://firstmonday.org/htbin/cgiwrap/bin/ojs/index.php/fm/article/viewArticle/967/888 (Accessed 15 August 2011).

Whitley, M. T. (1929) 'Children's interest in collecting', *Journal of Educational Psychology*, vol. 20, no. 4, pp. 249–61.

Wohlwend, K. E., Zanden, S. V., Husbye, N. E. and Kuby, C. R. (2011) 'Navigating discourses of place in the world of Webkinz', *Journal of Early Childhood Literacy*, vol. 11, no. 2, pp. 141–63.

Reading A
Yu-Gi-Oh!, media mixes and everyday cultural production

Mizuko Ito

Source: 'Technologies of the childhood imagination: Yugioh, media mixes and everyday cultural production', in Karaganis, J. (ed), 2007, *Structures of Participation in Digital Culture*, New York, Social Science Research Council, pp. 88–111.

The Yu-Gi-Oh! manga series has spawned a television animation, an immensely popular card game, at least 10 video game versions, and character goods ranging from T-shirts to packaged curry to pencil boxes. All project Yu-Gi-Oh! into different sites of consumption, play, spectatorship, and social action.

Yu-Gi-Oh! is similar to the media mixes of Pokémon and Digimon in that it involves human players who mobilize otherworldly monsters in battle. There is a difference, though, in how this fantasy is deployed. In earlier media mixes, such as Pokémon, the trading cards are a surrogate for 'actual' monsters in the fantasy world: Pokémon trainers collect monsters, not cards. In Yu-Gi-Oh!, Yugi and his friends collect and traffic in trading cards, just like the kids in 'our world'. The activities of children in our world thus closely mimic the activities and materialities of children in Yugi's world. They collect and trade the same cards and engage in play with the same strategies, rules, and material objects. Scenes in the anime depict Yugi frequenting card shops and buying card packs, enjoying the thrill of getting a rare card, dramatizing everyday moments of media consumption in addition to the highly stylized and fantastic dramas of the duels themselves. In Japan during the period when I was conducting fieldwork, Yu-Gi-Oh! cards were a pervasive fact of life, a fantasy world made manifest in the pockets and backpacks of millions of boys across the country. A 2000 survey of 300 students in a Kyoto elementary school indicated that, by the third grade, every student owned some Yu-Gi-Oh! cards (Asahi Shimbun, 2001).

Hypersociality

Yu-Gi-Oh! demonstrates how pervasive media technologies in everyday settings integrate the imagination into a wider range of sites of social activity. Far from the shut-in behavior that gave rise to the most familiar forms of anti-media rhetoric, this media mix of children's popular culture is wired, extroverted, and hypersocial, reflecting forms of sociality augmented by dense sets of technologies, signifiers, and systems of exchange. David Buckingham and Julian Sefton-Green (2004) have argued in the case of Pokémon that 'activity – or agency – is an indispensable part of the process rather than something that is exercised post hoc' (p. 19). The image of solitary kids staring at television screens and twiddling their thumbs has given way to the figure of the activist kid beaming monsters between Game Boys, trading cards in the park, text messaging friends on the bus ride home, reading breaking Yu-Gi-Oh! information emailed to a mobile phone, and selling amateur comics on the Internet. This digitally augmented sociality is an unremarkable fact of life for the current generation of kids in urban Japan. With the majority of Japanese accessing the Internet through mobile phones and with the rise of the handheld Game Boy as the preferred platform for gaming, computer and TV screens are no longer privileged access points to the virtual and the networked world.

Congregating with their Game Boys and Yu-Gi-Oh! playing cards, kids engage in a form of hypersocial exchange that is pervaded by the imagination of virtual gaming worlds. Buzzing with excitement, a group of boys huddles in a corner of their after-school center, trading cards, debating the merits of their decks, and talking about the latest TV episode. A little girl rips open a pack of cards at a McDonald's, describing their appeal to her baffled grandparents. A boy wears a favorite rare card around his neck as he climbs the play equipment at the park, inciting the envy and entrepreneurialism of his peers. As their mother completes her grocery shopping, a brother and sister walk into an elevator dueling with coupled Game Boy Advance machines. When Yu-Gi-Oh! players get together, (hyper)social exchange involves both the more familiar discursive sharing of stories and information and the material exchange of playing cards and virtual monsters.

Hypersocial exchange is about active, differentiated, and entrepreneurial consumer positions and a high degree of media and technical literacy, rather than the one-way street connoted by the term mass media or mass culture. This builds on the sensibilities of kids who grew up with the interactive and layered formats of video games as a fact of life and who bring this subjectivity to bear on other media forms. The interactivity, hacking, and first-person identification characteristic of video gaming is integrated with cardplay and identification with narrative characters. Players collect their own cards and monsters, combining them into decks that reflect a personal style of play, often derived from the stylistic cues presented by the manga characters. Pokémon decisively inflected kids' game culture toward personalization and recombination, demonstrating that children can master highly esoteric content, customization, connoisseurship, remixing, and a pantheon of hundreds of characters (Buckingham & Sefton-Green, 2004; Yano, 2004) – an environment of practice and learning that Sefton-Green has called a 'knowledge industry' (2004, p. 151). These more challenging forms of play have also attracted a wide following among adults.

Like most popular forms of anime content, Yu-Gi-Oh! has an avid following of adult fans, often called *otaku*, the Japanese term for media geek (Greenfeld, 1993; Kinsella, 1998; Okada, 1996; Tobin, 2004). Adult *otaku* communities are the illegitimate offspring of the Yu-Gi-Oh! media empire, and exist in uneasy relationship with the entertainment industries that create Yu-Gi-Oh! content. They exploit gaps in both dominant systems of meaning and mainstream commodity capitalism, using tactics that circumvent the official circuits of mass marketing and distribution. With the advent of the Internet, *otaku* communities found their communications medium, an organizing ground for special-interest fan communities and a site for distributing alternative content and grey market goods. Cultural remix is about the appropriation and reshaping of mass cultural content as well as its revaluation through alternative economies and systems of exchange.

One kind of *otaku* knowledge is known as *sa-chi*, or 'searching', methods by which card collectors identify rare card packs before purchase. I find myself out at 1 a.m. with a group of card collectors, pawing through three boxes of just-released cards. The salesperson is amused but slightly annoyed, and it takes some negotiating to get him to open all three boxes. My companions pride themselves on the well-trained fingertips and disciplined vision that enables them to identify the key card packs. They teach me a few tricks of the trade, but clearly this is a skill born of intensive practice. After identifying all the rare, super-rare, and ultra-rare cards in the store, they head out to clear the other neighborhood shops of rare cards before daybreak, when run-of-the-mill consumers will start purchasing.

Single cards, often purchased in these ways, are sold at card shops and on the Internet. In city centers in Tokyo such as Shibuya, Ikebukuro, and Shinjuku, there are numerous hobby shops that specialize in the buying and selling of single cards, and which are frequented by adult collectors as well as children. These cards can fetch prices ranging from pennies to hundreds of dollars for special-edition cards. Street vendors and booths at carnivals will also often have a display of single-sale Yu-Gi-Oh! cards that attract children. Internet auction sites and Yu-Gi-Oh! websites, however, mediate the majority of these player-to-player exchanges. The total volume is extremely large. One collector I spoke to purchases about 600 packs of cards in each round of searches and could easily make his living buying and selling Yu-Gi-Oh! cards.

Children share the same active and entrepreneurial stance, cultural fascinations, and interests as the adult gamers, but they lack the same freedom of movement and access to money and information. The rumor mill among children is active although often ill informed. All the children I spoke to about it had heard of search techniques, and some had half-baked ideas of how it might be done. Children create their own local rules, hierarchies of values, and microeconomies among peer groups, trading, buying, and selling cards in ways that mimic the more professional adult networks. Despite adult crackdowns on trading and selling between children, it is ubiquitous among card game players. Once mobile phones filter down from the teen to the elementary-school-age demographic, these exchanges are likely to be central to an expanded range of communications between kids exchanging information, beaming character art, and cutting deals during their downtime in transit and at home in the evenings.

Another arena of *otaku* cultural production, which I will mention just briefly here, is the publication and selling of amateur comics, often derived from mainstream content such as Yu-Gi-Oh!.

Unlike the world of the card and video game *otaku*, the manga *otaku* are dominated by working-class girls (Kinsella, 1998, p. 289), with much of the content featuring boy–boy relationships idealized by a feminine eye. For example, Yu-Gi-Oh! fanzines often feature romantic liaisons between Yugi, Kaiba and Yugi's best friend, Jounouchi (Joey in the English-language version). Unlike professional cultural production, fanzines center on tight-knit communities of peers that both create and buy amateur manga. Artists sit at their booths and chat with artists and readers who browse their work. Comic Market is the largest show of its kind, but a greater volume of zines changes hands through a more distributed exchange network that includes the Internet, regional events, and events focused on specific form of content, such as a particular manga series or genre. There are an estimated 20,000 to 50,000 amateur manga circles in Japan (Kinsella, 1998; Schodt, 1996). Most participants are teenagers and young adults rather than children, but these practices are an extension of childhood practices of drawing manga and exchanging them among friends (Ito, 2006). As in the case of the card *otaku*, manga *otaku* translate childhood imaginaries into alternative adult networks of amateur cultural production and commerce.

Unlike spectacular narratives of good and evil told on the TV screen, the buzz of competitive exchange between kids in the park, the furtive rounds of nighttime collectors, and the flow of cards, monsters, and fanzines through Internet commerce and street-level exchange point to a peer-to-peer imaginary that is heterogeneously materialized and produced through highly distributed social practices. The Yu-Gi-Oh! imaginary exceeds the sanctioned networks and contact points of mainstream industrialists and the hegemonic narratives they market to supposedly passive masses of children. While the Internet has taken center stage in our theorizing of new forms of communication and relationality, media mixes in children's content, below the radar of mainstream adult society, have been quietly radicalizing a new generation's relationship to culture and social life.

References

Buckingham, D. and Sefton-Green, J. (2004) 'Structure, agency, and pedagogy in children's media culture', in Tobin, J. (ed) *Pikachu's Global Adventure: The Rise and Fall of Pokémon*, Durham, NC, Duke University Press.

Greenfeld, K. T. (1993) 'The incredibly strange mutant creatures who rule the universe of alienated Japanese zombie computer nerds', *Wired*, vol. 1, no. 1 [online], http://www.wired.com/wired/archive/1.01/otaku. html.

Ito, M. (2006) 'Japanese media mixes and amateur cultural exchange', in Buckingham, D. and Willett, R. (eds) *Digital Generations*, Mahwah, NJ, Lawrence Erlbaum.

Kinsella, S. (1998) 'Japanese subculture in the 1980s: otaku and the amateur manga movement', *Journal of Japanese Studies*, vol. 24, pp. 289–316.

Okada, T. (1996) *Otakugaku nyuumon [Introduction to Otakuology]*, Tokyo, Ota Shuppan.

Schodt, F. L. (1996) *Dreamland Japan: Writings on Modern Manga*, Berkeley, CA, Stonebridge.

Sefton-Green, J. (2004) 'Initiation rites: a small boy in a Poké-world', in Tobin, J. (ed) *Pikachu's Global Adventures: The Rise and Fall of Pokémon*, Durham, NC, Duke University Press.

Shimbun, A. (2001) *Otousan datte Hamaru*, Tokyo.

Tobin, S. (2004) 'Masculinity, maturity, and the end of Pokémon', in Tobin, J. (ed) *Pikachu's Global Adventures: The Rise and Fall of Pokémon*, Durham, NC, Duke University Press.

Yano, C. R. (2004) 'Panic attacks: anti-Pokémon voices in global markets', in Tobin, J. (ed) *Pikachu's Global Adventures: The Rise and Fall of Pokémon*, Durham, NC, Duke University Press.

Reading B
Creative production in the digital age

Patricia G. Lange and Mizuko Ito

Source: 'Creative production', in Ito, M. (ed), 2010, *Hanging Out, Messing Around, and Geeking Out*, Cambridge, MA, MIT Press, pp. 243–91.

What constitutes 'creative work' is contested by scholars. The term traditionally has been used to describe 'imaginative' or 'expressive' work, where 'expressive' refers to sharing aspects of the self (Sefton-Green 2000, 8). Our understanding of what constitutes creative production includes imaginative and expressive forms that are also shaped by kids' individual choices and available media. The influx of digital media into everyday life is reshaping these understandings, particularly our assumptions about the relation between media production and consumption. Media theorists have argued for decades that media 'consumption' is not a passive act and that viewers and readers actively shape cultural meanings (Buckingham, 2000; Dyson, 1997; Eco, 1979; Jenkins, 1992; Kinder, 1999; Radway, 1984; Seiter, 1999b). Contemporary interactive and networked media make this perspective difficult to ignore. Developments in the technology sector in the past decade have pushed this understanding into common parlance and consciousness. 'Web 2.0', 'user-generated content', 'modding', 'prosumer', 'pro-am', 'remix culture' – these buzz words are all indicators of how creative production at the 'consumer' layer is increasingly seen as a generative site of culture and knowledge. A decade ago, creating a personal webpage was considered an act of technical and creative virtuosity; today, the comparable practice of creating a MySpace profile is an unremarkable achievement for the majority of U.S. teens. As sites such as YouTube, Photobucket, and Flickr become established as fixtures of our media-viewing landscape, it is becoming commonplace for people to both post and view personal and amateur videos and photos online as part of their everyday media practice. In turn, these practices are reshaping our processes for self-expression, learning, and sociality.

In the case of young people, new media production is framed by ongoing debates about the appropriate role of media in young people's lives. Our discourse about media and creativity is framed by a set of cultural distinctions between an active/creative or a passive/derivative mode of engaging with imagination and fantasy. Generally, practices that involve local production – creative writing, drawing, and performance –

are considered more creative, agentive, and imaginative than practices that involve consumption of professionally or mass-produced media – watching television, playing video games, or even reading a book. In addition, we commonly make a distinction between active and passive media forms. One familiar argument is that visual media, in contrast to oral and print media, stifle creativity, because they do not require imaginative and intellectual work. Popular media, particularly television, have been blamed for the stifling of childhood imagination and initiative; in contrast to media such as music or drawing, television has often been demonized as a commercially driven, purely consumptive, and passive media form for children and youth.

Today, these long-standing debates about media, kids, and creativity are being reframed by the proliferation of new forms of digital media production and social media. What is unique about the current media ecology is that photos, videos, and music are closer at hand and more amenable to modification, remix, and circulation through online networks. In the past few years, it has become common for personal computers to ship with a basic kit of digital production tools that enable youth to manipulate music, photos, and video. In addition to the new genres of creative production that are being afforded by digital media-creation tools, we see networked publics as affording a fundamental shift in the context of how new media are created and shared; media works are now embedded in a public social ecology of ongoing communication (Russell et al., 2008). As is common when new media capabilities are introduced, it takes some time for literacy capacity to build and for people to come together around new genres of media and media participation that make use of these capabilities. Given that multimedia production tools have become mainstream as consumer technologies only in the past decade, we are now at a transitional moment of interpretive flexibility with regard to literacy and genres associated with the creation of digital music, photos, and video. The practices that we describe [here] need to be situated as part of this transitional moment, when youth are experimenting with new digital cultural forms and, in interaction with adult mentors and parental guidance, are developing new forms of media literacy.

Judged by the standards of traditional media production, many new genres of digitally remixed derivative works would be considered inferior to original creations that did not rely on appropriation of content produced by others. Contrary to this view, Marsha Kinder points out the historical specificity of contemporary notions of creativity and originality. She suggests that children take up popular media in ways that were recognized as creative in other historical eras. 'A child's reworking of material from mass media can be seen as a form of parody (in the eighteenth-century sense) …' (Kinder, 1991, p. 60). In a similar vein, Anne Haas Dyson (1997) examines how elementary-school children mobilize mass-media characters within creative-writing exercises. Like Ellen Seiter (1999a), Dyson argues that commercial media provide the 'common story material' for contemporary childhood, and that educators should acknowledge the mobilization of these materials as a form of literacy. These theorists point to the more socially embedded and relational dimensions of creative production that are in line with much of what we see proliferating on the Internet today. …

Most of the content creation that youth engage in is a form of personal media creation that is focused on documenting their everyday lives and sharing with friends and family. In some cases, this everyday personal media production serves as a jumping-off point for developing other kinds of creative interests. In other cases, youth express interest in developing highly technical media skills from an early age. Yet both commonplace and exceptional cases in media production share certain commonalities, and the boundary between 'casual' and social media production and 'serious' media production is difficult to define. Although friendship-driven and hanging out genres of participation are generally associated with more casual forms of media creation, they can transition quickly to messing around and geeking out. Conversely, the relationships that youth foster in interest-driven creative production can become a source of new friendship and collegiality that is an alternative to the kinds of friendships and status regimes that youth must inhabit at school. We can see this in the social energies that young people bring to online discussions with their interest-based friends as well as in conventions and meet-ups where youth are sharing their lives as well as their creative work.

All these cases demonstrate the growing centrality of media creation in the everyday social communication of youth. Whether it is everyday photography or machinima, youth are using media they create as a way of documenting their lives and as a means of self-expression. These cases also demonstrate the centrality of peer-based exchange in motivating creative work and providing a learning context. Peers are fellow creators youth see as knowledgeable audiences who have shared investments in the work, and with whom they have a relation of reciprocity. Peers view and comment on their work and vice versa. This may be the given peer group of local friends or family, or it may be a specialized creative community. Teens consider what their friends will think of their MySpace profiles, and video creators hope fellow makers will appreciate the craft that went in to their work. In both these cases, networked publics enable kids to connect with others in ways that facilitate sharing and peer-based learning. Even when the initial impetus for media production comes from family, school, or after-school programs, a prime motivator for improving the craft lies in the network of peers who serve as audiences, critics, collaborators, and coproducers in the creation of media.

School programs can provide an introduction to creative production practices that kids may not otherwise have exposure to. In most programs, however, the audience for production is limited to the teacher and possibly the class. In addition, most classroom projects are not driven by the interests of the participants themselves. By contrast, the examples we have found in youth recreational and hobby productions indicate a different dynamic. When youth have the opportunity to pursue projects based on their own interests, and to share them within a network of peers with similar investments, the result is highly active forms of learning. In after-school programs where youth have the opportunity to showcase their work to a broader audience of creators and aficionados, they can gain validation for their work in ways similar to what we have observed online. For example, Dilan Mahendran's study (Hip-Hop Music Production) found that youth hip-hop creators in the program he studied distributed their works to larger audiences and participated in a range of public performances and competitions. The case of hip-hop demonstrates the power of amateur and small-scale communities of media production to support aspirational trajectories that rely on reputation in more niche or local contexts. Online networks enable young people to find these niche audiences in ways that were not historically available to youth. Although it is rare for youth to be able to reach a scale of audience that rivals professional media production, many are able to reach beyond the boundaries of home, local activity groups, and families in finding appreciative audiences for their work.

References

Buckingham, D. (2000) *After the Death of Childhood: Growing Up in the Age of Electronic Media*, Cambridge, Polity.

Dyson, A. H. (1997) *Writing Superheroes: Contemporary Childhood, Popular Culture, and Classroom Literacy*, New York, Teachers College Press.

Eco, U. (1979) *The Role of the Reader: Explorations in the Semiotics of Texts*, Bloomington, IN, Indiana University Press.

Jenkins, H. (1992) *Textual Poachers: Television Fans and Participatory Culture*, London, Routledge.

Kinder, M. (1991) *Playing with Power in Movies, Television, and Video Games*, Berkeley, CA, University of California Press.

Kinder, M. (ed) (1999) *Kids' Media Culture*, Durham, NC, Duke University Press.

Radway, J. (1984) *Reading the Romance: Women, Patriarchy, and Popular Literature*, London, The University of North Carolina Press.

Russell, A., Ito, M., Richmond, T. and Tuters, M. (2008) 'Culture: media convergence and networked', in Varnelis, K. (ed) *Networked Publics*, Cambridge, MA, MIT Press.

Sefton-Green, J. (2000) 'Introduction: evaluating creativity', in Sefton-Green, J. and Sinker, R. (eds) *Evaluating Creativity: Making and Learning by Young People*, London, Routledge.

Seiter, E. (1999a) 'Power Rangers at preschool: negotiating media in child care settings', in Kinder, M. (ed) *Kids' Media Culture*, Durham, NC, Duke University Press.

Seiter, E. (1999b) *Television and New Media Audiences*, Oxford, Oxford University Press.

Chapter 6

Researching children's lives offline and online

Martyn Hammersley

Contents

In this chapter, you will:

- examine some of the main ways in which researchers have set about exploring the lives of children and young people

- gain an understanding of key methodological arguments surrounding these methods

- consider some of the conflicting views regarding how researchers should carry out investigations

- explore the opportunities in, and barriers to, studying the online activities of children and young people, as compared with their offline activities

- come to understand the value and the complexities of combining study of online and offline lives

- examine some of the ethical issues arising in research with children and young people, and the different perspectives that can be adopted towards these.

1   Introduction

This chapter will explore some of the ways in which researchers go about studying the lives of children and young people, as illustrated by research discussed in earlier chapters of this book. It is designed to review key methodological issues associated with this research. In particular, it will compare what is involved in studying children's and young people's lives offline and online, thereby recognising the significant impact of new media and digital technologies (Livingstone, 2009). The development of these technologies, and the online activities and forms of communication they facilitate, has not only generated new topics for investigation, but also opened up new sources of data for researchers. Take, for example, the case of social networking sites. These offer places for children and young people to 'hang out', meet new people, flirt, blog, write diaries, post pictures and art work, share music and videos, and so on. What they produce here will provide important insights into their lives; for example, Boyd (2010) discusses how relationship break-ups are now frequently enacted publicly online. These sites also offer a means by which researchers can establish and sustain online contact with young people. At the same time, it should not be assumed that patterns of social interaction online are completely different from, or unrelated to, those that take place offline; or that the methods available to study them are totally different.

The chapter will begin by looking at research referred to in earlier chapters that has studied the lives of children and young people offline. In particular, we will compare the use of participant observation and interviews.

2 Researching children and young people offline

Researchers have traditionally gained information about people's lives in more or less the same ways that all of us do in everyday life: by asking questions, watching and listening to what people do, using available documents, and so on. However, the particular form these methods take in research, and the uses made of them, depend to a considerable extent on the questions being addressed, and also on the disciplinary and methodological traditions within which researchers work. These are quite diverse.

A variety of terms are used in the literature to distinguish between the array of approaches that researchers can adopt in studying childhood and youth. For example, in Chapter 2 there is an outline of what is referred to as 'the folklore tradition', which is illustrated by the work of Opie and Opie (1997) on playground games. This sort of work has been of considerable importance in promoting the idea of children's oral cultures, and documenting how these changed over the course of the twentieth century. Another kind of work mentioned in the early part of Chapter 2 is ethnography. The author refers to her own study of children's play at home as 'ethnographic' (Woodyer, 2010), and also discusses other ethnographic studies such as that of the lives of children in a Sudanese village by Katz (2004).

2.1 Ethnography, participant observation and interviews

Historically, the term 'ethnography' referred to the sort of research carried out by anthropologists, but the label is now also used in many other disciplines, and this has led to some variability in its meaning. The most common form of ethnography involves in-depth study of a particular setting or a small number of settings, such as street corners, neighbourhoods, villages, towns, workplaces, schools or youth clubs. Furthermore, this is usually done through participant observation by the researcher in these settings: observing what happens, usually playing a marginal role, talking to people informally as well as sometimes more formally in interviews, and doing this over a relatively long period of time. In addition, there could be audio or even video recording of particular events or interviews, or the analysis of documents, photographs and artefacts.

Activity 1   The folklore and ethnographic traditions

Allow about 20 minutes

Look again at the description of the folklore tradition in Chapter 2. Compare this sort of research with the brief account of ethnography that has just been provided and with what you have learned about this kind of work in other chapters. On this basis, answer the following questions:

- What are the similarities between these two kinds of research in terms of what they aim to do and how they set about doing it?

- What are the differences between them?

Comment

Both folklore studies and ethnography involve the study of cultural phenomena through eliciting accounts or engaging in observation. Historically, there was quite a close relationship between the development of folklore studies and anthropological work. In its late nineteenth-century form, anthropology was often primarily concerned with the collection of artefacts and the recording of stories and myths that had been passed down between generations. However, in the twentieth century, anthropological work shifted its focus towards studying contemporary patterns of social life, although the interest in myths and artefacts did not disappear.

This shift can be illustrated by a story about Franz Boas, one of the pioneers of anthropological fieldwork, who was the PhD supervisor of Margaret Mead. In the course of fieldwork he wrote in his diary:

> I had a miserable day today. The natives held a big potlatch again [a gift-giving ceremony found among Indian groups living in the North West of America]. I was unable to get hold of anyone and had to snatch at whatever I could get. Late at night I did get something (a tale) for which I had been searching – 'The Birth of the Raven'. ... [Next day:] The big

> potlatches were continued today, but people found time to tell
> me stories.
>
> (Quoted in Rohner, 1969, cited in
Pelto and Pelto, 1978, p. 243)

Commenting on this extract, Pelto and Pelto remark: 'Most anthropologists today would be overjoyed at the prospect of observing a full-blown potlatch and would assume that crucially important structural and cultural data could be extracted from the details of the ceremony' (Pelto and Pelto, 1978, p. 243). We might add that, by contrast, folklorists would probably agree with Boas's priorities, being more interested in collecting stories; though it should be said that, in fact, Boas's interests extended well beyond this.

As this indicates, folklore studies tend to focus on specific types of cultural object and their character, such as games, nursery rhymes, myths and fairytales. Furthermore, the main interest has been in discovering varieties of the same cultural feature occurring across many different groups of people, spread geographically, or preserved over long periods of time. It is also important to note that these cultural objects are effectively regarded as separable from the immediate contexts in which they occur.

By contrast, ethnographers tend to be interested in a wider range of phenomena – in terms of both beliefs and behaviour – and in how particular cultural phenomena relate to other aspects of people's lives *in the here and now*. A good illustration of this ethnographic approach, referred to in Chapter 2, is Gregor's (1977) discussion of the game of 'Women's Sons' (*teneju itai*) played by children of the Mehinaku in Brazil. In contrast to the folklore orientation, his focus is very much on how the game was played in a particular context at a particular time, who played which roles, the children's attitude towards it, and how participation in the game related to the wider culture, for example what role it may have served in preparing them for later life in their society.

There are also differences in the sort of data that folklorists and ethnographers tend to rely on. We can see this by looking at how the Opies went about collecting information about children's games. They requested help through a national newspaper, getting responses from teachers who then elicited children's written accounts of the games they played. While folklore study of children's culture has also involved direct observation, this has usually amounted to seeing children perform particular games especially for the researcher, rather than observing the spontaneous behaviour of children in play settings. There is a direct contrast in this respect between the work of the Opies and the ethnographic approach of Thorne (1993), also referred to in Chapter 2, who spent a great deal of time observing how children organised their games in a school playground, and who focused on what this could tell us about their attitudes and orientations, in particular how gender divisions are acted out through games.

I noted earlier that, while ethnography has been the central approach to research amongst anthropologists, it is also now used by many other kinds of social scientist. One area where it has been particularly common is in the study of youth cultures, which was the subject of Chapter 4. This field of work has been rather more influenced by the disciplines of sociology and cultural studies than anthropology, and one effect of this has been that the sorts of work labelled 'ethnographic' in those disciplines have often departed from the anthropological model in various respects. In particular, participant observation has not always been the main source of data, with primary or exclusive reliance sometimes being placed on interviews, or even on the study of typical styles of personal appearance, analysis of media reports and other documents. Indeed, some accounts have been based only very lightly on empirical evidence. At the same time, there have also been substantial ethnographic studies.

Activity 2   Milltown Boys
Allow about 40 minutes

Among the ethnographic studies referred to in Chapter 4 is Williamson's (2004) account of the 'Milltown Boys'. This is of considerable interest from a methodological as well as a substantive point of view. It reports what is sometimes referred to as a 're-study'. In the 1970s, the author carried out an investigation of the lives of a group of teenage boys growing up in a South Wales working-class community, collecting data over a three-year period. He lived in the community himself, and spent a great deal of time with the boys, in their various activities, and also talking informally with them. Some 25 years later, he tracked down as many of them as he could find in order to discover what had happened to them subsequently and to document their current lives through interviews. The extract from his interview with 'Spaceman' quoted in

Chapter 4 comes from this later re-study, with the informant reflecting back on his earlier life.

On the basis of the above information, and that provided in Chapter 4, consider the following questions:

- Should Williamson's 'revisiting' of the Milltown Boys be classed as an ethnography?
- Do you think there would be any significant differences in reliability between the findings of his two studies, the first one and the later re-study, given the different kinds of information on which they draw?

Comment

In response to the first question, Williamson's original study has many of the features that would normally be associated with an ethnography. Indeed, it even matches the anthropological ideal that the researcher should live for a lengthy period of time in the community. Many ethnographic studies in other disciplines do not involve this. Indeed, it would, of course, be impossible were the focus on a workplace or an educational institution – while the ethnographer could live in the local area, many of the people he or she is studying would be unlikely to do so. However, it is by no means always done even where a particular neighbourhood or community is being investigated. In addition, the sorts of data Williamson employed, in particular participant observation of the Boys' everyday activities, and his attempt to elicit their own perceptions and views, fit with the ethnographic model.

By contrast with this reliance on participant observation, Williamson's later re-study necessarily depended almost entirely on interview data for information about his informants' lives in the period since his original study, and about their attitudes and activities today; though, in the course of contacting and interviewing them, he did visit some of their homes, and the pubs and clubs they frequented. Whether or not Williamson's re-study counts as ethnographic would probably be a matter of dispute among qualitative researchers. Some commentators insist that ethnographic work must always involve long-term participant observation as its centrepiece, whilst others routinely include studies that rely solely on one-off interviews. Others take a view somewhere between these positions.

In my view, the issue of what counts and does not count as ethnography is less important than being aware of the range of different sorts of method used by, and data available to, researchers; along with the implications of this for the kinds of research question they can address, and the reliability of the evidence they produce.

With regard to the second question, Williamson had little choice but to change his primary research method in the re-study: the Milltown Boys no longer operated as a group by that time, not all still lived in the same community and indeed many had lost contact with one another. Nevertheless, we can still ask about the reliability of his informants' accounts in their interviews with him. While he was in the advantageous position of being able to capitalise on previous relationships with the men, and on his knowledge of their activities and environment in the past, he had very limited access to the details of their current lives outside of what they told him in the interviews. This contrasts with the original study, for which he could compare what they said with what he had observed them do, and also compare the accounts of different boys about the same events, over a relatively long period of time.

Williamson's study raises the issue not just of what counts as ethnography, but also of what constitutes *good* ethnographic work, or good research more generally. In the case of ethnography, this is often discussed partly in terms of variation in the role that a researcher plays: in particular, how 'close' he or she gets to the people being studied, how much time is spent in the field on a daily or weekly basis, how long the fieldwork lasts, and so on. For example, in the course of an article about research on skinheads in the UK, an extract from which formed Reading A for Chapter 4, Nayak refers to an influential discussion of skinheads by Pearson (1996), noting in passing that it had been based on 'fragmentary observation' (Nayak, 1999, p. 74). Later he refers to 'the majority of skinhead studies' as constituting 'a sociology of appearances' (Moore, 1994. p. 15), in being 'frequently based on secondary data and media reporting' (Nayak, 1999, p. 75). The implication here is, of course, that, in this field at least, there are doubts about the reliability of findings from studies that do not deploy lengthy, close-up participant observation.

This highlights an important feature of an ethnographic orientation: the idea that closeness to the social phenomena studied, in other words 'being there' (Geertz, 1988), is essential: it is assumed that only by being able to observe and talk to the people concerned directly, over a considerable time period, accompanied perhaps by participation in their activities, will a researcher be able to understand what they do and why. This is one of the grounds for some commentators' reluctance to call interview-based studies ethnographic; although an analogous argument can be developed about the kind of interview used by qualitative researchers compared with those characteristic of survey research. The general assumption is that closeness to the people being studied, in literal or metaphorical terms, will maximise the quality of the evidence produced.

There is something to be said for this argument, in that closeness means that the amount and diversity of (at least some kinds of relevant) evidence is maximised. However, we should note that 'closeness' on its own will determine neither whether fruitful research questions are addressed, nor how sound and well-evidenced the answers are likely to be. Studies based on flimsy evidence can sometimes generate productive questions and hypotheses, while those relying on detailed data from close-up contact can be pedestrian and not very illuminating. It might be argued that the best studies are likely to combine a thoughtful, creative questioning approach with detailed ethnographic investigation, but as we saw in the case of Williamson's re-study this is not always possible; and, as we shall see later, interviews can have considerable advantages.

As noted earlier, a great deal of qualitative research today, whether or not it is labelled 'ethnography', relies primarily, or exclusively, on interview data. Much quantitative work also depends for its evidence on eliciting accounts from people, notably through questionnaires – whether administered face-to-face, sent by post, carried out over the phone, or online. Such accounts can take a variety of forms, and the mode of elicitation may have important implications for their validity and value. For example, in the case of interviews we can identify two particularly important respects in which they can vary:

1 They may be relatively informal or formal. At one end of this spectrum they may be snatched conversations taking place alongside or around other activities, while, at the other, they will be meetings specially prearranged for the purposes of asking questions, and insulated as far as possible from surrounding activities.

2 They can be highly structured or relatively unstructured. A structured interview involves closed questions with interviewees being asked to choose from a set of pre-specified answers, as in the case of fixed-choice questionnaires. By contrast, in unstructured interviews the questions are open-ended, and for the most part they will be designed to invite informants to talk at length about matters that could be relevant to the research topic. This is, of course, a

dimension, with more semi-structured kinds of interviewing between these two poles.

What our discussion here has indicated is that both participant observation and interviewing can vary in important ways that could be relevant to the reliability of the evidence produced, and the validity of the inferences drawn from it.

Activity 3   Relatively unstructured interviews

Allow about 20 minutes

Look at some of the examples of data from relatively unstructured interviews reported in earlier chapters. For example, in Chapter 2 there are extracts from interviews with Joshua, Stephen and Matthew, that were part of Woodyer's (2010) research on children's play in domestic settings; there is an extract from an interview with Samantha from Epstein's (1997) work on children's school-based cultures and heterosexuality; and one from an interview with a group of girls from Tucker's (2003) research, relating to intimidation by other children. There is also a brief extract from an interview with Stephen in Reading C. In Chapter 4, the reading by Nayak (1999) contains several extracts from this sort of interview.

What would you say are the strengths and weaknesses of relying entirely on relatively unstructured interviews in researching the lives of children and young people?

Comment

Strengths

It is important to remember that perceptions, beliefs, attitudes and reasons cannot be simply read off from observed behaviour. Nor can they always be elicited in relatively short informal interviews, or in highly structured ones. By contrast, in principle at least, relatively unstructured interviews allow the researcher to explore in depth how people see the world and their reasons for action. It may take considerable time to build trust with informants – particularly, for example, in the case of adults interviewing children – in order to gain access to their views and experiences, and to understand them. Furthermore, since the direction in which the conversation goes in relatively unstructured interviews is more under the control of the informant than in structured interviews, it is likely that things will be mentioned that are relevant to the research that the researcher would not have thought to ask about. This is also often a feature of group interviews, where what one participant says will stimulate others. Another point, this time about interviews in general, is that they can provide us with information about events and people in the past that the researcher cannot now observe, and about what goes on in settings to which he or she cannot get access.

Weaknesses

To start with, we should note that interviews are a particular form of social interaction that makes specific demands on participants, and sometimes the latter may be unable or unwilling to meet these. For example, very young children may struggle to understand interview questions if they have no experience of being interviewed before, while adolescents may sometimes refuse to conform to the requirements of an interview, as may some adults.

Equally important, interviewees may not tell the truth; for example, they may put up a 'front' in order to create a particular image of themselves. As a result, there may be significant differences between what they say to the interviewer about their lives and what they actually do, or what they say in other contexts. In addition, they may not be able to provide the information asked for: sometimes interview questions address matters that informants do not have information or views about, yet people may provide speculative accounts or invent responses because they feel obliged to answer, or are embarrassed to refuse. This is sometimes especially the case with young children. Furthermore, even when the questions are about their own behaviour, people may not be able to provide accurate information – after all, we are not fully aware of much of what we do. In the case of retrospective studies, such as that of Williamson, where informants are asked to provide biographical information about past events in their lives, there is also the issue of memory: we know that we do not always remember the past accurately.

Finally, comparing relatively unstructured interviews with more structured ones or the administration of questionnaires, the latter maximise the chances that information about the same topics will be obtained from all respondents, and allow accounts to be elicited from a larger number of respondents.

2.2 The radical critique of interviews and constructionism

The weaknesses mentioned in my comment on Activity 3 are not the only criticisms that have been made of reliance on interview data: what is sometimes called the 'radical critique' of interviews has also been influential (Murphy et al., 1998; Rapley, 2001; Potter and Hepburn, 2005). This challenges the routine use by researchers of interview data as a 'window on the world beyond the interview' or as a 'window into the minds of informants' (Dingwall, 1997; Silverman, 1997; Atkinson and Coffey, 2002). In effect, what is rejected by this critique is almost all previous social science use of interviews, including in the field of childhood studies.

The radical critique argues that treating interview data as transparent in this way neglects the sociocultural processes through which this data has been generated. We must recognise, so the argument goes, that, rather than simply being an expression of the experience or of the views of informants, interview data is co-constructed with interviewers: it is shaped by what information the latter supply about their research, the questions they ask, their verbal and non-verbal responses to answers, and so on. With a different interviewer, or even the same interviewer on a different occasion, what the informant says would vary, perhaps in ways that are highly significant for the research.

Furthermore, informants' accounts will draw on the particular cultural resources that are available to them, selecting these as judged to be appropriate in the particular circumstances: ways of speaking will be adopted that formulate people, places and actions in one way rather than another. For this reason too, if the interview were to be 'run again' at a different time, or in a different place, or with a different interviewer, the data generated might be different. Moreover, it is argued, even when the data is substantially the same, this will reflect the influence of the cultural resources employed as much as any reality 'behind' the accounts provided, either what goes on in situations beyond the interview or in the heads of informants.

In short, accounts supplied in interviews, or for that matter via questionnaires, never provide unmediated access to people's beliefs and attitudes, or to real-world events that they have witnessed. At best, critics argue, in order to draw any conclusion from interview data about these matters, it is necessary first to examine the interview process in detail, the cultural resources which informants deploy, and so on, in order to try to 'discount' the influence of these things. However, the radical critics push through here to a much more radical conclusion: that interview data cannot be used as evidence about things like attitudes or events, and that we cannot 'discount' the influence of the medium of the interview.

The radical critics argue that it is a mistake to think of attitudes, social events or activities as existing independently of how language is used to formulate them on particular occasions by particular people, whether in interviews or in other contexts. In these terms, social phenomena are constructed in and through discursive practices (ways of speaking or writing) rather than standing outside of those practices. While this may seem puzzling, or even fanciful, it does make sense of the fact that where different people give accounts of 'the same event' there are often discrepancies among these that are hard to resolve, and that arise from the different interest they have in the scene, or the different concepts they use to think about it. This is often referred to as the Rashomon effect, after a famous Japanese film, directed by Akira Kurosawa, which explored this phenomenon.

Widdicombe and Wooffitt (1995) applied this radical critique of interviews to the study of youth cultures. They report that one of the issues that they originally wanted to investigate in studying punks:

> was the extent to which an individual's social identity as a member of a specific subculture was tied to ways in which that individual compared him or herself to other members of their own group and with members of other groups. ... Consequently, we treated people's accounts as being somewhat 'transparent' insofar as we assumed that they would reveal the workings of psychological processes which underpinned the individual's perceptions of him or herself in relation to others. However, once we realized that language use is itself a form of social activity, it became untenable to treat accounts as transparent representations of inner mental events, like cognitive processes or attitudes, and so on. Instead, we began to examine accounts which dealt with comparisons between the individuals and other members of the group, or other groups, to see how these comparisons were constructed, and to try to discover the kinds of interpersonal or inferential work which were being addressed through these accounts.
>
> (Widdicombe and Wooffitt, 1995, p. 2)

When the authors say here that it is 'untenable to treat accounts as transparent representations' because 'language use is itself a form of social activity' what they are challenging is the idea that the primary purpose of language in human life is to describe and explain actions, events, processes and structures that exist independently of it. Rather, they insist, language is used to *do* things: to make promises, accusations, apologies; to challenge, excuse, claim or deny membership in some group; to disparage or praise; and so on. So we must pay attention to what it is being used to do, rather than treating it as representing an independently existing world.

There is an important implication of this argument: rather than analysing what people say in interviews as simply telling us about their experience, lives and attitudes, we should attend to the *work* that any descriptions and explanations they provide are designed to do. Moreover, as already noted, this work is likely to be contextually related to the activities of the interviewer, and in the case of group interviews to those of fellow participants. Processes of co-construction are central.

Still, the argument here is that what is being co-constructed is not *just* interview data, but also and simultaneously the social phenomena being talked about. For instance, as in the case of Widdicombe and Wooffitt's interviews about punks, when informants discuss whether or not they are punks, or what it is to be a punk, they are – *through this talk* – constructing punk culture, along with their own identities in relation to it, rather than simply describing these things. This points in the direction of a rather different kind of qualitative inquiry from folklore studies, ethnography and most interview-based research, towards one or another kind of discourse analysis, where the focus is specifically on the discursive practices people employ and how the social world is constituted through their use. (An outline of different types of discourse analysis can be found in Wetherell et al., 2001, if this is of interest.)

Activity 4   Transcription of interviews
Allow about 20 minutes

Look back again at the interview extracts quoted in Chapters 2 and 4 and the associated readings. How much information do these extracts provide about the way in which the data has been generated in the interview situation, for example through its co-construction by interviewer and interviewee?

Comment

One of the criticisms made of interview studies by the radical critics is that they do not usually employ the sort of detailed transcription that is required in order to understand the ways in which what people say is shaped by the interview process. This has implications both for the kind of analysis that can be carried out by the researcher, and for what access readers have to the process of data construction, and therefore their ability to assess the interpretations made of the data.

There is some variation between the extracts in this respect. In Chapter 2 the interview extracts from Woodyer's research are presented as part of a continuous account in reported speech, but with direct quotations from the words of the informants. Here, we get a very selective sense of what the informants said. At the same time, in the case of the interview with Joshua especially, we are given some indications of the interview process, notably where Woodyer mentions *how* comments were made (for example 'he laughs', 'he responds firmly', 'he giggles', 'he says smugly'), and her own reactions ('I chuckle'). Other extracts in that chapter and in Chapter 4 are presented in the more conventional 'playscript' format. This gives us lengthier extracts from what the informants said, showing the consecutive turns in some short conversational sequences. However, we do not know what happened before these sequences, and this might have affected them, or what happened after them. Furthermore, it seems likely that these turns have been tidied up, with any overlap and pauses eliminated, along with backchannel responses from the researcher (such as, 'uhuh'). Furthermore, in these particular extracts we are given little or no information about non-verbal behaviour.

The key question is, though, how much, and what kinds of information, are required in order for sound analysis to be carried out, and for readers to be able to assess the likely validity of the conclusions drawn? This is a matter of dispute, and is likely to vary according to the interview data concerned, the research questions being addressed, and the conclusions presented by the researcher.

Returning to the arguments of Widdicombe and Wooffitt, punk culture, like other youth subcultures, is not simply a matter of people talking to one another, or to outsiders, about who they are and what they do. Even more relevant, it might be argued, is how they dress and what they *do*: for example, there are certain distinctive activities that punks engage in, from producing or enjoying particular kinds of music or art that reflect an anti-authoritarian, nihilistic attitude to the taking of hard drugs. However, the argument that Widdicombe and Wooffitt and others make here effectively implies that these activities, like the accounts given in interviews, are simply cultural performances. Moreover, they are situated and variable, rather than taking the form of standardised, entirely ritualised patterns of action engaged in by a distinctive set of people who are, as it were, all signed-up members of a well-defined punk community.

What is involved here is a shift in the focus of inquiry away from trying to use what young people say in interviews about their attitudes and behaviour in order to construct a model of a particular subculture to which they belong, how it arose, why they chose to identify with it, and so on, to a concern with *how young people construct subcultural identities in and through how they act in interviews, and in other contexts.* From this point of view, there is no reason why what people do in other contexts should be given any methodological priority over what they say (and, through saying, do) in interviews. Furthermore, interviews have some advantages: for the kind of discourse analysis proposed, we need a research method that allows us to generate an accurate record of discursive practices; and audio- or video-recorded interviews do this. They would be preferable from this point of view to participant observation, where this relies on field notes that do not capture the discursive practices involved in a detailed and entirely reliable fashion. Ironically, in these terms, the interview is rehabilitated, but it is used in a way that is quite different from most other interview studies: the focus is entirely on the discursive practices displayed in interview talk.

The arguments behind the radical critique of interviews we have outlined here draw on an underlying set of ideas, sometimes labelled constructionism, that has much wider application, methodologically and theoretically, than the question of how (or whether) interview data can legitimately be used by researchers. As you have seen, it also challenges traditional kinds of participant observation, such as that of Williamson, as a source of data about youth cultures, or about anything else. If it is true that subcultures exist only in and through interactional performances of one kind or another, then the idea of identifying members of some youth culture, and then engaging in participant observation with them in order to describe and explain their lives, becomes impossible: it falls at the very first hurdle, since how are we to identify who are skinheads or Lolitas or punks, other than by ourselves employing the discursive practices that are conventionally used to identify members of these groups? Doing this would trade on, rather than analyse, the discursive, situated work in which people engage for this purpose. Moreover, if we then provide an account of 'what skinheads do' or 'what Lolitas do' we would again simply be deploying the discursive practices available to do this while at the same time effectively pretending that we were describing behaviour that exists independently of those practices. Instead, constructionists argue, we must focus on these discursive practices themselves, seeking to document their character and how they function.

So, on this argument, we can only study the discursive (and other) practices through which people identify (and self-identify as) skinheads or Lolitas, and through which they characterise the features of these distinctive subcultures. It is argued that this is not just a matter of studying language use, because the phenomena with which researchers have traditionally been concerned, such as the games which children play or the subcultures in which young people participate, are intrinsic to the discursive practices that constitute them. Documenting these practices involves simultaneously documenting the phenomena; indeed, on the constructionist argument, there is no other means of doing this. Note, however, that the character of these social phenomena is now understood in a very different way from how they are conceptualised by most social research, and indeed from how they are treated by most of us in our everyday lives. Indeed, if followed through fully, constructionist arguments seem to suggest that researchers themselves constitute the social phenomena they claim to study through what they choose to observe, the questions they ask, how they interpret the data they collect, draw conclusions from this, write their research reports, and so on: that social phenomena do not exist independently of the discursive practices of researchers any more than they do independently of the discursive practices employed by the people researchers study.

All this is difficult terrain, and you may have found it hard to follow the argument in places. Moreover, resolving the debates between constructionists and their opponents is even more challenging. It is worth noting that constructionism, in various forms, is currently very influential among researchers working with children and young people, and in other fields too; even if its radical implications are not always followed through to the end. Moreover, as we shall see, it has interesting implications for the study of the online activities of children and young people. After all, a contrast is frequently drawn between virtual reality online and 'real life' offline. Yet, on the basis of constructionism it appears that this is spurious: what happens offline is no less cultural performance than what happens online. In the next section we will consider how children's and young people's online lives can be researched.

Summary of Section 2

While researchers use the same sorts of methods we all do in seeking to understand the social world, how they select and employy these methods will reflect the particular methodological tradition within which they work.

As regards the offline lives of children and young people, observation and interviewing are among the main sources of data employed by researchers. These involve contrasting advantages and disadvantages.

In evaluating ethnographic or participant observation studies, one criterion often used is how close the researcher managed to get to the people being studied, in terms of observing their everyday lives. For this reason, such studies are often regarded as superior to those based entirely on interview data.

There has been some more radical, constructionist criticism of interviews, which suggests that they cannot be used as a source of information about the world beyond the interview. Instead, the focus should be on the discursive practices displayed in informants' talk.

These constructionist arguments extend beyond the use of interviews, suggesting a radical re-specification of the focus of research towards the analysis of cultural performances.

3   Researching children's and young people's lives online

The various chapters of this book have discussed a wide range of online activities in which children and young people engage. Moreover, it has been noted that, over the past couple of decades, children and young people in many societies have not only increasingly engaged in online games and online modes of communication, but also that aspects of these have been incorporated into their offline activities as well.

As noted earlier, the new digital media have provided researchers with new sorts of data, both textual and visual, as well as new phenomena to investigate, notably online communities of various kinds. We will identify a variety of methods that researchers employ in this field, but initially a fundamental distinction can be drawn between two broad strategies. First, there is the use of online methods by researchers to elicit information about the online (and perhaps also the offline) lives of children and young people: for example, using email, social networking sites, or conferencing to make contact with people and carry out interviews, administer questionnaires, or to elicit diaries or blogs. The second strategy involves researchers studying 'naturally occurring' online data for research purposes. We can see this distinction as analogous, in some ways, to that between relying on the elicitation of accounts and employing participant observation, which we discussed earlier.

Activity 5 Investigating online activities

Allow about 15 minutes

Select a particular type of online activity, such as one of those mentioned in earlier chapters, and consider how you would go about investigating it.

List the strategies that you can think of which could be used to provide data about children and young people's participation in this activity. Then think about how you might obtain data about their motives for participation, and their attitudes towards various aspects of the activity and other people involved in it.

Finally, consider what further data might be required to identify what they may be learning through their participation.

There is no specific comment for this activity. The issues it raises will be covered in the remainder of this chapter.

If we look at studies of children's and young people's involvement in new digital technologies, we find a variety of methods employed. These include the following:

1   The recruitment of children and young people as informants offline to elicit accounts from them about their participation in online activities. This was one of the strategies employed by Willett: young people were approached through media studies teachers at two schools, and they were interviewed offline in groups, although permission was also sought to access their personal pages. In addition, individual follow-up interviews were conducted, offline, with some of the young people (Willett, 2009).

2   Eliciting accounts from children and young people online about their online activities. Marsh (2010) used this strategy, initially gaining access to children via a primary school but then setting up an online questionnaire for them to fill in about their internet use. This included:

> asking children to identify if they used virtual worlds outside of school and, if so, how often. Questions also focused on the nature

of children's activities when using virtual worlds, that is, if they shopped, played games, read the in-world texts and chatted to friends. Many of the questions were multiple-choice to enable ease of completion. However, some more open questions were also asked, such as 'What do you like about playing in virtual worlds?'. Children were invited to complete the survey when they attended ICT lessons in the IT suite, which each class in the school did twice a week. The IT teacher in the school frequently used on-line surveys … and therefore the practice was not unfamiliar to the children. (Marsh, 2010, p. 28)

3   The study of children's and young people's participation in particular online sites by the researcher engaging in 'participant observation' there. This was the approach adopted by Treseder in a study of 'pro-ana' websites, which are concerned with exchanging ideas about dieting and that, in some cases, actively promote 'pro-anorexia' views (Hammersley and Treseder, 2007).

4   The introduction of a new online activity and the elicitation of accounts, by one method or another, to investigate children's or young people's experience of it. This seems to have been what was involved in a project reported by Jackson et al. (2008), who used a variety of strategies to investigate children's use of the BBC Adventure Rock website.

5   The offline observation of children's online participation and how this meshes with their offline activity. This was the approach adopted by Wohlwend et al. (2011), who set up cameras in an after-school computer club to record how the children used the Webkinz website.

Each of these strategies has advantages and disadvantages, both as regards what it is and is not likely to give access to, and in terms of the reliability of the evidence it will probably generate for answering particular research questions. For example, how reliable would information be about internet use provided in response to a questionnaire, as compared with researchers actually observing participation? While the third strategy may provide reliable information about the nature of online participation, it is unlikely to offer much evidence about motivation and attitudes. Finally, none of these methods will usually supply strong evidence about what learning is taking place. (Of course, it is possible to combine these strategies, in one way or another, and some of the studies mentioned do this.)

We could also ask about the relative advantages of eliciting answers to questions online versus in face-to-face interviews. Face-to-face communication is often viewed as being natural and direct, whereas online communication raises questions even about exactly with *whom* one is communicating: whether it is one person or more than one, whether they have the personal and social characteristics that they claim, or that they are assumed to have, and so on.

"On the Internet, nobody knows you're a dog."

Figure 1   A cartoon by Peter Steiner

However, the immediacy and reliability of face-to-face contact can be exaggerated, since our communications with one another in this mode are necessarily mediated by cultural and linguistic forms of non-verbal and verbal behaviour. We do not literally see and hear the other person 'for who he or she really is'; in fact, the very idea of doing this is open to question – would we be in immediate contact if we could see the other person's brain and the electrical discharges occurring there? This is clearly not the case.

Nevertheless, it could be argued that there is an important sense in which face-to-face communication provides us with a wider range of information about the other person than is available in online communication, or for that matter in communication by phone or by post. We not only have access to the words people use, not only do we hear their voices saying them with particular inflections and emphases, but we also see the paralinguistic behaviour surrounding their communication (facial expressions, gesture, etc.), their direction of gaze, and also any activities they are simultaneously engaging in that could be relevant to understanding what they say.

In some respects, this argument is similar to the one we explored in relation to ethnographic studies, where closeness to 'the action', and the people involved in it, is seen as supplying a broader range of information than is available via more 'remote' forms of research, such as reliance on interviews and, even more, on questionnaires. Yet, as we saw, this kind of argument can be undermined by constructionism, and this approach has sometimes been applied to the study of online communities too. From this point of view, in order to understand patterns of social interaction in these contexts we do not need to know who the people involved 'really' are, in terms of their offline personal characteristics and lives; indeed, there is no reason to privilege their identities in these other contexts as 'real' – as we noted earlier, from a constructionist perspective these too are 'performances'. What should be the focus is how children and young people construct identities in and through the discursive practices they deploy online *and elsewhere*. For example, being an emo online (see Chapter 4) is simply performing there in the appropriate way, it does not depend on who you are or what you are like offline. Similarly, one can analyse the ideology of 'thinness' promoted by some of those running 'pro-ana' websites without needing to consider whether or not they are 'in fact' anorexic. If all action, and all social phenomena, are cultural performances, then those that take place online can be investigated in their own right just much as can those that occur offline; the latter should not be privileged.

Activity 6   Virtual ethnography

Allow about 20 minutes

A considerable body of online research, some of it concerned with children and young people, labels itself 'virtual ethnography', 'online ethnography' or 'webnography' (Markham, 1998; Hine, 2000). On the basis of our earlier discussions of the nature of ethnography, and of constructionism, what do you think the arguments might be for and against the idea that ethnography can be 'virtual'?

Comment

One answer would be that, in effect, virtual ethnography is simply a form of participant observation: researchers participate in online sites and watch others' participation in them. The implication here is that online sites can be treated as equivalent to offline sites, like playgroups, schools or colleges, and studied as places where distinctive social processes occur. Since what is being investigated is virtual (though still real), participant observation must also be 'virtual'. Given that embodied activities do not happen in this type of setting, conventional participant observation is not feasible. In these terms, online participant observation can be treated as a legitimate form of ethnography.

In response to this it might be argued that an ethnographic approach would demand that we understand how the participation of people online fits into their offline lives: that we should not treat the online/offline distinction as given, as if what people do online and offline were completely unrelated. For example, if Wohlwend et al. had only been collecting online data about the children's participation in the Kidkinz networking site, they would not necessarily have been aware that the children knew one another 'in the real world', and that they were interacting together offline in ways that shaped their online activities.

What is most important, once again, though, is not whether it is legitimate to talk about 'virtual ethnography' but rather to understand what different sorts of research strategy can provide access to, and what they may obscure. A further illustration is provided by a discussion of some girls' use of the Bebo social networking website (Willett, 2009; Ringrose, 2010). If the researchers had restricted themselves to studying what occurred online they might have been inclined to assume that the personal pages of the girls were primarily designed as self-presentation aimed at the general audience of Bebo users. Yet, it becomes clear from this research that the girls used the site primarily to communicate with their offline friends; and, in fact, they altered one another's personal pages as part of their interpersonal offline activity. As Willett (2009, p. 287) comments: 'the readings and meanings that they contributed to

on-line content were markedly different to the way we might read them';
in other words, from how they would be read by someone simply doing
online participant observation. This nicely illustrates the value of
combining online and offline data.

Up to now, we have been concerned with various *methodological* issues
involved in researching children's and young people's lives offline and
online; in other words, those concerned with how we can best do
research in order to understand social phenomena. However, the *ethics*
of the research strategies we have been discussing is also an important
topic, and online research raises ethical issues in distinctive ways. We
will explore these in the next section.

Summary of Section 3

There is a variety of strategies by which researchers have studied
the online activities of children and young people.

While constructionism implies that these can be investigated by
relying entirely on online data without any attention to how those
activities fit into the offline lives of participants, in fact much
research has studied both.

There are advantages and disadvantages associated with the
various data collection strategies available for studying online
activities; these vary in significance depending on the research
focus and the people being studied.

---

4   Research ethics: offline and online

Children and young people are often classed, along with some other
groups, as vulnerable, and therefore as needing protection against harm
that might be caused through the research process. Of equal importance
is the widespread commitment among researchers in this field to respect
the autonomy of children and young people. In rather different ways,
these two principles (central to many discussions of research ethics) –
protection from harm and respecting autonomy – have led to an
emphasis on the importance of seeking informed consent for research.
As regards harm, the concern has often been with obtaining informed

consent from carers for children and young people, on the grounds that they may be more aware of dangers than the children and young people themselves. By contrast, the principle of respecting autonomy emphasises the need to gain informed consent from children and young people.

Activity 7   Informed consent

Allow about 20 minutes

The notion of informed consent has its origin in medical contexts, where it is usually insisted that patients must be provided with adequate information, and must consent on the basis of this, before they receive any major treatment. However, this requirement is also widely applied in psychological and social research.

Consider what would be involved in gaining consent in the following sorts of inquiry:

- a participant observation investigation of a group of young people, of the kind carried out by Williamson in his first study

- a study based primarily on observation of, and interviews with, young children, for example Woodyer's (2010) research on children's play in domestic settings, discussed in Chapter 2

- a study of the participation of young people in an online community, for instance on a 'pro-ana' website.

Comment

There are uncertainties surrounding what 'informed consent' means, and about its value (O'Neill, 2002). Some of these concern what it would mean to be 'informed', others are about what it means to 'freely consent'. Many of these issues come to the surface in thinking about the three sorts of research mentioned.

In the case of a participant observation study of a group of young people, based on the model of Williamson's research, some of the questions that can arise are about who should be approached for initial access to the group (a youth worker, a gang leader), and to what extent its members would be free to opt out of the research if other members insisted on participating, or vice versa. In effect, the group as a whole has to make a decision about whether to participate or whether to opt out, and there are different ways in which this might be done, some of them perhaps being ethically acceptable while others are not (e.g. a unilateral decision by the youth worker or the leader of the group might be regarded as ethically unacceptable). Related problems are caused by the fact that such groups are rarely well defined, in terms of who belongs and who does not and who can speak on their behalf, and these things may change over time. As a result, some participants may come to be observed by the researcher even though they have not formally agreed to participate.

With studies of young children, there are obvious questions about whether they will understand the information provided, and grasp its implications and the possible consequences, and therefore whether we can take their assent as truly indicating consent; though, in fact, this issue arises with participants of any age. In addition, we might ask whether informed consent from carers is also required if harm is to be avoided? If so, how should conflicts between the decisions of children and young people themselves and those of their carers be resolved? In the case of Woodyer's research, which took place in children's homes, continual negotiation of access was probably required, as well as careful attention not just to the issue of autonomy, but also to the protection of privacy.

In the case of online data, there are commentators who argue that anything that is publicly available on the web can be used by researchers without permission being sought. Others challenge this, insisting that research online comes into the category of human subjects research just as much as offline research, and should be subjected to the same ethical requirements. Of course, this argument may be given increased emphasis when the online participants being studied are children and young people. There are complex issues involved here, as the work of Willett (2009) illustrates:

> We promised our participants anonymity (we use pseudonyms and no images). Although we had permission to interview the pupils (from both parents and pupils), and we also had permission to view the interviewees' sites (many of which were set to public), we were viewing spaces which were clearly not meant for parents or teachers … Young internet users have 'mirror sites' which are shown to parents as a way of protecting their privacy, indicating the private nature of sites (although publicly available). Although most of the sites we viewed were public, some users chose not to share their sites with us (either keeping them private or not giving us their usernames). In many ways the sites were seen by their users as private to their peer group (although they were aware that anyone could access them), and the interviewees said they would find it strange if adults looked at their sites. To make things more complicated, although we had permission to view some sites, we did not have permission to view all the sites of

> the 'friends' of our interviewees or indeed the comments left by
> friends. However, it was difficult to make sense of
> interviewees' sites without looking at the sites of their peers.
>
> *(Willett, 2009, pp. 286–7)*

Where the online sites being investigated may involve and promote self-harm, as in the case of pro-ana sites, further difficulties are introduced in deciding what is and what is not ethical, and where the responsibilities of the researcher lie. Moreover, in this case not knowing the background characteristics of the participants, not least their ages, exacerbates the difficulties.

As the comment to Activity 7 indicates, the question of informed consent by no means covers all of the ethical issues that can arise in research on children and young people. Others include the protection of privacy, and also whether the researcher is obliged to report activity that could cause harm, whether to the person concerned or to others. For example, Holmes (1998) reports how one of the children she was studying said to her one day: 'Can I tell you something? I hate my life, I just want to kill myself' (Holmes, 1998, p. 25). A related issue in the study of youth cultures concerns whether there is an obligation on the part of the researcher to report illegal activity.

In all these cases there is a tension between maintaining confidentiality, and therefore respecting autonomy, and protecting people from harm, whether caused by the research or by factors external to it. In the example mentioned above, Holmes's solution to the problem was to report what the child had said to the teacher, so that support was provided without his being aware that the researcher had intervened. Many researchers would probably have done the same, but others might have sought the child's permission to pass on the information. There is room for disagreement here, as with most other ethical issues.

In part, the scope for disagreement reflects the fact that there is a range of different ways in which people (researchers included) approach ethical issues, and these will by no means always lead to the same practical conclusions. We will mention just one contrast here. On the one hand, there are those who emphasise what they see as absolute duties or rights that must always be respected by researchers. For example, they might argue that researchers must, in all circumstances, respect the autonomy of children, especially since there continue to be serious infringements of that autonomy in most societies today. A rather different approach can be labelled 'situated ethics'. Here the concern is to come to some conclusion about what would be ethically most satisfactory in the particular situation, this often involving compromises among competing values. This was perhaps the sort of approach that Holmes adopted in the example discussed above. It is also worth noting that the values taken into account in situational decision making may include those central to the research enterprise itself, so that often the focus may be on 'how to balance the needs of the research with those of the research subjects' (Berry, 2004, p. 327; Hammersley and Traianou, 2012).

Summary of Section 4

Researchers carrying out studies with children and young people have been particularly concerned to minimise the risk of causing harm and to respect their autonomy. This partly stems from the idea that they are more vulnerable than adults, and from a commitment to respecting their rights, rights that it is believed are infringed in many of the contexts in which they participate in most societies.

There is the potential for conflict between the principles of minimising the risk of harm and respecting autonomy, and other values are relevant as well, notably the need to protect privacy.

These problems take on distinctive forms in the study of online activities, not least because there are issues about 'who is who' online.

There are differing views about research ethics, and these can result in somewhat discrepant conclusions about what researchers should, and should not, do.

---

5   Conclusion

In this chapter I have explored some of the methodological and ethical issues involved in research on children and young people. These issues are highlighted by the differences between research conducted offline and that taking place online. We started by comparing the folklore and anthropological traditions, in terms of focus and strategies, and went on to examine the strengths and weaknesses of participant observation and interviews as sources of data. This led to a discussion of constructionist challenges to conventional uses of these methods, particularly interviews. We noted how constructionism seems to require a major shift in the research focus, for example away from youth cultures as patterns of activity and their associated values and attitudes, towards the study of the discursive and other practices through which these phenomena are ongoingly socioculturally constituted.

Constructionism also has implications for the study of online communities. It is sometimes argued that these should be treated not only as just as 'real' as offline behaviour, but also as quite independent of it. As such, the focus could be entirely on investigating the discursive practices through which online identities are constructed and sustained, challenged or revoked, and so on. At the same time, I showed that it may be misleading to speak of online and offline lives as if these were separate entities, since for many young people activities in the two environments are closely intertwined, thus implying that researchers must give attention to both.

In the final section we briefly considered some of the ethical issues that can arise in research on children and young people, especially the question of informed consent, and the rather different views that can be taken about these.

References

Atkinson, P. and Coffey, A. (2002) 'Revisiting the relationship between participant observation and interviewing', in Gubrium, J. F. and Holstein, J. A. (eds) *Handbook of Interview Research*, Thousand Oaks, CA, Sage.

Berry, D. (2004) 'Internet research: privacy, ethics and alienation: an open source approach', *Internet Research: Electronic Networking Applications and Policy*, vol. 14, no. 4, pp. 323–32.

Boyd, D. (2010) 'The public nature of mediated breakups', in Ito, M., Baumer, S., Bittanti, M., Boyd, D., Cody, R., Herr-Stephenson, B., Horst, H. A., Lange, P. G., Mahendran, D., Martinez, K. Z., Pascoe, C. J., Perkel, D., Robinson, L., Sims, C. and Tripp, L. (eds) *Hanging Out, Messing Around, and Geeking Out: Kids Living and Learning with New Media*, Cambridge, MA, MIT Press.

Dingwall, R. (1997) 'Accounts, interviews and observations' in Miller, G. and Dingwall, R. (eds) *Context and Method in Qualitative Research*, London, Sage.

Epstein, D. (1997) 'Cultures of schooling/cultures of sexuality', *International Journal of Inclusive Education*, vol. 1, no. 1, pp. 37–53.

Geertz, C. (1988) *Works and Lives: The Anthropologist as Author*, Stanford, CA, Stanford University Press.

Gregor, T. (1977) *Mehinaku: The Drama of Daily Life in a Brazilian Indian Village*, Chicago, IL, Chicago University Press.

Hammersley, M. and Traianou, A. (2012) *Ethics and Qualitative Research*, London, Sage.

Hammersley, M. and Treseder, P. (2007) 'Identity as an analytic problem: who's who in "pro-ana" web-sites?', *Qualitative Research*, vol. 7, no. 3, pp. 283–300.

Hine, C. (2000) *Virtual Ethnography*, London, Sage.

Holmes, R. (1998) *Fieldwork with Children*, London, Sage.

Jackson, L., Gauntlett, D. and Steemers, J. (2008) *Children in Virtual Worlds: Adventure Rock Users and Producers Study* [online], London, BBC and University of Westminister, http://www.bbc.co.uk/blogs/knowledgeexchange/westminsterone.pdf (Accessed 1 August 2012).

Katz, C. (2004) *Growing Up Global*, Minneapolis, MN, University of Minnesota Press.

Livingstone, S. (2009) *Children and the Internet*, Cambridge, Polity.

Markham, A. (1998) *Life Online: Researching Real Experience in Virtual Space*, Walnut Creek, CA, AltaMira Press.

Marsh, J. (2010) 'Young children's play in on-line virtual worlds', *Journal of Early Childhood Research*, vol. 8, no. 1, pp. 23–39.

Moore, D. (1994) *The Lads in Action: Social Processes in an Urban Youth Subculture*, Aldershot, Arena.

Murphy, E., Dingwall, R., Greatbatch, D., Parker, S. and Watson, P. (1998) 'Qualitative research methods in health technology assessment: a review of the literature', *Health Technology Assessment*, vol. 2, no. 16, pp. 1–260, http://www.hta.ac.uk/execsumm/summ216.htm (Accessed 31 October 2011).

Nayak, A. (1999) 'Pale Warriors: skinhead culture and the embodiment of white masculinities', in Brah, A., Hickman, M. and Mac an Ghaill, M. (eds) *Thinking Identities: Ethnicity, Racism and Culture*, Basingstoke, Macmillan.

O'Neill, O. (2002) *Autonomy and Trust in Bioethics*, Cambridge, Cambridge University Press.

Opie, P. and Opie, I. (1997) *Children's Games with Things*, Oxford, Oxford University Press.

Pearson, G. (1976) '"Paki-bashing" in a north east Lancashire cotton town: a case study and its history', in Mungham, G. and Pearson, G. (eds) *Working-class Youth Culture*, London, Routledge and Kegan Paul.

Pelto, P. and Pelto, G. (1978) 'Ethnography: the fieldwork enterprise', in Honigmann, J. (ed) *Handbook of Social and Cultural Anthropology*, Chicago, IL, Rand McNally.

Potter, J. and Hepburn, A. (2005) 'Qualitative interviews in psychology: problems and possibilities', *Qualitative Research in Psychology*, vol. 2, no. 4, pp. 281–307.

Rapley, T. (2001) 'The art(fulness) of open-ended interviewing: some considerations on analyzing interviews', *Qualitative Research*, vol. 1, no. 3, pp. 303–23.

Ringrose, J. (2010) 'Sluts, whores, fat slags and playboy bunnies: teen girls' negotiations of "sexy" on social networking sites', in Jackson, C., Paechter, C. and Renold, E. (eds) *Girls and Education 3–16: Continuing Concerns, New Agendas*, Maidenhead, Open University Press.

Rohner, R. (1969) *The Ethnography of Franz Boas*, Chicago, IL, University of Chicago Press.

Silverman, D. (1997) 'Towards an aesthetics of research', in Silverman, D. (ed) *Qualitative Research: Theory, Method and Practice*, London, Sage.

Thorne, B. (1993) *Gender Play: Girls and Boys in School*, Buckingham, Open University Press.

Tucker, F. (2003) 'Sameness or difference? Exploring girls' use of recreational spaces', *Children's Geographies*, vol. 1, no. 1, pp. 111–24.

Wetherell, M., Taylor, S. and Yates, S. (eds) (2001) *Discourse Theory and Practice*, London, Sage.

Widdicombe, S. and Wooffitt, R. (1995) *The Language of Youth Subcultures*, New York, Harvester-Wheatsheaf.

Willett, R. (2009) '"As soon as you get on Bebo you just go mad": young consumers and the discursive construction of teenagers online', *Young Consumers*, vol. 10, no. 4, pp. 283–96.

Williamson, H. (2004) *The Milltown Boys Revisited*, Oxford, Berg.

Wohlwend, K. E., Zanden, S. V., Husbye, N. E. and Kuby, C. R. (2011) 'Navigating discourses of place in the world of Webkinz', *Journal of Early Childhood Literacy*, vol. 11, no. 2, pp. 141–63.

Woodyer, T. (2010) *Playing with Toys: The Animated Geographies of Children's Material Culture*, unpublished PhD Thesis, London, University of London.

Acknowledgements

Every effort has been made to contact copyright holders. If any have been inadvertently overlooked the publishers will be pleased to make the necessary arrangements at the first opportunity.

Grateful acknowledgement is made to the following sources:

Figures

Cover image: Children dancing in the park, Paris, July 14th, 1992 (board), © Holzhandler, Dora (Contemporary Artist)/Private Collection/The Bridgeman Art Library; page 5: © Bridgeman Art Library/Private Collection; page 7: © Mary Evans Picture Library/ Alamy; page 11: © Victoria and Albert Museum, London; page 13: Thomas Gainsborough (1756), The Painter's daughters chasing a Butterfly. Copyright © The National Gallery, London; page 14: © Cameraphoto Arte, Venice/Art Resource, NY; page 17: © Barnardo's; page 18: © Barnardo's; page 22: © Topham Picturepoint; page 24: © Martine Franck/Magnum Photos; page 31: © Topham Picturepoint; page 57 (top): With permission of the University of Sheffield; page 57 (bottom): © Monkey Business Images/Dreamstime.com; page 58: © Jody Dingle/Dreamstime.com; page 59: © AF archive/Alamy; page 68: Katz, C. (2004), 'Playful work and 'workful' play', Growing up Global, University of Minnesota Press. Copyright © 2004 by the Regents of the University of Minnesota; page 70: © Michelle D. Milliman/Shutterstock; page 73: © Iona Opie; page 76: © Belinda Pretorius/Dreamstime.com; page 82: © Photowitch/Dreamstime.com; page 91: © Haizhongyang/ Dreamstime.com; page 93: © Lisa F. Young/Dreamstime.com; page 96: © Lisa F. Young/iStockphoto.com; page 113: © Matthew Brown/ iStockphoto; page 119: © Antonio Oquias/Dreamstime.com; page 123: © Jarenwicklund/Dreamstime.com; page 125: © Aprescindere/ Dreamstime.com; page 131: © Christopher Walker; page 134: © Martin Woodhead; page 136: Courtesy of Mary Jane Kehily; page 144: © Jane Conversano/Dreamstime.com; page 146: © Image Source/Alamy; page 150: © Hanhanpeggy/Dreamstime.com; page 156: © Michael Brown/Dreamstime.com; page 172: Reproduced by permission of Ashgate Publishing; page 182: © John Harris/Report Digital; page 186: © Hannes Bretschneider; page 188: Photograph by Montreal hip-hop artist Mickey Boston, Montreal, QC; page 194: © Picture Contact BV/ Alamy; page 195: © Lebrecht Music and Arts Photo Library/Alamy;

Text

Index